W9-CBQ-347

The Triumph
of the Lawyers

THE TRIUMPH
OF THE LAWYERS

Their Role in English Politics, 1678–1689

by *Michael Landon*

UNIVERSITY OF ALABAMA PRESS

University, Alabama

COPYRIGHT © 1970
UNIVERSITY OF ALABAMA PRESS
Standard Book Number: 8173-5401-8
Library of Congress Catalog Card Number: 69-15418
Manufactured in the United States of America

Acknowledgments

THIS BEING MY FIRST BOOK-LENGTH PUBLICA-
tion, I would like to dedicate it, with gratitude, to the many
fine ladies and gentlemen who taught me during my school-
boy and student days in Canada, England, and the United
States. I wish especially to dedicate it to the three men who
gave me my training as a historian: the late Mr. T. D. Craig,
Senior History Master at Eastbourne College, Eastbourne,
Sussex, England; Mr. H. G. Pitt, Tutor in Modern History
at Worcester College, Oxford; and Professor W. L. Sachse
of the University of Wisconsin History Department.

I am grateful to the American Philosophical Society for
the very generous grant that made it possible for me to carry
out research in various libraries and collections in England
during the summer of 1966. The Society's grant was supple-
mented by a grant-in-aid from the University of Mississippi
Committee of Faculty Research. Thanks are also due Professor Douglas Lacey, of the United States Naval Academy, for
the loan of his microfilm copy of the Roger Morrice diary,
and Professor G. Peter Browne, of Carleton University, Ot-
tawa, for much valuable advice concerning seventeenth-

century jurisprudence. Professor Basil D. Henning of Yale University very kindly allowed me to consult his files, at the History of Parliament Trust office in London, on the seven men with whom my work is most concerned. The city archivists of Chester and of Bristol were very courteous and helpful to me in going through their collections.

My colleagues in the history department of the University of Mississippi have all been helpful in one way or another, at one time or another, but particularly mention must be made of Professor John H. Moore, our present Chairman, and his predecessor, Professor J. O. Baylen. Two of my students, Mr. Robert Board and Mr. Carl Pitts, have helped me with my research and with the preparation of the bibliography. To my wife, Doris, I owe an enormous debt of gratitude for her patience, and for her kind and loving assistance, over the past few years.

University, Mississippi   MICHAEL LANDON
July, 1969

Contents

Preface

> . . . the Revolution Settlement was first and
> foremost the rule of law. It was the triumph of
> the Common Law and lawyers over the king,
> who had tried to put prerogative above the law.
> (G. M. Trevelyan, in *The Eng-*
> *lish Revolution, 1688–1689*)

NO MODERN TREATMENT OF THE GLORIOUS
Revolution, or of the tumultuous events that occurred in the
period from the Popish Plot hysteria of 1678 to the Trial of
the Seven Bishops in 1688, gives the Whig lawyers referred
to by Trevelyan anything more than passing mention. Even
Trevelyan himself, despite the statement quoted above, failed
to provide his readers with any information about the lawyers who were so active in bringing about the Revolution.
He tells us nothing of who the lawyers were or what they
did, precisely, that finally enabled them to "triumph." Some
nineteenth-century historians, such as Lord Macaulay and
Leopold von Ranke, examined the roles of the individual
lawyers rather more fully, but still far from exhaustively.
Chroniclers contemporary to the lawyers had a great deal to
say about the lawyers' political activities, and they evidently

considered the lawyers an important influence, but their accounts are quite apt to be biased. However, in the published documentary sources for the period itself—in the parliamentary debates, the reports of trials, the Historical Manuscripts Commission Reports, and the Calendars of State Papers—the lawyers speak for themselves at great length, and their speeches and actions are frequently reported and often commented on by others.

Although both Whigs and Tories finally combined against James II to bring about the Revolution, it was the Whigs who had been the consistent opponents of the Crown and its policies in the years from 1678 to 1688, and it was the Whigs who primarily shaped the Revolution Settlement of 1689. The purpose of the present work, therefore, is to examine the political activities of the most outstanding Whig lawyers of the period, in an effort to find out what sort of men they were, what they as lawyers did to further the Whig cause, how—if at all—they differed in their ideas and actions from the other classes of Whigs (such as the aristocrats and the London merchants), and finally, precisely what part they played in formulating the Revolution Settlement that Trevelyan claims was a triumph for them and for the system of law for which they stood. By doing so we will test the accuracy of Trevelyan's statement and, at the same time, it is hoped, remedy what seems to be a serious deficiency in our knowledge of the political history of a crucial period in the evolution of the modern constitutional framework of Great Britain.

The Triumph
of the Lawyers

1

The Legal Profession and Politics in Seventeenth-Century England

THE BARRISTERS-AT-LAW OF THE LATER SEVenteenth century belonged to a profession that was both lucrative and honorable, and one that attracted into its ranks some of the ablest men of the age. Then, as today, the education and professional accreditation of barristers of the Common Law courts was controlled by the four societies of jurists housed in the four great "Inns of Court": the Inner Temple, the Middle Temple, Lincoln's Inn, and Gray's Inn. These societies appear to have originated in the fourteenth century in much the same way as did the "halls" of Oxford and Cambridge. They were founded by groups of students who banded together for mutual protection and support, came to be controlled by their elder members, and eventually developed into corporations of "Masters of the Law," the "readers" and "benchers," who housed and taught students of the law.

Theoretically, the Inns of Court had the status of independent, voluntary societies over which the state had no more authority than it had over any other corporation or college. But by the sixteenth century they had acquired a monopoly control over admission to the bar, and the Tudors were not the sort of rulers who would leave unregulated bodies that were of such key importance in the administration of public justice. Although Sir William Dugdale, the great seventeenth-century historian of the Inns of Court,[1] could find no ordinance affecting these institutions from either the Crown, the Privy Council, or the judges prior to the reign of Mary I, from that time on such ordinances are fairly frequent.[2]

In 1574 the judges, obviously seeking to limit the number in the profession, ordered:

> no more in number to be admitted from henceforth than the chambers of the houses will receive after two to a chamber. Nor that any more chambers shall be builded to increase the number; saving that in the Middle Temple they may convert their old hall into chambers not exceeding ten.

And seeking to control admission to the bar they ordered:

> None to be allowed to plead before the Justices of Assizes except he be allowed for a pleader in the Courts of Westminster, or shall be allowed by the justices of Assizes to plead before them.[3]

To the same end they ordered in 1596, with the assent of the governing bodies of the four Inns, that "there be in one year only four outer barristers called in any one Inn of Court," though in 1615 the number was raised to eight. They added that "no fellow of these Societies should wear any beard above a fortnight's growth." In 1604 it was ordered, over Attorney General Sir Edward Coke's signature, that "none be hereafter admitted into the Society of any house of Court that is not a gentleman by descent"—presumably another attempt to limit numbers. Finally, in 1615 a religious conformity in the profession was assured by an order that "every gentleman of the several Societies . . . who shall not receive the communion by the space of one year together, shall be expelled *ipso facto*." By the early seventeenth century, then, the barrister's position was firmly regulated—at least on paper—both as to quantity and to quality, and was preeminent among the professions that might appeal to a young gentleman of ability who had his way to make in the world.

An examination of the Inns' admission registers for the period with which we are concerned makes it clear that law students were recruited, almost without exception, from among the sons of the dominant social and political class of the country, the landed gentry. Our examination is confined to those three Inns whose published registers cover the whole of the seventeenth century.[4] Taking as a sample the entrants in the last nine months of the years 1604, 1634, 1654, and 1669, if we consider the rank in society of the entrants' fathers (or their own rank if, as is sometimes the case, that is given instead) we find a similar proportional distribution in each of the years and in each of the Inns. This is reflected in the overall totals :[5]

Peers or sons of peers	2
Baronets or sons of baronets	21
Knights or sons of knights	50
Esquires or sons of esquires	258
Gentlemen or sons of gentlemen	182
Sons of jurists	35
Commoners or sons of commoners	18
	566

In addition to the ranks listed above, an archbishop's son entered the Middle Temple in 1604, a colonel's son entered the same institution in 1654 (a sign of the times, perhaps), and a merchant's son in 1669. This last, together with the eighteen commoners who were apparently accepted, is evidence that Coke's order of 1604 limiting admission to the Inns to "gentlemen by descent" was not too rigidly observed.

Not all or even a majority of those who entered one of the Inns ever intended to become barristers. A nodding acquaintance with the Common Law would be a useful asset to any gentleman who intended to enter public life or even for one who planned to stay at home, manage his estates, and probably serve as a justice of the peace. Serious apprentices of the law were, therefore, considerably outnumbered among the students in the Inns by young gentlemen who simply sought to add a finishing touch of law to their general education. The convenient situation of the Inns—on the western edge of the City of London and on the way from the City to the center of government at Westminster—was probably an additional attraction to young men of ambition. John Evelyn tells us in his diary for 1699 that his recently deceased brother had gone to the Middle Temple as a youth "as gentlemen of the best quality did, but without intention to study the law as a profession."[6]

Neither the Lincoln's Inn register nor that of Gray's Inn tells us which of their entrants actually went on to be called to the bar. Only the Middle Temple register gives this information. Of their entrants in the four nine-month periods under consideration approximately one in five went on to be called. The one peer's son was among these but doubtless the majority of peers' sons did not go on to be called. Twenty-five percent of the baronets' sons, nineteen percent of the esquires' sons, and thirty percent of the gentlemen's sons went on to be called. As one might expect, the highest percentage of those going on to be called is found among the sons of judges and barristers: sixty-one percent. What is a little surprising is that not one of the four in the Middle Temple sample whose fathers were apparently not of the rank of gentleman—and who might, therefore, have been expected to want to make a career of the law—went on to be called. Perhaps they merely wished to acquire the smattering of law that would be useful in business, or perhaps they saw the Inn as a place where useful social contacts might be made —possibly they possessed both motives.

Those students who did in fact wish to become barristers normally had to be members of their Inn for seven years before they could be called to the bar—the same number of years that was traditionally required to be served by most apprentices in trade or industry and that was (and is today) required to qualify for a master's degree at Oxford or Cambridge. A few were called earlier "of grace," usually because they had previously spent some time at one of the other Inns. They had, as it were, "transferred credits." Most of the students were admitted while in their later teens and were called to the bar in their early twenties. For example, future Lord Chancellor John Somers entered the Middle Temple in 1669 at the age of eighteen.[7] The future Solicitor General William Williams entered Gray's Inn in 1650 at the age of sixteen.[8] However, considerable deviation from the norm appears to have been permitted on occasion. That William Turner, son of Edward Turner who was a bencher of the Middle Temple and Speaker of the House of Commons (1661–1671), was admitted to the Middle Temple in June, 1669 at the tender age of ten and was called to the bar "of grace" just four years later, presumably was due to his father's influence.[9]

The majority of those entering the Inns appear to have come to them from the universities of Oxford or Cambridge. Of the seventy-five who entered the Middle Temple with John Somers in the last nine months of 1669, ten came from Cambridge and thirty-three came from, or in a few cases later went on to, Oxford.[10] Most of them had not taken degrees at the university but had merely spent a year or two putting the finishing touches to their general education before going on to study the law.

After completing his seven-year apprenticeship the student was then ready to be "called to the bar." This process was administered by the officials of his Inn, originally by the readers. But with the decline of that office in the seventeenth century, admission came to be conferred by the benchers of the Inns.[11] However, his call to the bar did not admit the new barrister immediately to the fullest privileges of his profession. A rule of 1615 which laid it down that "for the time to come no outer barrister [may] begin to practise publicly at any Barr of Westminster until he hath been three years at the Barr" was confirmed by an order of the Lord Chancellor and the twelve judges in June, 1664, which gave as the reason "that the over early and hasty practice of utter barristers doth make them the less grounded and sufficient, whereby the law may be disgraced, and the client prejudiced."[12] Presumably, this period was spent by the novice barrister sitting in on trials as an assistant to a senior barrister.

Westminster Hall, where the highest courts of the kingdom, the King's Bench, the Common Pleas, the Exchequer, and the various equity courts, were located, and where, consequently, the seventeenth-century barrister spent a great deal of his time, was still a large, open chamber, two hundred and fifty feet long and seventy feet across. The judges of one court could look out over the heads of the immediate spectators, over the throng of fashionable lawyers, book and broadside-sellers, and other loiterers thronging the main body of the hall, to where their colleagues were presiding over other courts. Winter drafts moving unimpeded through the hall caused the legal profession to suffer a great deal from rheumatism and colds. However, the lawyers could perhaps find some consolation in the thought that similar discomfort had been suffered by their distinguished predecessors over many generations. The Court of Common Pleas being the worst affected, it was proposed during the 1660s to move the court into a back room, but the suggestion was quashed by the chief justice of the court, Sir Orlando Bridgman, on the grounds that such a move would infringe the provision in the Magna Carta which promised that Common Pleas would always be held *in certo loco,* and hence to shift its location by even a few feet might give rise to uncertainty. Apart from the continual drafts, down to as late as 1841 the building was subject to periodic flooding caused by the overflowing of the River Thames.[13]

In addition to the time he spent in Westminster Hall, a barrister would spend a certain part of each year riding on circuit; that is, accompanying the royal justices as they moved from county town to county town, conducting the assize at each of them. Just as in Westminster Hall, the novice could not expect to make much profit at first, but would usually appear in his first few years merely in the capacity of a junior assistant until, in time, he became known locally and achieved seniority among the barristers on a particular circuit. For this reason barristers generally kept to the same circuit throughout their careers. Roger North, himself a lawyer, whose biography of his elder brother, Francis North, Lord Guilford, is one of the major sources for the history of the legal profession in this period, tells us that "success in circuit business" was "a cardinal ingredient in a lawyer's good fortune."[14] It paid, therefore, to persevere in spite of the hardship of long days in the saddle hurrying from assize town to assize town, the hazard of heavy eating and hard drinking with overgenerous local hosts, and the need to study carefully the idiosyncrasies both of one's own seniors at the bar and of the different judges, the better to play up to their individual whims and fancies.[15]

Despite the initial difficulties, the prospects of a young barrister in the seventeenth century were bright. "If the common lawyer be sufficiently able in his profession," promised a contemporary writer, "he shall want no practice, if no practice no profit."[16] He need not depend entirely on his earnings in Westminster Hall and on circuit. Additional income could be derived from presiding over local public or private courts, such as manorial courts or borough or city courts, or by obtaining a position as recorder of a corporate town. Lucrative jobs with great possibilities for future preferment were also to be obtained under the judges or under the court officials of Westminster Hall. Legal assistants were required by the Lord Keeper of the Great Seal as secretaries for Chancery business and spiritual promotions, to serve on commissions of the peace, and to administer injunctions and dockets. Legal staff were also employed by the Lord Treasurer's office, the Customs House, the Chancellor of the Exchequer's office, the Principality of Wales office and the offices of the several royal duchies, the Court of Wards, the attorney general's office, and the solicitor general's office. For job openings in the royal household itself the writer advised the young barrister to "examine further the black book in the exchequer."[17] Francis North, for example, while still a junior barrister on the Norfolk circuit, served as chairman of a commission "for dividing the great level of the fens" in accordance with an Act of Parliament. Shortly thereafter he was preferred by the Bishop of Ely to be judge of the Royal Franchise Court of Ely.[18]

Heneage Finch, a future solicitor general, once estimated

his barrister's gown to be worth £20,000 to him.[19] Francis North, we are told by his brother, had been practically penniless as a law student, but in 1671, after ten years at the bar, he had saved £6,000.[20] John Somers was earning £700 a year at the bar in the 1680s.[21] John Maynard, admittedly at a somewhat later age, earned the same amount on one circuit in 1648.[22] But if an able lawyer could earn a small fortune in private practice at the bar in the seventeenth century, the law officers of the Crown, by a combination of Crown and private practice, could earn a very large fortune. Sir Francis Winnington's fee-book[23] shows that in 1671, when he held the appointment of standing-counsel to Prince Rupert, though he received a retainer of only £10 from the prince, in the four terms of that year he earned £1,790—exclusive of his earnings while on circuit and during the vacations. From 1672 to 1674, while he held the position of attorney general to the Duke of York, in addition to his salary from the duke of £160 and the £140 salary he received from the Crown as a King's Counsel, he earned well over £3,000 per year. In 1675, his first year as the king's solicitor general, his official salary was only £70 per year, but he earned a total of £4,066. This included, besides £459 in fees for royal patents passing through his hands, a £50 fee from the colony of Virginia, an occasional £50 as a retainer from the Duke of York, and an annual payment of £8 from the City of London at Christmas. But by far the greater part of his earnings came in the form of fees from private clients, including such figures as Lord Salisbury, the dukes of Ormonde and Richmond, and the Herbert family, to whom he was related by marriage.[24] Although the attorney general's salary was only £81 6s. 8d. a year, Roger North tells us that the office was worth £2,000 a year more than the far more exalted office of chief justice of the Court of Common Pleas.[25] Since the salary of a justice was £1,000 a year, it may be reckoned that the position of attorney general would bring its holder almost £3,000 more than he could have expected to earn as an ordinary barrister in private practice. The highest official salary attainable in the legal profession was the £4,000 paid to the Lord Chancellor; but of course neither he nor the judges, if they conducted themselves properly, could earn any perquisites of office, nor could they engage in private practice. Therefore, their earnings were not so great as those of the law officers of the Crown. Their duties were not so arduous as those of the law officers, however, and their positions carried far more honor and prestige.[26]

It was during the seventeenth century that the hierarchy of the law officers of the Crown evolved into the form that it has retained to the present day. One noteworthy development was the rise of the order of "King's Counsels." Holdsworth claims to find the origin of such a class at least as far back as the beginning of Elizabeth's reign, but he admits that the office first received official recognition in 1604 when Francis Bacon, who had complained that his position in relation to the Crown was that of "a kind of *individuum vagum,*" received a patent from King James appointing him "our councillor at law or one of our Counsel learned in the law."[27] Thus a new order in the legal profession was established at the very beginning of the century, mainly at the expense of the medieval "order of the coif," the "Serjeants-at-law," who were appointed from among the most distinguished members of the bar and from whose ranks new judges were selected. Holdsworth tells us that by the later part of the century, the "K.C.'s" were ceasing to be actual Crown officials and were being appointed "out of favour more than merit in the profession." The law officers naturally were reluctant to consult men promoted on such grounds,[28] and the office of King's Counsel quickly became what the office of serjeant had long been, an honorary (though salaried) position carrying no privileges beyond that of preaudience at the bar over ordinary barristers (but after the attorney general and the solicitor general). The abolition of the "order of Serjeants" by the Judicature Act of 1873 was finally to leave the K.C.'s as the unchallenged elite of the English bar.

Even more noteworthy than the rise of the order of K.C.'s was the increase during the century in the power of the offices of attorney general and solicitor general. As early as the thirteenth century there are references to *attornati regis*, but it was not till Edward IV's reign that a single "King's attorney" was appointed—an appointment which down to Henry VIII's reign was always for life or "during good behaviour," but which after 1509 was always "during pleasure" only. It is also during Edward IV's reign that we first find mention of the "King's solicitor." This appointment continued to be "during good behaviour" until after the Restoration, when it was also made "during pleasure" only. The technical medieval distinction between an attorney and a solicitor was gradually disappearing in the sixteenth century, and both offices were always, in fact, held by barristers so that the gap between them lessened considerably. At least from 1509 both officials were summoned ex officio to Parliament by individual writs of attendance to act in an advisory capacity to the House of Lords. After 1530 the custom was generally followed of having the solicitor general automatically succeed the attorney general in his office. In the seventeenth century the two offices came to assume their modern prominence, their holders becoming the chief legal advisors and deputies of the Crown, giving legal advice to all the departments of the state and representing them, when necessary, in the courts. From 1566, when the queen's solicitor,

Richard Onslow, was elected to the House of Commons and eventually chosen as Speaker, the solicitor general could sit, and often did sit, in the lower House, despite his writ of attendance to the Lords. But, although the attorney general's connection with the Lords was precisely the same as that of the solicitor, not until the appointment of Francis North in 1673 was an attorney general suffered to sit unchallenged in the Commons. After the Revolution, Henry Pollexfen, William III's first attorney general, and his successors, George Treby and John Somers, sat in successive parliaments without ever being questioned.[29]

Roger North suggests that there was a certain amount of competition for business between the attorney general and the solicitor general, both of whom were entitled to draft patents for the Great Seal.[30] But the rise to prominence of these two officials led to a much more important competition with—and to the final downgrading of—the serjeants, who, even as they were being ousted by the King's Counsels from their long-established positions as the undisputed leaders of the bar, now lost, besides, their equally long-established position as the chief legal advisors of the Crown. Accounting for the usurpation Holdsworth explains that it was basically because in a century of change and development, the king needed counselors who could adapt themselves to new categories of business. The serjeants were purely lawyers; the offices of attorney general and solicitor general satisfied the need of the Stuart kings for counselors who were both lawyers and politicians.[31]

Those who practice the law almost inevitably become interested in politics. In the seventeenth century the greatest political issues were constitutional ones and, therefore, of particular interest to lawyers. It is not surprising then that nearly all the outstanding men of the profession during the age were also very active politically, nor is it very surprising that in the political controversies that divided Englishmen between 1603 and 1689 the great majority of the Common Lawyers should have sided with the opposition to the Crown.

The basic question at issue, of course, was the location of sovereignty in the state. A bone of contention between the Crown and the barons in the later middle ages, the question had lain dormant during the Tudor period because the basic agreement as to policy that existed between ruler and the majority of subjects made it irrelevant. But it arose again immediately on the accession of James I in 1603 because James openly and loudly proclaimed that sovereignty belonged to the king by Divine Right at the same time that large numbers of his politically active subjects found themselves in profound disagreement with him over the three main issues that were to keep the sovereignty dispute at or near the boiling point for more than three-quarters of a century: religion, finance, and foreign policy. The common lawyers could not agree with the absolutist Divine Right claims of these Stuart kings, for it was their firm conviction that the ultimate sovereign of the English state was the law itself, which allowed certain powers and privileges to the subjects.

James I was not hostile to the Common Law so long as it fulfilled the role that he envisaged for it. In fact, he claimed that "as a king I have least cause of any man to dislike the Common Law for no law can be more favourable and advantageous for a king, and extendeth further prerogative than it doeth."[32] While it was certainly true that the law was jealous of the royal prerogative, it was also jealous of the rights of the subject. The man most active in drawing this latter truth to James' attention was Sir Edward Coke.

A dutiful servant of Queen Elizabeth as Speaker in the

Parliament of 1603 and later as her attorney general, Coke was kept on in the latter capacity by King James, whom he served equally dutifully by energetically prosecuting Sir Walter Raleigh and also the Gunpowder Plot conspirators. After being elevated, however, to the chief justiceship of the Court of Common Pleas, in June, 1606, Coke emerged as a staunch champion of the independence of the judiciary. Removal to the chief justiceship of the King's Bench in October, 1613 and admission to the Privy Council did nothing to mellow him. After Coke's encouragement of indictments of Lord Chancellor Ellesmere and other Chancery officials for what he regarded as trespassing upon the preserves of the Common Law, James finally felt himself compelled to dismiss his talented but uncooperative chief justice in June, 1616.[33] This was a tactical error on the king's part, for it left Coke free to devote all his time to those literary efforts of his that were ultimately to contribute a great deal more to the undermining of Stuart absolutism than his independent stand as a judge could ever have done.

Coke's great contribution to the development of English law and constitutional theory in the seventeenth century was his research into and codification of the old medieval Common Law, with the result that a knowledge of that law was made readily available to his contemporary colleagues and to their successors. Claiming that Sir Thomas Littleton's *Treatise on the Laws,* published in 1481 just a few years prior to the accession of the first Tudor, was "the most perfect and absolute work that ever was written in any human science,"[34] Coke presented seventeenth-century lawyers with the medieval law that, properly understood and used, could be a powerful weapon against the Renaissance ideal of the monolithic state in which an absolute king held sway by means of a large and efficient civil service and a powerful army. The medieval Common Law was well adapted to such a role because it had developed amidst the medieval struggle for supremacy between kings and barons. The precedents established by the old baronial opposition could now be utilized by the new opposition of country knights and squires and their aristocratic and mercantile allies.

The first eleven of Coke's thirteen *Reports* of medieval and Tudor case law were published by him between 1600 and 1615. His four general discourses on the common law, the *Intsitutes,* were written after his retirement from the bench. The first of these, a commentary on Littleton, was published in 1628; but the second, a commentary on thirty-nine major statutes, the third, a commentary on the criminal law, and the fourth, on the jurisdiction of the various courts, had to wait till a more favorable political climate prevailed and thus were not published until 1641. His last two *Reports* likewise had to wait till 1655 and 1658, respectively, before being made available to the public.[35]

Coke's two chief concerns were that the civil law courts, evolved from the Council and from Chancery, and considerably strengthened by the Tudors in order to suppress over-mighty and factious subjects, should not be allowed to overwhelm the Common Law courts; and that the admitted prerogative rights of the Crown should not be permitted to trespass on the legal rights of the subject. In his *Fourth Institute* he wrote of the powerful prerogative court of Star Chamber: "of all the high and honorable courts of justice, this ought to be kept within his proper bounds and jurisdiction." He presented a great deal of evidence to refute the common charge that the court was a Tudor innovation, but at the same time he emphasized that it ought to be restricted to its original medieval function as a supplement to the Common Law courts rather than being allowed to replace them.[36]

In the House of Commons debate on the Petition of Right in 1628, Coke led the attack on the Lords' amendment that would have inserted into the preamble to the Petition a proviso expressing Parliament's "due regard to leave entire that sovereign power, wherewith your majesty is trusted, for the protection, safety and happiness of your people." "This," Coke explained,

> turns all about again. Look into all the petitions of former times; they never mentioned wherein there was a saving of the king's sovereignty. I know that prerogative is part of the law, but 'Sovereign Power' is no parliamentary word. In my opinion it weakens Magna Charta, and all the statutes; for they are absolute, without any saving of "Sovereign Power"; and should we now add it, we shall weaken the foundation of law, and then the building must needs fall. . . . Let us hold our privileges according to the law: that power that is above this, is not fit for the king and people to have it disputed further.[37]

Coke's career as a leader of the opposition in the parliaments of 1620, 1624, 1625, and 1628 was of great consequence for future English constitutional development. As Holdsworth has pointed out:

> It cemented the old standing alliance between Parliament and the common law; it enlisted in favour of the Parliament that superstitious reverence which men felt for the common law, and it strengthened that note of legal conservatism which is the distinguishing characteristic of the constitutional struggles of the seventeenth century, and the secret of their successful issue.[38]

Thus an alliance was formed between the lawyers and the parliamentary opposition. When, as often happened, Parliament was not in session, then the lawyers had to carry on the struggle in the courts of law. Up until 1688, however, their efforts to oppose the Crown without parliamentary backing were to prove, as we shall see, almost totally ineffectual.

Coke's revival and exposition of medieval Common Law was reinforced by the scholarship of another great lawyer of the early seventeenth century, John Selden (1584–1654), whose *Dissertatio ad Fletam; Notes on Fortescue's De Laudibus*, and *Tracts* on the office of the Lord Chancellor, on the legal jurisdiction of Parliament, and on the privileges of the baronage (written at the request of the House of Lords) were widely read by lawyers[39] and served to emphasize further the limitations on, as well as the extent of, the Crown's prerogative.

An interpretation of the prerogative that very much favored the Crown was not, however, without its advocates in the legal profession in the early seventeenth century. The most noteworthy of these was undoubtedly Francis Bacon, later Viscount St. Albans (1561–1626), who was Coke's greatest rival in the legal controversies of James I's reign. Bacon had been as ready as anyone to insist on the limitations on the Crown's prerogative power in the latter years of Elizabeth's reign. But under James I he came to espouse the common Renaissance idea of state reforms carried out by an enlightened King and Council. His enthusiasm for the idea blinded him to the intellectual limitations of James I and his inability to win the hearts of his subjects—traits possessed by all the members of England's Stuart dynasty except Charles II. It also caused him to underestimate the degree of opposition to James, so that he optimistically hoped that

King and Parliament could work together in mutual harmony for the nation's welfare.[40]

Bacon expressed his views on the ideal relationship between the Crown and Parliament in a speech he drafted for the opening of Parliament in 1620:

> It is no doubt great surety for kings to take advice and information from their Parliament. . . . But in those things that are *arcana imperii,* and received points sovereignty [sic], as making of war or peace, or the like, there they are to apply their advice to that which shall be communicated unto them by the king; without pressing further within the veil.[41]

Like James himself Bacon stressed the function of the law as defender of the prerogative. In his essay "Of the Office of a Judge" he urged, in rather picturesque terms, that English jurists be ever ready to defend the Crown's rights:

> . . . Solomon's throne was supported by lions on both sides. Let them be lions, but yet lions under the throne: Bewaring how they attack, or weaken any part of the Royal Prerogative.[42]

The unfortunate Earl of Strafford, a generation later, who was not a lawyer (though in his youth he had spent some time as a student at the Inner Temple), had essentially the same conception of the preeminence of the prerogative and, also like Bacon, placed too much faith in the ability of a Stuart monarch while underestimating the strength of the parliamentary opposition.

After the Restoration in 1660, the Baconian concept of the alliance between the prerogative and the law was held by such notable figures as Heneage Finch (1621–1682), first Earl of Nottingham, who was Charles II's Lord Keeper from 1673 to 1675 and Lord Chancellor from 1675 until his death; and Francis North (1637–1685), Lord Guilford, who became Lord Keeper on the death of Nottingham. But neither Bacon nor those great men who later reflected his constitutional views were believers in royal absolutism. While Bacon, in his same essay on the judicial office, insisted that English judges must let their decisions be governed by *raison d'état* ("Matter of State"), he qualified that statement by adding that:

> I understand by Matter of State not only whatsoever touches the Rights of the Crown, but whatsoever introduceth any unsafe alteration, or dangerous precedent; or manifestly oppresseth any considerable portion of the people. And let no one weakly conceive that just laws and true politicks have any antipathy: For they are like the spirits and sinews, one moves with the other.[43]

So it would seem evident that all the great lawyers of seventeenth-century England were basically in agreement that ultimate sovereignty lay with the law. Where the champions of the "Rights of the Crown" differed from the champions of the rights of the subject was over the distribution of power. One set looked at the law and saw certain powers allotted by it to the king; the other set looked and saw certain powers—in some cases, unhappily, conflicting powers—allotted to the people in Parliament. Similarly all the lawyers would probably have agreed that the exercise of sovereignty belonged jointly to King, Lords, and Commons. They would have differed, however, on the precise role and powers of each of the three constitutional entities in regard to the others.

The ambivalence of the legal profession with respect to the great constitutional questions of the century is seen in the attitude of the Inns of Court towards the political crisis of 1638 to 1642, which led to the outbreak of Civil War. Justice Robert Berkeley had declared in the Ship Money

Trial (1638) that it was "utterly mistaken" to hold that "in case the monarch of England should be inclined to exact from his subjects at his pleasure, he should be restrained, for that he could have nothing from them but upon a common consent in Parliament." He conceded that "there peers and Commons may . . . , amongst other things, make known their grievances, if there be any, to their sovereign and humbly petition him for redress." "But," he went on:

> the former fancied policy I utterly deny. The law knows no such king-yoking policy. The law itself is an old and trusty servant of the king's; it is his instrument or means which he useth to govern his people by. I never read nor heard that Lex was Rex; but it is common and most true that Rex is Lex, for he is . . . a living, a speaking, an acting law. . . .[44]

On the other hand, in May, 1642 the Lords and Commons in Parliament were to reply to the royal proclamation declaring their Militia Ordinance to be invalid:

> The high court of parliament is not only a court of judicature, enabled by the laws to adjudge and determine the rights and liberties of the kingdom . . . but it is likewise a council to provide for the necessities, prevent the iminent [sic] dangers, and preserve the public peace and safety of the kingdom . . . And what they do herein hath the stamp of the royal authority although his majesty, seduced by evil counsel, do in his own person oppose or interrupt the same. . . .[45]

While the framework of the state was being thus split asunder, as each side asserted its supremacy over the other and its right to administer the affairs of the country alone, the "Gentlemen of the four Innes of Court" were to be found in the middle trying to effect a reconciliation and reunion.

In their petition to the House of Commons in 1641 they

urged the members to "serve God's annointed, his immediate Vicegerent, our true and lawfull Soveraigne Lord the King, in his person and all his Regall dignities and lawfull immunities, without any impeachment of his Regality, in whose honour the reputation of three Kingdomes depend." But they also urged them "to ratifie and confirm all things . . . that we may thereby live in these . . . turbulent times with as much peace to our conscience, with as much dignity to our Nation, in as true love and obedience to our lawful Soveraigne, and with as much libertie and liberality of our fortunes, as our fore-fathers heretofore have done."[46] This petition hardly constituted an endorsement of Berkeley's statement in the Ship Money Trial. The gentlemen expressed their viewpoint even more clearly on December 30, 1641 when they assured the House of Commons, which had been perturbed by the news that five hundred armed men from the Inns had marched to Whitehall to offer their services to the king, that the lawyers and law students could be depended on to be quite impartial:

> that they had onlie an intent to defend the King's person, and would likewise to their uttermost alsoe defend the Parliament: being not able to make distinction betweene the King and Parliament. . . .[47]

The political chaos of the two ensuing decades naturally gave rise to a body of constitutional literature written by nonlawyers. In the *Art of Lawgiving* (1659), James Harrington, though himself a layman, reflected the view of most lawyers of the period when he asserted that:

> Where the Sovereign Power is not . . . entire and absolute . . . there can be no government at all. It is not the limitation of Sovereign Power that is the cause of a commonwealth, but such a libration [balance] or poise of Orders that there can be in the same no number of men

having the interest, that can have the power; nor any number of men having the power, that can have the interest to invade or disturb the government. As the Orders of Commonwealths are more approaching to, or remote from this Maxim . . . so are they more quiet or turbulent.[48]

The sovereign power, the lawyers would say, was entire and absolute—it was the law; and England was governed, under the law, by a balance of three "Orders"—King, Lords, and Commons.

Thomas Hobbes, in his *Elements of Law* (1650), however, moved by his anxiety that there be a strong and stable form of government, asserted that sovereignty was indivisible. A balance of orders was impractical, in Hobbes' judgment, for if the three orders were in agreement, the individual citizen was no freer than he would be under a single despot, whereas if they did not agree then a condition of civil war would ensue (as had happened in 1642), nullifying the whole purpose of government (i.e., protection of lives and property). Condemning the "confusion in our understandings, that cannot find out readily to whom we have subjected ourselves,"[49] Hobbes listed four criteria by which the absolute sovereign might be identified:

(1) a man that could not be, of right, punished or an assembly that could not be, of right, dissolved.

(2) The man or assembly that might at pleasure make or abrogate laws.

(3) The man or assembly that had the original right of appointing magistrates, judges, counselors or ministers.

(4) He who might lawfully perform an act that no other member of the commonwealth could.[50]

Under the English Constitution these criteria could only be met by the king.

Shortly after the Restoration, Chief Justice Sir Matthew Hale (1609–1675) wrote two tracts in refutation of Hobbes' work.[51] The first of these, "Of laws in General and the Law of Reason," was in answer to Hobbes' attack on the importance that Coke and others attached to medieval law. Hobbes was in favor of the imposition by the sovereign of an organized code of laws, comprehensible to any intelligent layman, based on a rational analysis of the needs of the modern state, a policy similar to that which would be advocated by Jeremy Bentham a century later. Hale argued in reply that reason was certainly necessary to a lawyer, but that, as in any other profession, training and experience were also needed. He went on to argue that in the difficult task of judging the reasonableness of a law we should consider that the presumption is in favor of laws by which "a kingdom hath been happily governed four or five hundred years."[52] The second of these tracts deals with Hobbes' view "Of Soveraigne Power." Hale obviously understood Hobbes' tract to imply that sovereignty rested in the king, and he expressed agreement in a passage that actually implied his belief that the ultimate sovereignty belonged to the law:

> No good subject that understands what he says can make any question where the Soveraigne Power of the kindom resides. The laws of the land . . . teach us that the king is the only supreame governour of his realme.[53]

"Incident to that supreame power" the king had six "greate powers of sovereignty": firstly, he had the sole power of making peace and of declaring war; secondly, he had the right to mint coin; thirdly, he had the power to pardon public offenses; fourthly, he had the administration, either personally or by delegation, of all common justice both civil and ecclesiastical; fifthly, he had control over the militia and the raising of any other armed forces; and sixthly, he had the power of legislation. But, nevertheless, there were "certaine qualifications." Although the laws had no coercive power over the king, they did have a "direct power" over him because he was bound by his coronation oath and by laws that "concerne[d] the liberties of his subjects" which "in many cases hinder[ed] the kinges acts and [made] them void if they [were] against law." His control of the armed forces was limited because he could not make the militia serve outside the kingdom and money for other forces had to be approved by Parliament, and his legislative power was limited by the need for parliamentary consent.[54] So that, although Hale does not say so in as many words, he too evidently believed that the power of government was divided among King, Lords, and Commons and that sovereign over them all was the law. As the custodian of the law, the legal profession had the awesome responsibility of being the custodian of the ultimate sovereignty of England.

In this period after the Restoration some progress could certainly be seen to have been made in the storm-filled years that had elapsed since 1603. Parliament had sufficiently asserted its rights that even James II at the height of his power never dared to claim what Charles I's judges had claimed on his behalf in the Ship Money Case—that the king could, for reasons of state, completely override the privileges of Parliament. The abolition of the great prerogative conciliar courts of Star Chamber and Ecclesiastical High Commission left the Common Law courts supreme—and unchallenged in their supremacy. But the old sources of dispute between the Stuarts and their subjects—finance, foreign policy, and religion—continued to cause trouble, and so the question of the location of ultimate sovereignty in the state remained a vital one. In spite of what Trevelyan says, the Common Law had really triumphed as early as 1660, though it was to come under severe attack again in James II's reign. The question of the next three decades would be whose *interpretation,* whose *version* of the law would triumph, that favored by the Crown and its agents who naturally favored strong royal power, or that of the Crown's lawyer opponents, who naturally favored considerable limitations on royal power.

The law in the seventeenth century, like the legal profession, was in a state of evolutionary development. No doubt this is true of the law in every century, but the developments of the seventeenth century were particularly rapid. It has been conclusively demonstrated by J. C. Gray[55] and others that it was Coke who was the real originator of the modern power of precedent in English law. Although Bracton cites many precedents, and later writers such as Fleta, Fortescue, and Littleton cite a few case decisions, their citations were evidently intended to be illustrative rather than authoritative. The same is true of the decisions reported in the *Year Books* covering cases from the late thirteenth down to the early sixteenth centuries. But Coke, in his *Reports,* cites literally thousands of decisions gleaned from previous centuries. Because of their antiquity, and because he approved of them, Coke cited them as authoritative. By the end of the century most lawyers were treating these decisions as authoritative and binding—because Coke had so considered them. In the eighteenth century the doctrine of *stare decisis,* whereby a judicial decision as a precedent carries great weight in the same court in which it was delivered and in all coordinate courts and is absolutely binding on all inferior courts, would be endorsed by Blackstone and so become a cardinal principle of Anglo-American law. Down through the seventeenth century, however, the precedents provided to lawyers by Coke and other legal reporters were regarded as merely persuasive rather than binding, as precedents are in civil law to this day. The lawyer politicians, therefore, vied with each other in matching precedent for precedent, each group seeking to confer the authority of antiquity on its particular interpretation of the law. The courts, of course, decided which precedent prevailed.

Another formative factor affecting the development of the Common Law in the seventeenth century was the Renaissance theory of "natural law." It was generally agreed that a nation's laws ought to conform to certain self-evident, or logically determinable, rules for the ordering of a human society, perceivable through the faculty of reason possessed by all mankind. Inasmuch as it was God who had endowed all men with that faculty, the system of natural law could even be regarded as God-given. Coke patriotically regarded the English Common Law as being the very embodiment of human reason and, therefore, altogether congruent with natural law. He even argued that the Common Law courts could set aside a parliamentary statute if it were contrary to reason, though this notion proved unable to prevail against the doctrine of parliamentary supremacy.[56] And so again we find the lawyers arguing that their particular interpretation of the law is the one most in accord with "natural" or "fundamental" law, and again it is the courts that decide among them.

In the Common Law courts of Westminster Hall, whose justices held their positions at the king's pleasure, the Crown could generally be sure, down to 1688, that only interpretations of the law favorable to the royal prerogative would receive judicial endorsement. Over and above the ordinary law courts, of course, there existed the "High Court of Parliament," its actions governed by the *lex et consuetudo parliamenti*, a branch of the law into which no lesser court normally ventured to trespass. In the seventeenth century

Parliament had still not clearly determined the difference between the judicial and the legislative functions in government.[57] Lawyers and members of Parliament still felt that the law was something that was discovered, clarified, and declared rather than something that was newly made. Parliamentary statutes were regarded as statements of what the law was or, in accordance with natural law, ought to be, rather than as enactments of innovations. Though only the House of Lords exercised the normal judicial function of trying cases, the House of Commons nonetheless considered itself to be a court higher and more honorable than any of the courts of Westminster Hall, and a court whose decisions should be binding on such inferior courts. But this High Court of Parliament had three parts to it—King, Lords, and Commons—and any opinion of the Commons as to what the law was, or ought to be, could only be enforced if both Lords and King concurred. The king could create new peers and seat them in the House of Lords; the king appointed the spiritual peers, the bishops; and the king decided when Parliament met and when it was prorogued or dissolved. And so in this court, too, interpretations of the law that sought to limit the royal prerogative had little chance of prevailing.

But, if the Crown controlled the courts that decided which interpretations of the law were to be accepted, an equally important factor affecting the politico-legal situation in the period 1660–1688 was that the majority of the common lawyers were sympathetic to the opposition, and a good many of them were to be found in its ranks. Roger North tells us that:

> . . . so few Gentlemen of the Law were noted for loyalty (I use the word of that time) that it was made a Wonder at Court that a young lawyer should be so. The Reason was because, at the Time of the Restauration, the Profes-

sion, that commonly follows the Encouragements, was not well furnished with Cavaliers; and the chief Practice fell into the Hands of those who before had the Vogue; although some of them, by Virtue of the Act of Indemnity, escaped practising at the Crown Bar, as Defendants for themselves. This made it a fashion, for those that rose up under them, to be against the Court; for they would allow none else to be good Lawyers: which was a Prejudice that only great Abilities, with some Favour, could rise up against.[58]

Besides Roger North's brother, Lord Guilford, and the Earl of Nottingham, the only other lawyers of real ability to be found on the side of the Court in the period around 1680 were Sir Robert Sawyer, who served as attorney general from February, 1680 to December, 1687, and Heneage Finch, Nottingham's son, who was solicitor general from January, 1679 to April, 1686. And George Jeffreys—upon whom both Charles II and James II leaned more heavily than any other individual for legal support—although he has had his defenders,[59] probably owed his rise to the highest legal offices more to his zeal in the service of the Court than to his knowledge of jurisprudence or his forensic skill.

But North's explanation as to why the majority of lawyers were "against the Court" must be qualified. Although the legal profession had, not unnaturally, cooperated with the various governments of the interregnum, they surely could not, with their training, have approved of the irregular and chaotic manner in which the state, even when Cromwell was at the height of his power, was run. They could only have been relieved when the old tripartite division of powers— King, Lords, and Commons—was restored; and they must have hoped that now at last, even though a Stuart was king, the law would be sovereign. They were to be disillusioned, and eventually to drift one by one into active opposition until James II was left, in the latter part of his reign, with only two lawyers of note to represent his interests in Westminster Hall, George Jeffreys and a renegade Whig, William Williams.

The structure of politics in Restoration England had two major divisions. One was the Court, presided over by the king himself and including his handpicked advisors and favorite companions, his civil servants and professional consultants, the prelates of the Church of England, and those members of the nobility whose wealth and social standing automatically entitled them to be with the monarch. At the local level, in the towns and counties, the Court could depend on usually uncritical support from the "old cavaliers." These were gentlemen of long lineage, but often (because of the Civil Wars) of small fortune. They took pride and found consolation in identifying themselves with the Crown and with the Church of England for which, they believed, King Charles the Martyr had died, and they were often resentful of the new men in their neighborhoods, men of wealth and local power, many of whom had supported the Roundhead cause and prospered because of it. The second group, the "Country," as it was sometimes called, was made up of those members of the politically active classes who for lack of power or of "favour" were excluded from the closed circle of the Court: the landed gentry and their brothers and sons (not the "old cavaliers" but including some ex-cavaliers who felt that they had been insufficiently compensated by the Crown for their sacrifices on its behalf), the professional men, and the merchants of the towns and cities. Nonconformists, resentful of their status as second-class citizens, normally adhered to the Country cause. When powerful courtiers such as the Earl of Shaftesbury or the Duke of Buckingham fell from favor at Court they could bring pressure to bear on the king by organizing and leading a "Country Party" in opposition to his policies and thus, perhaps, compel him to readmit them to his inner councils. It was the Court, of course, that governed and administered England. If the men of the Country party—which by 1679 was being called the "Whig" party—wished to have some influence on the government and some voice in the formulation of its religious, financial, and foreign policies, they could only do so in Parliament through their elected representatives in the House of Commons.

As we have seen, some few lawyers, either because of "great Abilities" or "some Favour," were employed by the Court and were, therefore, loyal to the Court—or "Tory" —cause, and upholders of the royal prerogative. Having been reared in the tradition of Coke and Hale, however, the Tory lawyers would go only so far in their championing of the power and privileges of the Crown—as James II was to discover. The great majority of lawyers, of course, belonged in the Country category, and it is not surprising that they preferred to interpret the law in such a way as to stress the power and privileges of Parliament. Nor is it surprising that attempts in June, 1681 to draft addresses in Gray's Inn and the Middle Temple thanking King Charles for his declaration justifying the dissolution of what was to be his last parliament were violently rejected "both by bench and barr."[60] Holdsworth summed it up when he said: "They stood for the supremacy of the law, and of the rights and privileges of Parliament. In other words they formed the backbone of the party which came to be called Whig."[61]

In the following chapters we shall examine, in as much detail as the sources will permit, the part played in the political struggles of 1678–1689 by the lawyers who were the most active in the Whig cause.

2

The Whig Lawyers

IN THE DECADE 1678–1689 THE STRUGGLE between Crown and opposition reached a new height of intensity. It began with the attempt by the Whigs, led by the Earl of Shaftesbury, to win control of the government and exclude the Duke of York from the succession to the throne by taking advantage of the furor, from 1678 to 1681, over the alleged Popish Plot to murder the king. A period of reaction followed, from 1681 to 1685, during which the Whigs, their backs to the wall, saw many of their leaders executed for treason or else driven into exile overseas. In the period from 1686 to 1688, however, King James II finally carried reaction too far, overreaching himself to the extent that he so alienated the Tory champions of the Crown that they combined with the Whigs to bring about the "Glorious Revolution."

In considering the political role of the Whig lawyers in this eventful period, we will examine particularly the part played by seven men: Robert Atkyns, William Jones, John Maynard, Henry Pollexfen, George Treby, William Williams, and Francis Winnington. There were, it is true, other outstanding lawyers who could be called "Whig" in the period under consideration. Henry Powle (1630–1692), who was called to the bar from Lincoln's Inn in 1654 and became a Bencher of the Inn in 1659, was very active in the prosecution of the Popish Plot, strongly supporting the impeachment of the Earl of Danby and opening the evidence for the House of Commons in their impeachment of Lord Stafford before the House of Lords. However, he played a very moderate part in the Exclusion crisis, and after 1681 he withdrew almost entirely from politics and spent his time traveling abroad or in the practice of his profession, only to reemerge briefly upon the political scene in 1689 when he was chosen as Speaker of the Convention Parliament. In 1690 he accepted the appointment of Master of the Rolls.[1] John Somers (1651–1716) was called to the bar from the Middle Temple in 1676 and was a protégé of both Winnington and Pollexfen. He wrote, or at least helped to write, several of the important Whig pamphlets of the period, as we shall have cause to note,[2] but he did not emerge upon the open political stage until the Trial of the Seven Bishops in June, 1688. After that he went on to play an important part in the counsels of the Convention Parliament, though the importance of his contribution to that assembly's deliberations has been exaggerated in some accounts.[3] Besides these two great men the contributions of other lawyers, such as Richard Wallop (1616–1697) and John Holt (1642–1710), to the Whig cause during our period will be noted; but the political activities of the seven lawyers first named will be this writer's chief concern, because he feels that they were the most important and that their careers were the most representative of the Whig lawyers of the period.

All of the seven, like the great majority of their colleagues, belonged to the class of lesser landed gentry. All came from the western half of the country; three of them were from Devonshire. The eldest, John Maynard (1602–1690), was descended from several generations of Devonshire landowners and was a cousin of the Elizabethan seadog Sir Francis Drake. His father, Alexander Maynard of Tavistock, had been a barrister before him. The next eldest, Robert Atkyns (1621–1709), came of an old Gloucestershire family and was also a lawyer's son. His father, Sir Edward Atkyns, Sr., had served on all three of the high courts at different times during the interregnum. William Jones (1631–1682) came of a Somersetshire family. His father, Richard Jones, had represented that county in the Parliament of 1654. Henry Pollexfen (1632–1691) came of an ancient family of Sherford in Devonshire. William Williams (1634–1700) came of a Welsh family that was said to be descended from Cadrod Hardd, a tenth-century Anglesey chieftain. His father, Hugh Williams, was Rector of Llantrisant in Anglesey and proprietor of an estate, Caeau Gwynion, brought into the family by his wife. Francis Winnington (1634–1700) came of an old Cheshire family, though his father was actually a landowner of Powick, near Worcester. George Treby (1644–1700), a cousin of Henry Pollexfen,[4] was the son of Peter Treby, a landowner of Plympton Saint Maurice in Devonshire.[5]

John Maynard was graduated from Exeter College, Oxford, with a bachelor of arts degree in 1621, entered the Middle Temple in November of the same year, and was called to the bar in November, 1626.[6] Though he did not become a bencher of his Inn until 1648,[7] he had already made a name for himself some years before. He was for a while a protégé of William Noy, Charles I's attorney general from 1631 to 1634,[8] but the year 1641 found him wholeheartedly allied with the parliamentary opposition to the Crown. Member of the Long Parliament for Totnes in Devon,[9] he was one of the managers for the Commons in the impeachment of the Earl of Strafford and took that opportunity to express his views on the supremacy of the law. "It is true, my lords," he exclaimed, "that treason against the person of a prince is high treason, and the highest treason that can be to man, but it falls short of this treason against the state." He charged Strafford with having boasted, while president of the Council of the North, that "some of the justices . . . are all for law, but they shall find that the king's little finger is heavier than the loins of the law," and, while lord lieutenant in Ireland, "that neither law nor lawyers should question anything that he ordered."[10] By "treason against the state" Maynard obviously meant treason against the law.

Later, in a speech given at the Guildhall shortly after the attempted arrest of five members of the House of Commons, Maynard stressed the importance, if religion and the law were to be preserved, of upholding the privileges of Parliament:

> Master Speaker the only meanes to preserve and injoyne the sincere and pure teaching of God's word and pious discipline by wholesome Lawes enacted and made for that purpose, is by a Parliament, by that great and wise Councell expert in the sciences of good government of either a Church or common-Wealth.[11]

He went on to stress the importance of maintaining a strong House of Commons as a check against the powerful lords and bishops of the upper house. Shortly thereafter Maynard was one of those who conducted the prosecution of Archbishop Laud.[12] And in the summer of 1643 he was a lay member of the Westminster Assembly, which laid the foundations of later Anglo-American Presbyterianism.[13]

As one might expect of a lawyer, Maynard's championing of parliamentary privilege and religious reform was not carried to the point of advocating the abolition of the monarchy. In 1648 he resisted strongly the suggestion that Parliament should no longer negotiate with the king. In the subsequent debate concerning the army's remonstrance demanding justice against the king, Maynard is described as "arguing as if he had taken fees on both sides, one while magnifying the gallant deeds of the army, and then 'firking' them for their remonstrance, as tending to the destruction of the kingdom and the dissolution of the government."[14] Nevertheless, when the abolition of the monarchy was a *fait accompli,* Maynard seems to have settled down happily under the Commonwealth. Though he successfully defended the "Leveller," John Lilburn, in July, 1653,[15] he was created a serjeant the following February, and during the brief Protectorate of Richard Cromwell, Maynard served as his solicitor general. In 1640 Maynard had been appointed recorder[16] of Plymouth and sat in the Commons for that borough from 1656 to 1658. He was elected to the Convention parliament of 1660 for the borough of Beeralston in Devonshire, which he also represented during the long life of the "Cavalier" parliament.[17] He may be supposed to have welcomed the Restoration, ending as it did a period of near anarchy. He was made a King's Serjeant on November 9, 1660 and was knighted a week later.[18] For the next two decades he played no prominent part in politics except that he appeared as one of the Earl of Clarendon's defenders in the impeachment proceedings of 1667. Some of this time was devoted to preparing and editing his *Reports des Cases Argue & Adjudge en le temps del' Roy Edward le Second,* which was published in 1678. He evidently continued to make money at his profession. In addition to the Abbey House at Tavistock, where he had been born and which he rented and occupied, he also owned the manor of Beeralston, where he worked a silver mine, though without much success, and founded a charity school for eight free scholars. Beeralston was a parliamentary borough, and Maynard could always be sure of one of its two seats if he could not get elected elsewhere. Toward the end of his life he was able to purchase a magnificent mansion in Ealing, "Gunnersbury," which served for a while in the eighteenth century as a royal residence.[19]

Robert Atkyns, after some time spent at Sidney Sussex College, Cambridge, entered Lincoln's Inn in October, 1638, whence he was called to the bar in 1654.[20] He took his first step towards a political career in 1656 when he was elected member of Parliament for Carmarthen. In the Parliament of 1659–1660 he represented Evesham in Worcestershire. Though not a member of the Convention parliament, he was elected to the Cavalier parliament for Eastlow in Cornwall. He does not appear to have been very active in debate, however,[21] and finally gave up his seat in 1672 on his appointment as a justice of the Court of Common Pleas.[22]

In spite of his services to the Protectorate, Robert's father, Edward Atkyns, was appointed Chief Baron of the Exchequer and knighted by Charles II.[22] Some of the favor enjoyed by the father was evidently extended to the son, for Robert Atkyns was one of sixty Knights of the Bath given the accolade by King Charles on his coronation day.[23] The royal favor was further extended, unto the third generation, in September, 1673 when Charles, on a visit to Bristol, where Atkyns had been recorder since 1661, knighted his son, Robert Atkyns, Jr., together with the sons of several other leading citizens.[24] In June, 1662 Charles approved Atkyns' appointment as the queen's solicitor general.[25] In 1665 he was one of the commissioners appointed by the Crown to collect the extra tax money that Parliament had voted to meet the expenses of the Dutch war.[26]

So much royal favor seems to have enabled its fortunate recipient to amass a considerable fortune, for in May, 1671 we find a fellow tourist reporting from Saumur (in the Loire valley of France) that Atkyns was to be seen there "with his lady, a coach and six horses, a pack of hounds and half a dozen stable horses. . . ."[27] In that same month Atkyns received a royal appointment as "Receiver General" of all rates and duties granted by a parliamentary act levying certain impositions on proceedings at law.[28] In the two years that he held the office, before passing it on to his son in May, 1673, Atkyns made £1,000 profit from it.[29]

Atkyns was elevated to the rank of a serjeant-at-law on April 24, 1672, and shortly thereafter was appointed a justice of the Common Pleas.[30] He had already apparently been noted by some of the king's advisers as a potential enemy. The month before his elevation to the bench, Sir Robert Carr, chancellor of the Duchy of Lancaster, had written to Secretary of State Sir Joseph Williamson that, though he had not ever "believe[d] over well of Atkyns," he was "glad he is preferred thinking it will prevent his being in a place wherein he might do the king more disservice."[31] Presumably, Carr was referring to Parliament. Perhaps his enigmatically unfavorable report was due, in part at least, to complaints reaching the government during the previous decade that the Quakers in Bristol and the surrounding area were pursuing their sectarian activities almost completely unchecked.[32]

In June, 1676 Atkyns reportedly came very close to joining Sir William Ellis in being removed from the Common Pleas bench, apparently for having tacitly favored a petition from the City of London calling for a new parliament.[33] However, it was not until February, 1680, when his place on the bench was taken by Baron Thomas Raymond (who was promoted from the Exchequer), that Atkyns finally received notice of his dismissal from the Lord Chancellor.[34] On June 14, 1689 Atkyns testified before the House of Commons that his dismissal had been due to the hostility felt towards him by the two men who were then chief justices, Sir William Scroggs and Sir Francis North, because of his expressed objections to pensions for members of Parliament, his denial of the king's authority to censor books by proclamation without parliamentary approval, and his defense of the people's right to peaceably petition.[35] In 1680, faced with the crisis over Exclusion, Charles must certainly have wanted a bench of judges who would be as amenable to his will as possible. Scroggs and North must have persuaded the king that Atkyns' legal and political views made it unlikely that he would cooperate.

Little is known of the early career of William Jones. He entered Gray's Inn in May, 1647,[36] and it may be assumed that he was called to the bar the customary seven years later, in 1654. For the next seventeen years we know of him only what Roger North tells us: that by the later 1660s he had "the capital practice" at the King's Bench bar;[37] and John Evelyn's testimony that in 1677, faced with a legal problem, Evelyn thought it best to consult "that famous lawyer, Mr. Jones of Gray's Inn."[38] But despite his own high reputation, Jones was made exceedingly jealous, according to Roger North, by Attorney General Geoffrey Palmer's open patronage of Francis North, who was made a K.C. in 1668.[39] When Palmer died in 1670, he was succeeded in office by the solicitor general, Sir Heneage Finch.[40] Jones and North both aspired to the vacant solicitorship. However, neither one of them got the office at first, for it went to Sir Edward Turner, Speaker of the House of Commons. A year later, when Turner was promoted to Chief Baron of the Exchequer, the Duke of Buckingham used his influence with Charles on Jones' behalf, but the vacant office finally went to North. Jones had to be content with a K. C.[41] In November, 1673, when Finch was promoted to Lord Keeper, North became attorney general and Jones succeeded him as solicitor.

The final incident of this rivalry occurred in December, 1674 when Jones and North vied with each other for the vacant chief justiceship of the Common Pleas, following the death of John Vaughan. Buckingham's influence with the king had considerably diminished by this time, and so it is not surprising that North once again carried off the prize, with Jones once again following behind in North's footsteps, being given the attorney generalship. According to Roger North, Jones was driven by his deep disappointment at his failure to win out over Francis North on this occasion to make "the whole Scope of his future Government of himself" the securing of a position on the bench. It was for this reason, he says, that Jones after this began to associate more and more with the opposition to the Court.[42]

Following the breakup of the cabal and the rise of Danby to preeminence in the government, Jones' patron Buckingham had by the mid-1670s allied himself with the Earl of Shaftesbury in opposition to the Crown.[43] It is not altogether suprising, therefore, to find Jones also moving in opposition circles by this time. In February, 1676 Lord O'Brien[44] reported to Secretary of State Williamson that the attorney general was one of a "knot" of London critics of the government, headed by Sir Thomas Player,[45] that met in a certain coffee house almost every Sunday night. "These people,"

O'Brien claimed, "rely much on the Attorney's opinion in all things. They say frequently, He is a brave man."[46]

Whatever Jones' personal political sympathies may have been, he was still the chief law officer of the Crown and as such an instrument of Crown policy. When Charles became alarmed at the growing use of coffee houses for allegedly seditious meetings and decided to issue a proclamation for their suppression,[47] it was, ironically, Jones' task to draft the document. Roger North delights in telling us that on this occasion Jones' opposition associates, with mock seriousness, threatened him with parliamentary impeachment.[48] In January, 1676 Jones countered the king's action by presenting him with an opinion that coffee house licenses, once issued for a specific period, might not be revoked until that period was up.[49] Charles then had a second proclamation issued postponing the execution of the first until the following June. In the end the first proclamation never was enforced, though some of the more offensive coffee houses failed to receive new licenses when their old ones expired.[50] Meanwhile, Jones' close sympathies with the opposition made it likely that the time would eventually come when the king would no longer find it possible to employ him or when he himself would find that he could no longer serve the king with a clear conscience.

The two Devonshire cousins, George Treby and Henry Pollexfen, do not appear to have played much of a part on the national political scene before 1678. Pollexfen entered the Inner Temple in 1651, was called to the bar there in 1658, and was admitted as a bencher in 1674.[51] He evidently wasted no time in making a name for himself in his profession, for he is mentioned in Raymond's *Reports* as early as

1662—the earliest year in which he could have been admitted to plead at the bar of Westminster Hall.[52]

George Treby, unlike his cousin, spent some time at a university, matriculating at Exeter College, Oxford, in July, 1660. He entered the Middle Temple in October, 1663 and was called to the bar in June, 1671.[53] He appears to have spent the better part of the next few years engaged in legal and political activities in his home county. In the first week of March, 1677 his efforts were finally rewarded by victory in a by-election, and he entered the House of Commons as one of the two burgesses from his home town of Plympton. An attempt by his opponent to dispute the validity of his election met with no success.[54]

Treby's correspondence of 1677 reveals that he was working at the time with members of the Pollexfen family and other kinsmen and friends to further "the good cause" in Devonshire.[55] The precise nature of the "cause" is enigmatic, but it apparently involved a struggle by opponents of the Court in Devonshire against the power of Devonshire "Cavaliers" and above all an attempt to gain control of parliamentary seats in the county. The Pollexfens and the Trebys must have been, nominally at any rate, members of the Established Church,[56] but they probably worked in alliance with local nonconformists. Roger North, a Tory whose opinions in these matters must, therefore, be taken with a large grain of salt, described Pollexfen as "a fanatic, and (in the country) frequenter of conventicles; and one more notorious of this character was not to be found."[57] Of Treby he said that he was "no fanatic; but of the fanatic party, true as steel. His genius lay to free-thinking, and . . . made the scriptures and christianity, or rather all religion, a jest. . . ."[58]

Treby was appointed recorder of Plympton in 1678[59] and,

with his seat in Parliament, appears to have been useful as a liaison between the London and the Devonshire elements of Shaftesbury's followers.[60] In London itself he was active in opposition circles. In November, 1677 he came to the notice of the government when between four and five hundred copies of an "unlicensed and dangerous book," Bacon's *Historical Discourse of the Uniformity of the Government of England,* were seized in his chambers in the Middle Temple by officials of the Stationers' Company.[61] It is not clear from the records, however, whether Treby had the books because he was engaged in defending their owner, the bookseller John Starkey, or because he was intending to distribute them. Since he does not appear to have been proceeded against in any way, the former explanation appears to be the more likely.

William Williams matriculated at Jesus College, Oxford, in November, 1650, but in the very same month he also entered Gray's Inn, whence he was called to the bar in 1658.[62] During the ensuing decade he practiced the law in his native North Wales and in the adjoining English counties to such good effect that in 1665 one of his clients referred to him as "the leviathan of our laws and lands." During this period he also considerably added to his prospects by marrying Margaret Kyffin, a Denbighshire heiress.[63]

In April, 1667, at the age of thirty-three, he was elected by the mayor, sheriffs, and alderman of Chester to be recorder of their city—the metropolis of North Wales and the adjacent area of England. His wife's family connections may have been a factor in his obtaining the position, but it was undoubtedly mainly due to his own local reputation as "a very acute young gentleman." Sir Geoffrey Shakerley, the royal governor of Chester Castle, writing to Secretary Williamson in support of the mayor's request that Williams' election be confirmed by the Crown, testified that the recorder-elect was "a very ingenious man, and true son of the Church."[64]

William's election was confirmed by the Crown on April 20.[65] On July 16, he became a freeman of Chester. After his name on the roll, he was described as *"in lege eruditus."*[66] In the following years we find Williams writing from Wales to advise the mayor as to how best to deal with the activities of some "contumacious Quakers" in the city.[67] We also find Williams himself receiving a letter from the government warning him and the city justices of the peace not to interfere with the excise beer-gauger in the performance of his duty.[68] It seems likely that he had the possibility of his future election to Parliament in mind when he worked in London in 1671 to have the king agree to remit some of the outstanding taxes due from Chester. But his efforts were to no avail, and the money had to be paid the following year.[69]

The death of one of the members of Parliament for Chester, Mr. Thomas Ratcliffe, made a by-election necessary in February, 1673. It was reported to Secretary Williamson, before the election, that "the Royal party" could count on the support of two-thirds of the voters, while "the fanatics" would get the votes of the other third; but that the royalist vote was in danger of being split between two candidates, Williams and Colonel Robert Werden, who was a Gentleman of the Bedchamber to the Duke of York. Adherents of the Court had hoped that Williams "might have been taken off by means of the Lord Chancellor," but nothing had come of it, and he refused to withdraw his candidacy. The only reason that Williamson's correspondent could give for such obstinacy was that "he is a Welshman."[70] It seems most likely that it was this dispute between Williams and the

Court supporters in Chester that caused him to transfer his allegiance to the opposition. He wanted to get into Parliament, but since the Court party had another candidate, who had a prior claim to their support, he would leave the Court party and go elsewhere.

Williams' opponents professed themselves to be shocked by his ruthless campaign methods. He combined promises with threats. He promised that, if he were elected, he would pay the £40 debt still owing from the city to the king, that he would lend the city £500 for seven years free of interest, and that he would do most of his spending in Chester. On the other hand, he threatened that, if he were not elected, he would make "foreign artisans" free of the city, and that all those who voted against him would be disenfranchised and would be loaded with taxes without relief as long as he was the recorder.[71] On polling day, February 10,

> the writ was opened . . . , a poll desired and the court adjourned from the Hall to a field called the Roodee. The Recorder immediately after the adjournment threw off his gown leaped on men's shoulders, and commanded his party to carry him to the field . . . which caused such a crowd that nine men were smothered going down the stairs and many others crushed, some of whom are since dead.[72]

The throwing off of the gown was almost symbolic. The uniform of law and order was shed in preparation for the hurly-burly of practical politics. Williams was never again to depart so drastically from law and order.

Despite the fact that Williams had the support of the two sheriffs who were conducting the poll and that he enfranchised fourteen men during the course of the election so that they might vote for him, Werden was declared elected with a majority of fifty.[73] Williams would have to wait to enter into national politics. Even so we can see that, by 1673, Williams was not only a very able and successful lawyer but also a very ambitious man, one who had made an excellent marriage to an heiress, had secured the highest legal office in his part of the country, and was now resolved to enter Parliament. If the charges reported above, all of which admittedly were made by his opponents, are even partially true, we can see that he was a determined and ruthless politician and that, if the political group to which he belonged was unable or unwilling to further his ambition, he would abandon it and join the opposition.

Francis Winnington is reported to have spent some months at Trinity College, Oxford[74] before entering the Middle Temple in November, 1656. He was called to the bar *ex gratia*, less than four years later, in February, 1660. He became a bencher of his Inn in June, 1672 and reader and treasurer in the autumn of 1675.[75]

According to one contemporary account,[76] Winnington's forensic talent "consisted rather in speaking fluently, than in speaking Eloquently, and he knew how to Wrangle, better than how to argue." This same account implies that it was the lucrative profits of the profession that attracted the Worcester lawyer; and, indeed, as we have seen, by 1671 he had built up a lucrative practice.[77]

His influential connections probably helped him along the road to affluence. His first wife, Elizabeth, was a member of the illustrious Herbert family,[78] which probably assisted him in achieving by 1671 the position of "Standing Counsel" to Prince Rupert.[79] In 1672 he was appointed attorney general to the Duke of York, and in December of the same year he was knighted.[80] In January, 1673 he was appointed a K. C.[81] In November of that year it was rumored that he would succeed Sir Francis North as solicitor general.[82] The appointment went to Sir William Jones, however, and Winnington had to wait until December, 1674, when he was appointed to the solicitorship on Jones' promotion to the office of attorney general.

Apart from these lucrative professional appointments, Winnington was rewarded in June, 1674 with the reversion, upon the death of the Queen Mother, of rents worth £33 10s. 4½d. from the royal manor of Bewdley, near Worcester, where he was later to make his home.[83] He was also given the reversions, which were to fall due in 1735 and 1742, of ninety-nine-year leases on other lands and tolls belonging to the same manor.[84]

Winnington began his parliamentary career in February, 1677, when "by the King's command" he was chosen burgess for the royal borough of New Windsor in a by-election.[85] The solicitor general presumably was expected to add strength to the pro-Court party that the Earl of Danby was then building up, by means of influence and bribery, in the House of Commons.

Comparing the backgrounds of these seven men, we find that two of them—Maynard and Atkyns—were the sons of lawyers, though only one of them—Jones—had a father who had played an official role in national politics as a member of Parliament. We find that four of them—Maynard, Pollexfen, Treby, and Winnington—were members of the Middle Temple; two of them—Jones and Williams—were members of Gray's Inn; and one—Atkyns—was a member of Lincoln's Inn. Five of the seven—Maynard, Treby, Williams, Winnington, and Atkyns—had spent some time at a university, the first four at Oxford and Atkyns at Cambridge, but only Maynard completed the requirements for a bachelor of arts degree.

There is little or nothing in their respective backgrounds that can account for these seven lawyers having become particularly active in the Whig cause in the period 1678 to 1689. In considering the Inns to which they belonged, it may be noted that while only one of them belonged to the Inner Temple, which produced such notable Tories as the Finches, George Jeffreys, and Robert Sawyer, three of them did belong to the Middle Temple, which produced those staunch Tories Francis and Roger North. Four of the five who had attended a university had been to Oxford—the university of Laud and Clarendon—and only one had been to Cambridge —the university of Milton and Cromwell. Two things they all had in common. One is that they were all from the West or Southwest of England, both strongly royalist areas during the Civil War, but where cavalier influence had been enormously weakened by punitive taxation and other reprisal measures following the parliamentary victory. The other fact in common is that they were all lawyers. We have seen in the previous chapter how the political philosophy of the seventeenth-century lawyers was ultimately irreconcilable with the philosophies and policies of the Stuart kings. But the explanation for these seven particular lawyers having been among the opponents of the Court during all or most of our period of interest, instead of being ranged alongside the Finches, the Norths, Jeffreys, and Sawyer in its support, is only to be found, it seems, by examining their individual characters and the circumstances of their individual careers.

Pollexfen and Treby belonged to related families that were engaged in a local power struggle against the cavalier element in Devonshire. Williams, in 1673, had gone over to the opponents of the Court in Chester apparently because that was the quickest way to get elected to Parliament. Atkyns had commenced his career high in royal favor, and in 1677 continued to occupy the high position of a justice of the Common Pleas—though he was already becoming less and less secure in that position, owing to his constitutional scruples. Maynard, despite his Roundhead background, was a King's Serjeant in 1677 and having little to do with politics —that timid caution which is nearly always apparent in his political behavior kept him out of controversy. Jones' ties with his patron Buckingham had caused him to become involved with the opposition, but in 1677 he was still the senior law officer of the Crown. Winnington, his deputy, had been closely connected with the Court throughout his career and in 1677 continued to enjoy royal favor.

In June, 1677 Solicitor General Winnington, together with Serjeant Maynard, assisted Attorney General Jones in arguing the case for the Crown against an attempt by the Earl of Shaftesbury to secure his release from the Tower by means of a writ of habeas corpus. He had been imprisoned by the House of Lords for "high contempt," together with the Duke of Buckingham and Lords Salisbury and Wharton, because they had insisted that the long prorogation between November, 1675 and February, 1677 had automatically caused the parliament to be dissolved under a statute of Edward III requiring that parliaments be held at least once a year.[86] The earl, whose leading counsel was Williams, was unsuccessful in his bid for freedom;[87] but, though he returned temporarily to the Tower, his political career was by no means over. Before two more years had passed the king would be forced to take Shaftesbury into the government, and the earl would be close to becoming the most powerful man in England. Issues were to arise and crises to be precipitated that would force men to take sides. Both sides would call upon the lawyers to provide legal and constitutional arguments to back up their respective positions, and both sides would come to feel that those who were not for them must be against them. It was to become professionally and politically unwise, if not impossible, for outstanding lawyers to remain neutral—to keep out of the struggle between Court and Country, between Tory and Whig.

3

King, Lords, and Commons

CHARLES II'S SECOND, OR "PENSIONARY," parliament assembled for its seventeenth and final session on October 21, 1678 in the midst of national near-hysteria. This was the result of the horrific revelations made by Titus Oates of a "Popish Plot" to assassinate the king, massacre all Protestants, and put the Catholic Duke of York on the throne, and of the sensational discovery of the body of the apparently murdered Sir Edmund Bury Godfrey, the magistrate before whom Oates had made his first depositions. To the Whig opposition, led by the Earl of Shaftesbury, this opportunity must have seemed heaven-sent. The Old Presbyterians, resentful of the legal penalties against nonconformity and feeling that their liberties had been betrayed after the Restoration; the "Country" opposition, resentful of the small clique of apparently corrupt ministers, headed by the Earl of Danby, who surrounded the king, and desirous of a much greater voice, through Parliament, in the conduct of affairs; and finally the adventurers who attacked the ministers in order that they might supplant them—all now had, at last, found a cause that every loyal English Protestant could understand and approve, a cause that could carry them to victory at the polls and perhaps ultimately right into the royal closet itself.

The fact that the Duke of York was a Catholic, that his secretary, Coleman, was supposed to be one of the leading plotters, and that suspicion was being directed towards the queen meant that the friends of the Court were compelled to play down the whole matter. The leaders of the government, guiltily aware that under the smoke put up by Oates there smouldered the very real and dangerous fire of the secret treaties with Louis XIV, were in an embarrassing position. The Whigs, on the other hand, had nothing to lose and everything to gain. The government could be attacked for neglecting the security of the realm, while the opposition proved their loyalty by ruthlessly exposing in Parliament every facet of the treasonous plot and representing themselves as the true guardians of Crown, Church, and State.

The House of Commons was urged by the king, in his speech from the throne at the beginning of the session, to "leave the matter to the law,"[1]—presumably the king felt better able to handle the matter in his own best interests through his judges. The Commons, however, wasted no time in examining into the "damnable and hellish plot."[2] In this they were aided by Danby, who, contrary to the king's wishes but perhaps fearing more what they might do if left to their own imaginings, provided them with the main evidence that the government had gathered.[3] After petitioning the king to set a militia guard around London, the Commons set up committees to examine into Coleman's correspondence, to search the cellars of the Parliament House (where a mysterious knocking had been heard), and to search the fireworks store of a certain Monsieur Choqueux near the Savoy Palace.[4] The lawyers in the House were not employed in these matters, but as the Commons were, in fact, acting as the grand jury of the nation in the thorough examination of a plot, recourse to the lawyers soon became necessary. The names of William Williams, Serjeant Maynard, and Solicitor General Winnington appear in the list of members of committee after committee during this session,[5] notably of the committees set up to prepare the impeachments of the five popish lords implicated in the plot: the Earl of Powis and Barons Belasyse, Arundell, Petre, and Stafford.[6]

The House constantly found itself up against points of law that required professional clarification. For example, Captain Bedloe, a partner of Oates in the plot-mongering business, was worried because his pardon, in return for which he had offered to tell all he knew about Godfrey's murder (in which he himself claimed to have participated), did not specifically mention murder. Solicitor General Winnington informed the House with regard to this matter that:

> The pardon having passed the Seal, it is not to be mended by the Attorney General. But Mr. Bedlow may have a new pardon. If you doubt the insufficiency of this pardon, the King may grant another Warrant for one, and may let it be particular as to "murder"; for general words will not comprehend it.[7]

He was followed by Williams, who at the House's behest had been in consultation with Attorney General Jones over the matter and who spoke at some length on the precedents affecting it, finally ending by supporting Winnington's position.

One might have expected these lawyers, experienced in the sifting and weighing of evidence, to have had some doubts about the validity of Oates' testimony and to have expressed those doubts. William Williams had declared nearly two years before, when the liberty of a copartisan was at stake, that "men are not to be imprisoned upon notions,"[8] but now he and his colleagues, caught up in the national furor and with an eye to the main political chance, were prepared to hang men upon little better evidence.

It was Sir William Jones, of course, who in his capacity as attorney general had the duty of prosecuting most of those accused of involvement in the plot. Roger North tries to make it appear as though it were Jones himself who had fabricated the entire plot, and blames him for adding to the hysteria prevailing in London at the time by sending a message from his villa at Hampstead to his house in the city ordering his servants to move the firewood from his front cellar to the back "for fear of the fireballs of the jesuits." Jones' conscience, North felt sure, must have troubled him for having used "all the arts of his profession against the lives of so many poor men as he convicted to death for the plot."[9]

On October 18, 1678 in a report to the Privy Council on the evidence presented by Oates against the Jesuits accused of planning Godfrey's murder—William Ireland, Thomas Pickering, John Grove, and others—Jones the Whig reported his conclusion "that . . . this horrible and execrable Treason is fully and most Evidently proved not onely as to this most wicked Designe in general, but as to every one of the particular persons." However, the lawyer in Jones stressed that his findings were only valid "if the Testimony of Titus Oates bee to bee credited and that a single Witnesse in this Case of High Treason is sufficient."[10] A statute of 1552 had declared that two witnesses were needed to convict on a charge of treason. The relevant clause was generally considered to have been repealed by a clause in a later statute passed in 1554, but Coke and some other experts disagreed.[11] The courts, however, accepted the validity of Oates' testimony, and the problem of a second witness was settled the following month when Captain Bedloe added his testimony to that of Oates. Jones was thus enabled to prosecute the Jesuits successfully. He also led the prosecution in the judicial murder of Green, Berry, and Hill, Catholic servingmen whom Bedloe named as having actually carried out the murder of Godfrey.[12]

Serjeant Maynard appeared for the prosecution in the trial of the unfortunate Coleman and on November 28, in the House of Commons, lent all the prestige of his years and experience to the declaration that "Oates is not a liar."[13] All the Whig lawyers played a part in the prosecution of the unhappy "popish lords."

The papists, however, were for the Whigs but means to an end, that end being to remove Danby and the other ministers from about the king. William Williams particularly played a major role in bringing about the downfall of Secretary of State Sir Joseph Williamson and of Lord Treasurer Danby himself.

Two days before the beginning of the session in October, Williams had written to William Harvey, the mayor of Chester, advising him of what action to take towards some priests and Jesuits lately discovered in that city. He concluded his letter:

> The sudden death of sir Edmund Bury Godfrey, an active Justice of Peace in the county of Middlesex in the examination of persons about the late plott against his majesty, attended with many unhappy circumstances, must oblige all good subjects to search very strictly into subjects of this nature.[14]

The officials of Chester responded very satisfactorily to this call for vigilance. Early the following month they detained, because they were carrying no passports, a group of Irishmen who were returning to their country. They were found to be carrying commissions in the royal forces as well as other papers, all of which the mayor sent to Williams. The latter showed them to Secretary Williamson, whose signature appeared on the commissions, and Williamson wrote to the mayor explaining that the men had recently been dismissed from the royal service and that they ought to be permitted to continue their journey.[15]

But Williams had also shown the documents to his friends in the Commons. On November 19 he wrote to the mayor that: "these commissions have been the subject matter of much of the debate of the House yesterday . . ."[16] Cobbett records that on November 18:

> The Commons on being informed, that there were several commissions for Popish Recusants . . . not withstanding they had not taken the Oaths and subscribed the Declaration, according to the act of Parliament, and that they were countersigned by Sir Joseph Williamson, Secretary of State: the notice of this raised such a heat in the house, that they immediately sent Sir Joseph, as a member of their house, to the Tower.[17]

Williamson did not stay there long—the king procured his release within twenty-four hours—but he was sufficiently "compromised" that his eventual downfall was inevitable. He was dismissed from office the following February.

The prime target of the opposition leaders was, however, Lord Treasurer Danby. Powerful forces were combining at the end of 1678 against Charles' chief minister. He was no more hated by the Whigs than he was by the French government, which disliked having a man of his anti-French, pro-Anglican sentiments at the English king's side. On September 16 the French ambassador, Barillon, had written to Louis XIV that, although the opposition to Danby was very powerful, the treasurer had such a stranglehold on Parliament that a national revolt seemed the only conceivable outcome.[18] Now the Popish Plot scare offered an opportunity to unseat Danby by parliamentary action. Accordingly, Barillon was directed to offer his counsel and financial backing to the Whigs to the end that Danby might be destroyed and also that England might be rendered impotent on the international scene by internal political strife. By the gift of a pension the ambassador recruited a tool for Shaftesbury and his followers in the person of Ralph Montagu, a former ambassador in Paris and a personal enemy of Danby. Montagu possessed incriminating letters from Danby, written at the king's behest, on the subject of negotiating a French subsidy.[19]

Danby failed in an attempt to prevent Montagu from being elected to Parliament from Northampton and in a belated attempt to seize his papers on the ground that they contained treasonous material. Reading the transcript of the proceedings in the Commons on December 19, one gets the impression that the Whig leaders had all carefully rehearsed their parts. Their leader, Lord Russell, actually admitted that he knew what was in the letters that Montagu was about to produce to the House. After two of them had been read events moved smoothly to their preordained conclusion. Another opposition leader, Thomas Bennett,[20] said immediately: ". . . I would have the lawyers tell you, whether this you have heard be not worthy impeaching the Treasurer of Treason. . . ." Williams responded on cue: "Will any member aver this to be the Treasurer's letter?" After Montagu had done so, Williams began the denouncement:

> If this be his letter, there cannot be a more constructive treason than is contained in it. You have heard of Religion and Property apprehended in danger in several speeches. But when your laws are contemned by a Great Minister,

and they miscarry and are laid dead . . . [uproar]. Nothing ought to be imputed to the king, but this man, unless he clears himself upon somebody else must take the crime upon him. . . .[21]

There we have, summed up in a nutshell, an important part of the political philosophy of the Whig lawyers: religion and property are very important, but most important of all are the laws, for they guard all the rest. The trouble with the government is evil ministers—"nothing ought to be imputed to the king." This philosophy was to be expressed at much greater length in a pamphlet, "A Just and Modest Vindication of the Proceedings of the two last Parliaments of King Charles the second," put out by Sir William Jones and John Somers shortly after the dissolution of the Oxford parliament in March, 1681.[22] It stressed the necessity of the king's acting only on the advice of his council, so that "Reflections and Censures" could fall on ministers only, and the Crown itself could remain high in popular esteem and affection which was necessary for the stability of the state. They added that no minister could justify an unlawful act "under colour of the King's Commands, since all his commands that are contrary to Law are null and void; (which is the true Reason of that well-known Maxim, that the King can do no wrong)."

Williams moved for impeachment. Among those who followed him in denouncing Danby was Solicitor General Winnington. After the Whig leader Henry Capel, echoing Bennett, had said "if the gentlemen of the long robe will say this treason, I say so too, and shall think this a ground to impeach him," Winnington told the House that, although he had "a wife and children and some estate, and loyalty to [his] prince, and [hoped] to leave it to [his] posterity," nevertheless: "In this matter I shall deliver my opinion, and

I fear no man alive, let it fall where it will." There seemed to be a plot to destroy Parliament and the fundamental laws of the kingdom. The House should exercise its inherent judicial function and declare such activities to be treason. He, too, called for impeachment.[23]

The House finally voted, by 179 votes to 116, that there were sufficient grounds for impeaching the treasurer, and appointed a committee, which included Williams, Winnington, and Maynard, to draw up the articles. The matter was particularly recommended to "Lord Cavendish" (Russell's lieutenant in the House at this time) "and Mr. Williams,"[24] one political manager and one legal expert.

On December 21 Williams reported to the House six articles, prepared by the committee, accusing the treasurer "of High Treason, and other High Crimes, Misdemeanours and offences"; the House accepted all six after but little discussion.[25] On the 27th the Lords declined to commit Danby to the Tower;[26] and, in fact, his impeachment, as we shall see, was never to be successfully pressed. But the chief minister and, therefore, the Crown had finally lost that control of the House of Commons which the Crown had enjoyed since the Restoration. On December 30 the king prorogued the parliament and finally dissolved it on January 24, 1679.

The elections of February, 1679 showed that the anti-Court trend in the House of Commons reflected the general political trend in the country as a whole. Many of those elected in 1661 had lost their local standing and support. Many, of course, had long since died, and the Whigs made certain that the names of those who were known to have taken, or were suspected of taking, bribes from the Court were widely published. Williams was reelected to a seat for Chester. In January, at Danby's insistence, Winnington, having cast in his lot with the opposition, had been dismissed from his position as solicitor general. He was no longer considered a desirable representative for the royal borough of New Windsor, but he was elected to represent the city of Worcester in his own home district.[27] Treby worked successfully, both on his own behalf and for others, among the electors of Devonshire.[28] Also in Devonshire, Maynard was elected for both Beeralston and Plymouth; he finally decided to sit for the latter, a larger town that he had served as recorder since 1660.[29] The new House of Commons contained barely thirty or forty members upon whose vote the Court could rely.[30]

The king, now that Louis XIV had decided to support the opposition, had failed to get a new subsidy from France and was in a mood to be conciliatory. In his opening speech he reminded the new parliament, which assembled on March 6, 1679, that he had removed the popish lords from their seats in the upper house, that he had carried out the execution of several men convicted of involvement in the plot and in the murder of Sir Edmund Bury Godfrey, and "above all," that he had banished his brother the Duke of York from the kingdom. He then asked for funds to finance the disbanding of the army and for the payment of the fleet.[31] On one point Charles remained adamant. He refused to accept Sir Edward Seymour, a personal enemy of Danby, as Speaker of the Commons, despite several protests from the House. This action caused Williams to warn his colleagues, in what might perhaps be regarded as the keynote speech of the Exclusion parliaments, that:

> I have ever observed that prerogative once gained was never got back again, and our privileges lost are never restored. What will become of you when a popish successor comes, when in king Charles II's time, the best of

princes, you give up this privilege. When you have the oppression of a tyrant upon you, and all ill counsels upon you. Now you have none to struggle with, but ill counselors and a good prince. . . .[32]

A dissenting opinion was offered by cautious Serjeant Maynard, who expressed the fear that a quarrel with the king would merely cause the parliament to be again dissolved. He asked:

What is your evidence for the right that you pretend to? From Richard ii to Henry iv's time, there has been no denial of the Speaker that you have chosen. Because it has not been denied, cannot it be denied? Why do you let the Speaker excuse himself at the lord's bar, and not accept his excuse here. . . . This matter of right is not clear to me. But it is clear that we shall be ruined by a breach with the king.[33]

The breach was not to come yet. Moderation prevailed and, after a few days, a compromise was accepted by both King and Commons in the person of William Gregory, a moderate Whig.

Besides wanting to have at least some say in the appointment of its Speaker, the new House of Commons also showed a strong interest in seeing that the Court was prevented, as far as possible, from tampering with future elections. Because of the legal and constitutional aspects involved, the assistance of the lawyers would again be needed. When the customary Committee of Elections and Privileges, consisting of between four- and five-score members, was nominated on March 18, Treby was defeated in a bid for the chairmanship by Thomas Meres, who had been the Crown's nominee for Speaker.[34] However, Meres, perceiving in which direction the tide was flowing, very quickly aligned himself with the Whigs who, therefore, were presumably able to dominate the committee.[35] On March 19 the committee was ordered to take special notice of "all Miscarriages and undue Practices" on the part of local officials in the conduct of elections.[36] A week later Maynard and Winnington were among those named to a committee of some thirty members that was ordered to draft a bill for regulating elections and to consider particularly the judgment of the courts in the case of *Barnardiston* v. *Soame*.[37]

Sir Samuel Barnardiston, an opponent of the Court, had been a candidate in the by-election necessitated by the death of Sir Henry North, a member for Suffolk. He had received the greater number of votes, but a large number of his backers had been Dissenters and tradesmen. Sir William Soame, sheriff of Suffolk and a friend of the defeated candidate (Lord Huntingtower), had then made a double return on the grounds, rightly or wrongly, that many of Barnardiston's backers were not forty-shilling freeholders and were, therefore, not qualified to vote. On February 20, 1674 the House had voted to seat Barnardiston, who, in the following Trinity Term, sued Soame before the King's Bench for £3,000 damages, which according to Barnardiston's counsels, Solicitor General Jones and Serjeant Maynard, he had suffered because he had been prevented for a year from taking his rightful seat in Parliament and put to "great Expense and Charges" to assert his right. Chief Justice Hale and two out of the three puisne justices decided in Barnardiston's favor and allowed him £800 in damages and £98 in costs. In 1676, however, a Court of Exchequer Chamber, presided over by Lord Chief Justice North, who as attorney general had been leading counsel for Soame in the King's Bench hearings, decided six to two in favor of Soame, thus reversing the earlier verdict.[38]

The two dissenting justices in this latter hearing were Sir William Ellis and Sir Robert Atkyns. Atkyns' dissenting opinion, published after he had been dismissed from the Bench,[39] repeated Jones' and Maynard's argument before the King's Bench to the effect that, while the House of Commons alone had the right to control elections and had, in fact, decided in favor of Barnardiston over his opponent, yet the courts certainly had the right, even the duty, to compensate Barnardiston for the private wrong he had sustained. He cited Lancastrian and early Tudor statutes to show that a Knight of the County had a property right in the privileges and perquisites of his office.[40] Also, as had Jones and Maynard, he denied that a sheriff could claim judicial immunity in making election returns, because a sheriff was not then acting in a judicial capacity but merely in a clerical capacity.[41] But, Atkyns asserted, more significant than the wrong and injury done to the plaintiff was:

> the great Power and Interest of the Parties to the Action; and of those that concern themselves in the Example and Consequence of it, upon a politick Account, . . . there is a design to model the Parliament to the humour of the Court.[42]

It was this design that the House of Commons was concerned with in 1679.

Although consideration of election reform seems to have been allowed to lapse for a while, on May 1 the committee of March 26 was revived. William Williams specifically and all the lawyers in the House in general were added to the committee, which was again ordered to consider the case of *Barnardiston* v. *Soame* and to draft a bill for regulating elections. The drafting of the bill was particularly recommended to the care of Sir Robert Carr, Serjeant Maynard, and William Williams. A further committee, of some three dozen members including Williams, was appointed on the same day to search the Journals of the House for precedents for the punishment of local bailiffs and sheriffs guilty of making false election returns. But if the bill was ever even drafted no further action appears to have been taken with regard to it in the three weeks remaining before the parliament came to an end.[43]

Besides these constitutional struggles, the House resumed its role as a grand jury inquiring into the Popish Plot. On March 19 a committee was appointed to investigate the journals of the previous parliament and to report the next day on any unfinished business. On the 20th Winnington, the chairman, accordingly made his report, and it was resolved to appoint a "Committee of Secrecy" to collect information, prepare evidence, and draft articles of impeachment against the Catholic lords in the Tower. The same committee, to which Treby, Maynard, and Winnington were nominated, was further empowered to gain any more information that it could about the Plot and about the murder of Godfrey.[44]

Another order of the House on the same day, "that Mr. Speaker do send a letter to Mr. Williams and the rest of the members of the Long Robe that are now gone the Circuit, to summon them to attend the Service of the House,"[45] is symptomatic of a problem that had always troubled the House of Commons—that of enforcing attendance in the House on its lawyer members, who so often much preferred to be elsewhere earning fees.[46] An ordinance of Edward III's reign[47] had barred lawyers from membership in the Commons because, in an age when Parliament's functions were still primarily judicial, too many of them would have clients whose cases the House might be required to pass on. But the rule proved from the very first to be a dead letter, if for no other reason than the frequent need of the House for lawyers to provide it with legal information and advice, as now in the prosecution of the Plot. The fact that Williams alone is mentioned by name in the order seems to show that he was generally regarded as one of the leading legal experts in the House at this time.

Treby was made chairman of the Committee of Secrecy, which pursued its investigations with the aid of government funds to pay off informers.[48] While busy arranging for the popish lords' trials, Treby was also bothered, as politicians always are, with letters from home. A Mr. John Reepe of Plymouth wrote:

> because of the deep misery of many of mine, and many others' friends and relations, which they suffer, since the memory of living man, in Turkish slavery. I wish with all my heart you may be able to find some way to assist them.[49]

While his brother Henry wrote to ask:

> If Lord Peters [sic] is found guilty and his estate for-feited, and it be given to any person you know, or can make interest with. I desire you will endeavour to get me the office of collecting the rents of the manor of Brent, it being near me.[50]

One notes with pleasure that Treby did make some effort to help Mr. Reepe and his friends; it was no doubt politically wise to do so, though eighteen months later the ransom money still had not been made available, it having been delayed by the "Chancery gentlemen."[51] Brother Henry was doomed to disappointment: Lord Petre's impeachment was never carried through.

Another constitutional issue had been raised by the king's announcement on March 22 of a pardon under the Great Seal for Danby, a service which, as he reminded the Whigs, he had performed in 1677 for their leaders Shaftesbury and Buckingham.[52] Nevertheless, the announcement infuriated the opposition, who, it seemed, were to be balked of their biggest prey. It also raised the question, which was not to be finally answered until the Act of Settlement in 1701 : could a royal pardon be pleaded to an impeachment—the major constitutional weapon of the Commons in the seventeenth century?

Winnington, who bore Danby a particular grudge for having had him turned out of the solicitor general's office, expressed the feelings of the extreme Whigs in an angry speech which emphasized the limitations on the royal prerogative and as good as said that the monarch was but the paid servant of his subjects :

> The King cannot pardon treason against the government for then the government cannot be safe from evill ministers . . . a King should be a sanctuary of the people from oppressions of evill ministers but not a refuge of enemies to the government the protector of such an arch traitor as Danby. Sir, if Danby may be pardoned is this the way to secure Lawes and the Protestant religion? The King is a limited power, or ells he could not be as ours is, limitation is to the good and behoofe of the people, but if sheltering an open and notorious traitour, the minister of the present mischiefe, and common center in whom all the lines of ruine and confusion meet, is this for the good and behoofe of the people, prerogative is to abate the rigour of justice and not to illude and destroy it. If ministers may be pardoned at the prince's pleasure for all the wrongs that they do the people though the prince be sworne to protect the people from all wrongs, and is therefore trusted and paid there is no security in all our pretended free and legall Government, it is a mere cheate, we are all arrand [sic] slaves. . . .[53]

After a committee, headed by Winnington, had investigated the rather irregular procedure that had been used in granting the pardon, it was resolved to remonstrate by means of an "Humble Address" against the "Irregularity and Illegality of the Pardon."[54]

In this crisis Danby relied for advice primarily on Lord Chancellor Nottingham, who gave it as his opinion that nothing in the Common Law, the statute law, or the law of Parliament prevented the king from exercising his prerogative right of mercy by pardoning an impeached person. The argument that such pardons would prevent Parliament from exposing and punishing enemies of the state Nottingham countered by arguing that the king would have the least cause of anyone to protect such enemies.[55]

Henry Pollexfen, despite his connection with the opposition forces in Devonshire, was another of Danby's advisers. He was probably pleased to have such an eminent client, and the earl, for his part, probably thought it was a good idea to have among his counsel an able lawyer who had some influence with those who were out to destroy him. Pollexfen urged Danby to stand firmly on his pardon. He pointed out that the pardon was based on a royal prerogative that had never yet been successfully challenged, and that he could rely on the "King's interest" in the Lords to uphold it there. Even if the Commons were successful in outlawing such pardons, it could not be retroactive. If, on the other hand, the treasurer sought to defend himself by bringing out the full facts concerning the letters to France, "it would occasion many indecent reflections" on both himself and the king.[56] Pollexfen may have considered, even if Danby did not, that by pleading his pardon the earl was in fact tacitly admitting his guilt. Thus the minister would be hopelessly compromised while the honor of the monarch remained unsullied, which was always an important consideration with the opposition lawyers, if not with some other members of the opposition.

Winnington, meanwhile, sat as chairman of a committee which investigated the matter of "Secret Service" money paid to members of the previous parliament and reported his findings to the House on March 24. On the 25th he sat on the committee which drafted a bill of attainder against Danby to come into effect if he did not surrender himself by a certain date.[57]

On March 26, as part of the King's general policy of conciliation, Danby was compelled to resign the treasurership. The Commons bill of attainder against him having been commuted by the Lords to one of banishment, he finally surrendered to the Upper House, which committed him to the Tower, where he would remain for five years, a perpetual source of grievance to the Whigs.

A month later thirty leading members of the opposition, including Shaftesbury, the Earl of Essex, and the Marquess of Halifax, were included (together with thirty Tory supporters of the Court) in Charles' new, enlarged Privy Council. The Whigs not only controlled the Commons but also had a share in the king's council. They were next to seek to dispose of the Crown itself.

As Bishop Burnet pointed out,[58] the extremist Whig member of Parliament William Sacheverell first hinted at the exclusion of the Duke of York from the throne in the debate on Lord Russell's motion to address the king to ask that the duke be removed from his presence and councils on November 4, 1678. It is interesting to note that he mentioned it in a question put to the lawyers of the House:

> I have read a little in the Law, but I would have the Gentlemen of the Long Robe tell me, whether any degree or quality whatsoever, of a subject, can patronize any

correspondence with the King's enemies: or whether the King and the Parliament may not dispose of the Succession of the Crown. . . .[59]

No lawyer gave Sacheverell an answer right away, but the Whig lawyers, notably Winnington and Jones, were later to argue energetically in the affirmative.[60] For they and other Whigs felt that only Exclusion would suffice to save England from a despotism on the French model.

In April, 1679, however, Shaftesbury and the other new Whig councilors were not yet ready to talk of Exclusion. They preferred to consider possible limitations on a popish successor. The first Exclusion bill, which was introduced at this time in response to a report from Treby on the evidence that his Committee of Secrecy had gathered with regard to the duke's involvement in the Plot,[61] was backed by the rank and file members of the opposition who feared that too close association with the Court was making Shaftesbury and the other leaders inclined to adopt Tory views. Winnington's position at this time is rather enigmatic. On May 9 he made a speech on the Exclusion issue which was an odd mixture of procrastination and uncompromising firmness. He mentioned "the relation I have had to this great Prince, the duke of York." "But," he went on, "when I consider that the greatest thing in the world is at stake, I must argue to defend it." He stressed the importance of unity during the prevailing crisis and urged every member to show where he stood. There was to be no neutralism. But the goal of unity could best be achieved by putting Exclusion aside temporarily and concentrating on the trial of the five popish lords. Therefore, he suggested putting off discussion of Exclusion until after their trial, when it should be the very next piece of business, and then:

as this bill will be hard for the duke, so it is hard for us to be deprived of our civil liberties, which will be at the power of a prince that governs as the pope shall give his determination. When popery is introduced, but for one prince's reign, the pope will dispose of the royal family as well as of us; therefore when I speak against Popery, I speak for the royal family; and in speaking this, I speak for all good and virtuous men. If it be Exclusion or Banishment of the duke, let the Resolution be what it will, it is for our security.[62]

The House had sufficient confidence in Winnington to name him to the committee of reliable Whigs (of whom Williams was the only other lawyer) who were to draft a bill "to disable the Duke of York to inherit the Imperial Crown of this Realm."[63] But when this first Exclusion bill was voted on, on May 21, Winnington went out with the noes. The most likely explanation seems to be that he hoped to be taken back into the government. There was a rumor current at the time that, as part of the king's policy of conciliating the parliamentary opposition, the chancellorship was to be put into commission and that Winnington and Sir Robert Atkyns were to be among the commissioners.[64]

Williams and Treby voted for the bill. The cautious Maynard, perhaps diplomatically, was absent that day. The vote was 207 in favor and 128 against.[65] Six days later, however, the parliament was prorogued, and shortly thereafter dissolved.

When the second Exclusion parliament met on October 21, 1680 the Whig tide, which had threatened to engulf the throne, had already begun to ebb—though the Whigs may not have discerned the fact. Just a year before, when the parliament had first been called only to be prorogued from time to time for twelve months, Charles had apparently already made his irrevocable decision to oppose Exclusion.

The Whig councilors had been dismissed, rather to the relief of their followers, and the king had surrounded himself with Tory advisors who could be relied upon to back him up: Sunderland, Sidney Godolphin, and Laurence Hyde, who were later joined by the "trimming" Halifax, who transferred his allegiance away from the Whigs. The power of the purse was still great, however, so long as Louis continued to withhold subsidies from the king and to encourage the opposition. Therefore, Charles finally called Parliament into session in the hope of gaining more money for the fleet while refusing Exclusion.

The Commons at this time elected as their new Speaker, William Williams, who, as has already been noted, was probably the outstanding Whig lawyer in the two previous parliaments. He was not the only candidate. Henry Powle had been mentioned for the office and so had Treby, though the latter was eventually disqualified because of poor eyesight which would have prevented him from identifying members of the House.[66]

Why was Williams chosen? During his five years in the House he had shown a profound knowledge of parliamentary and legal procedure and constitutional precedent. He had always been fond of lecturing on the correct procedure to be followed. In March, 1678, for example, when Secretary Coventry protested that there was no precedent for addressing the king to ask him to prolong the session, Williams immediately referred him to an instance in Charles I's second year.[67] In June, 1678 he explained impatiently to the House, when they were discussing the recusancy of Sir Solomon Swale: "The question before you is not whether he be convicted, or not convicted of recusancy, but whether he is truly convicted or not in the exchequer of king's bench. . . ."[68] In October, 1678 he had reminded the House, when they were discussing a breach of the peace between two members, that: "By the Orders of the house, if you debate the censure they ought to withdraw."[69] In addition to being a seventeenth-century Erskine May, Williams had acquired much experience in the everyday activities of the House. He had been appointed to the Committee on Elections and Privileges only three days after first taking his seat.[70] He had served as chairman of several committees,[71] and on one occasion he had presided in the chair over a Committee of the Whole House.[72] Thus, in addition to having the necessary parliamentary knowledge, and being a reliable supporter of the Country party, he had presumably shown himself able to control the House in debate.

According to Williams' own account, he was told on October 19, just two days before Parliament assembled, that he was to be Speaker. The news was brought to him by Mr. Francis Charleton, member for Ludlow and a kinsman of Sir Job Charleton who had been Speaker in 1673.[73] The decision was presumably reached at a meeting of the Whig leaders. If so, the fact that news of it was brought to Williams by a messenger indicates that he was not himself in the inner councils of the party at this time. Probably a small group, something like a modern "shadow" cabinet, consisting of Shaftesbury, Buckingham, Cavendish, Russell, and one or two other aristocrats, made the important decisions.

Williams was nominated by Lord Russell,[74] and his seconder, following the pattern of Gregory's nomination, was almost certainly Lord Cavendish. Those two Whig leaders in the Commons had recently been ousted from the Privy Council, to which they had been appointed a month after Gregory's election, so that the precedent of nomination by non-privy councilors set in the previous parliament was continued. But now we should note the growth of a second precedent. Russell and Cavendish were able to nominate the Speakers because they controlled the votes of the vast majority of the members of the House. Thus in 1678–1680, when political parties were first beginning to acquire some sort of corporate entity, we see the development of two precedents that have controlled the election of the Speaker ever since: first, that the majority party has the right to make the nomination whenever the office falls vacant, and second, that the nomination is always made by two distinguished private members.[75] Under the modern constitutional system, of course, Russell and Cavendish would be disqualified from making the nominations in accordance with the first precedent, because as the leaders of the majority they would be in the government and so would not satisfy the requirements of the second.

The various accounts that we have of Williams' career all emphasize that he was elected to the chair "unanimously." But this was usually the case. Obviously there is little to be gained by the minority in opposing the choice of the majority, unless there is very good cause to do so; and the majority, for equally obvious reasons, will generally nominate someone who is widely acceptable. In February, 1673, when Sir Job Charleton had to resign from the chair on account of ill health, Edward Seymour was proposed by Secretary Coventry, seconded by Sir Robert Carr, Chancellor of the Duchy of Lancaster, and, after the customary show of reluctance, took the chair. Though the *Journal* does not say that he was elected unanimously, there is no record of any opposition to him.[76] When in February, 1678 Sir Robert Sawyer was nominated by Coventry and Secretary Williamson to replace Seymour, who had fallen ill, a second name was put in nomination. We do not have the names of the nominators nor the nominee, but it seems likely that, the numbers of the

Court and Country parties being just about equal, the latter felt that they had a good chance of having a candidate elected. This second nomination worried the House, which had to go back to the first year of James I to find a precedent. Finally, when the clerk of the House first put the name of Sir Robert Sawyer, it "was carried in the Affirmative by much the greater Number of Voices, without any division of the House."[77] There is no mention of any opposition to the election of Gregory in 1679.[78] Thus Williams' unanimous election may be regarded as being according to the rule rather than as an exception.

In other respects, however, the election of Williams was quite noteworthy. For one thing, although Welshmen had been attending Parliament for almost a century and a half, since the reign of Henry VIII, Williams was the first Welsh member to hold the office of Speaker.[79] It is interesting to note that his successor, Sir John Trevor, was also a Welshman. And Williams, as if to mark the occasion, did not make the customary modest speech protesting his unworthiness for such a great responsibility. Sawyer had:

> made a gratulatory speech to the house for their favour and respect; desiring their leave to intercede with his majesty to excuse him from undertaking so great and difficult an employment which . . . he conceived himself not able to perform.

Gregory had spoken in similar terms,[80] but Williams said:

> It were vanity in me by arguments from weakness and unfitness to disable myself for your service in this Chair at this time. The unanimous voice of the House calling me to this place precludes me, and leaves me without excuse. Whom the Commons have elected for this trust is to be supposed worthy and fit for it; wherefore I must acquiesce in your commands.[81]

He went on to tell them:

> that he was their own Minister, their own only, their own entirely, and that he expected no boon, but by their grace and favour, to depart as he came, when they should be pleased to command him.

The next day he went before Charles "with the air of one, who expected but disdained to court, his Majesty's approbation."[82] The king, presumably anxious to get his money, and not wanting a repetition of the crisis that had marred the opening of the previous parliament, granted it.

As Speaker, Williams was not able to participate in debates, and material is scarce by which we can discover much about his opinions or actions in the last two Exclusion parliaments. We do know that he kept in touch with his constituents, who had been so helpful over Williamson. Before the 1680 parliament met, he had written to the mayor and corporation thanking them for reelecting him. Apparently, he did not find it necessary actually to go to Chester and campaign. The following February he was writing again to arrange for his election to the Oxford parliament. On December 14, 1680 he wrote to the mayor asking for a list of all papists in Chester.[83] On December 23 he reported to the House that there were only thirteen on the list, none of them worth bothering about.[84]

One writer tells us that Williams "succeeded in degrading his office to a lower depth than any of his predecessors had found possible." He paints a picture which would seem to be an adaptation of the coarse and violent bully image customarily presented of Williams in the Trial of the Seven Bishops. He tells us that the Speaker "hounded the house on to its worst excesses":

> One of the vile witnesses at the Bar swore that Stafford had proposed the murder of the King; the members burst

forth into a roar of savage applause; with flaming face and hoarse voice, amid frequent oaths, Williams led the cheers.[85]

When this ignoble scene occurred, if it ever did, is hard to determine. The preparation of the evidence against Stafford was conducted by a committee of the House, with Williams out of the chair.[86] The trial itself, of course, was carried out by the Lords, though with the Commons present. According to Evelyn "the whole trial was carried on from first to last, with exceeding gravity."[87]

Not that Williams was not capable of invective. He told the kneeling Sir Francis Wythens, who was being expelled from the House for "abhorring":

> You being a lawyer have offended against your own profession, you have offended against yourself, your own right, your own liberty, as an Englishman. This is not only a crime against the living, but a crime against the unborn. You are dismembered from this body.[88]

To Sir Robert Peyton, expelled from the House for his alleged implication in one facet of the Popish Plot, he said:

> You are one of them that have played your own game and part; and that all men may take notice, you are a warning for all other members, and I hope here are none such. It shows that this parliament nauseates such members as you are.[89]

Strong words, yes; but they certainly are not coarse, nor were they brutal by seventeenth-century standards.

Peyton, a couple of months after his expulsion, challenged Williams to a duel. But for this the Speaker reported him to the Privy Council, which had him arrested and placed in the Tower.[90] Peyton had challenged the wrong man. Men of the robe would be at a disadvantage against young aristocrats brought up to arms, if dueling ever became a common feature of politics. This, plus the fact that his legal mind would naturally disapprove of settling differences by armed violence, is probably what had impelled Williams to propose in 1675 an act to make anyone fighting a duel incapable of pardon.[91]

Even as Williams was elevated to the chair of the House of Commons, Russell, Winnington, Titus, Bennett, and the other Whig leaders on the floor of the House were joined by an even more celebrated legal expert, Sir William Jones. The opposition leaders had been gratified by Jones' handling (as attorney general) of the Popish Plot. When Shaftesbury and the other Whigs had been ousted from the government in October, 1679, Jones had insisted on resigning with them.[92] Contemporary accounts differ as to his motives for resigning his lucrative office. Roger North—who sees all of Jones' actions in the latter part of his career as being motivated by a desire to get the better of his hated rival Francis North[93]— claims that Shaftesbury's lieutenant, Arthur Capel, Earl of Essex, persuaded Jones that ultimate victory must soon come to the Whigs, and that if Jones would openly throw in his lot with them, he should soon replace North as Chief Justice of the Common Pleas. Burnet, on the other hand, claims that Jones was offered the greater prize of the chancellorship if he would stay on. Both North and Burnet agree that Jones was "weary" of serving a Court with whose policies he could not in essence agree.[94] We can surely presume that he felt that the view of the constitution that he, as a common lawyer, believed in could at that particular juncture of affairs best be served by his leaving the government and entering Parliament. As Elkanah Settle rather romantically explained it:

> To Naked Truth's more shining
> Beauties true,
> Th' Embroidered Mantle from
> his Neck he threw.[95]

The Whigs were annoyed at Jones' refusal (in December, 1679) to sign a petition calling for an immediate session of Parliament.[96] But as a good lawyer and quondam law officer of the Crown he knew that the decision as to when to summon Parliament belonged irrefutably to the royal prerogative. By the time Parliament finally did meet in the following October, Jones was reported to be well in with the Whig leaders.[97] Ambassador Barillon reported to Louis XIV that if the Whigs ever managed to gain control of the government the former attorney general was certain to become chancellor, unless Shaftesbury wanted the position for himself.[98] In the meantime, Jones was returned to Parliament as comember (with Serjeant Maynard) for Plymouth,[99] on November 3, 1680, in a by-election. His appearance in the House of Commons among the champions of Exclusion did much to help that cause. William Temple recalled that the Exclusion movement benefited greatly from:

> Sir William Jones entering upon it so abruptly and so desperately as he did, if I mistake not, the first day he came into the house . . . which was sometime before the session began, having been engaged in a disputed election. And this person having the name of the greatest lawyer in England: and commonly of a very wise man; besides this of a very rich and of a wary or rather timorous nature; made people generally conclude that the thing was certain and safe, and would at last be agreed on all parts, whatever countenance were made at court.[100]

Jones and Winnington, sitting next to each other and working in close association, were the leading proponents of the second Exclusion bill.[101] For Winnington had now definitely come out for Exclusion and seconded the motion of Lord Russell for the bill,[102] which not only debarred James from the succession but declared him guilty of high treason if he should exercise authority or return to England after November 5, 1680.

Secretary Jenkins put the case for the Court on November 4. He claimed that the bill was contrary to natural justice because it condemned without conviction and did not give the injured party a chance to speak in his own defense. It was contrary to religion because it dispossessed a man of his right solely for a difference in a point of faith. What was more, the kings of England held their right from God alone, and no power on earth could deprive them of it. The passage of the bill would serve to make the monarchy elective. Finally, it was against their oath of allegiance, for by binding all persons to the king, his heirs, and successors, the oath included the duke as heir-presumptive.[103]

To these arguments Jones and Winnington countered on November 11 with the claim that the supreme law was the public good, and that the bill was, therefore, perfectly in accord with the principles of "natural justice." The bill, Jones argued, aimed not at the condemnation of the duke but at the protection of themselves. The basis of natural justice and religion was the preservation of the Crown and kingdom and overrode any individual interest. The oath of allegiance, he maintained, was intended to protect against popery, not to foster it, and he denied that it applied to the successor. Far from being opposed to the Anglican Church and religion, the bill aimed at protecting them. Against the argument that the bill would lead to civil war he claimed, incidentally answering Sacheverell's question of two years before, that

> to doubt that the legislative power of the nation, king, lords and commons, cannot make laws that shall bind any, or all the subjects of this nation, is to suppose that there is such a weakness in the government as must infallibly occasion its ruin.[104]

The Protestant majority, he went on, would ensure the upholding of the bill; there would be a much greater danger of civil war without it. The term "heir-presumptive," he informed them, was not to be found in the law books, and he finished with a warning that the nation would continue disrupted until all fear of a popish successor was removed.

Winnington expressed similar ideas:

> The King hath his right from God, and as supreme, is accountable to none; his person sacred and by our laws can do no wrong. If we should give all these qualifications to a successor, as hath been in some measure insinuated, it would make a strange confusion in the government. Life itself, to which a man hath as much right, as any successor can pretend to have to the crown, is taken away upon some forfeitures for the public good. And as there may be a forfeiture for life, so there may be a forfeiture of a right to the Succession. And to doubt that there is not an unlimited, uncontrollable power, residing somewhere in all governments, to remedy the exigencies that may happen, is to suppose there is such a weakness in this or any other government as that it must fall when a powerful fraction shall endeavour it. In this nation the power is in the king, lords and commons, and I hope they will make use of it to preserve the government upon this occasion. . . .[105]

Unfortunately for Whig hopes, the key phrase in all this was "kings, lords and commons." The king was opposed to Exclusion, and although he did not control the Commons in 1680 he did command a majority in the Lords. So that, although the Commons passed the second bill on November 11,[106] in spite of all Shaftesbury's efforts it was defeated in the Lords after a stormy debate by sixty-three votes to thirty.[107]

The prime mover of its defeat was Lord Halifax, who finally got the better of Shaftesbury in a forensic duel that lasted seven hours. Halifax cited the Duke of York's high reputation in Ireland and with the fleet. He urged the opposition to be content with legislating limitations to be imposed on the duke's power, if and when he became king, warned of the dangers of civil war if they persisted in their present extreme course, and finished by attacking them for their opportunistic political dealings.[108]

The disgruntled Commons solaced their feelings by passing a resolution on November 17 condemning Lord Halifax as an enemy of the king and kingdom and by beginning impeachment proceedings against Chief Justice Scroggs for undue leniency in the prosecution of the Plot, against Edward Seymour, the treasurer of the navy, for misuse of funds, and against Chief Justice North for his condemnation of the petitions[109] which earlier in the year had demanded a parliament.

During December and the first week of January bills were brought in against the English Roman Catholics as a class. One of these, drafted by Jones, Winnington, and three others, would have banned all Catholics from an area of twenty miles around London and would have forbidden them to ride horses or go armed anywhere in the kingdom. Another, drafted by Winnington alone, would have banished all "considerable papists" from the country. A third sought to facilitate the detection of the use of lands for "superstitious" (Roman Catholic) purposes. None of these bills ever got beyond the committee stage.[110] On the other hand, a bill to repeal the 1593 act against Protestant Dissenters, which aimed at winning the support of Nonconformists for the Exclusionist cause, was successfully passed through both Houses.[111]

Meanwhile, in the first week of December, 1680 the Commons successfully completed the impeachment before the Lords of the aged Catholic peer Lord Stafford. The lawyers were, of course, as active in these grand-jury functions as they had been in the constitutional ones. Treby's Secret Committee prepared the case against Stafford. Henry Powle, Jones, and Winnington managed the prosecution on behalf of the Commons. Serjeant Maynard opened for the prosecution and was ably seconded by Winnington, who "most eloquently aggravated the circumstances." After Treby had elicited from Oates and other eager witnesses full details of the treasons allegedly committed by the unhappy peer—he had, they swore, accepted a commission from the pope and plotted the assassination of the king—Jones summed up the case against him.[112] Lord Stafford was found guilty by his fellow peers and put to death on Tower Hill soon afterwards.

Shaftesbury's failure to get the Exclusion bill through the Lords served to discredit him with some of his followers. A group of the less scrupulous Whigs in the Commons began to treat separately with the Court, offering a generous tax appropriation in return for Exclusion and offices for themselves. The group was led by Montagu and encouraged by the Duchess of Portsmouth (the king's French mistress, who had a feud going with the Duke and Duchess of York), and favored the bastard Duke of Monmouth for the succession. Jones and Winnington were brought into this group by the promise of the chief justiceship of the Common Pleas and the attorney generalship, respectively.[113] Indeed, the king seems to have been anxious to enlist the support of the lawyers at this time, for Williams was offered the chief justiceship of Cheshire (Sir George Jeffreys having been recently ousted from that office at the demand of the Commons) and the attorney generalship.[114] Charles apparently made no objection to Treby's taking another post that Jeffreys was forced to give up in December, 1680, that of recorder of London, even though he had personally recommended Jeffreys for the post two years before and had paved his way into it by promoting the previous incumbent, Sir William Dolben, to the bench. The ambitious Winnington, however, was reportedly made very jealous by the appointment, considering himself more deserving of it.[115] In January the king bestowed on Treby the knighthood that would normally go to the holder of so prominent an office and in February commissioned him a justice of the peace for the cities of London and Westminster and for the counties of Middlesex, Surrey, Kent, Essex, and Devon.[116]

But Williams and Treby remained staunch Whigs, and Charles' irrevocable opposition to Exclusion prevented Montagu's scheme from having any chance of success. The Whig party once again closed ranks behind Shaftesbury. On January 7 resolutions were passed characterizing Halifax and other ministers as "Promoters of Popery" and "Enemies of the Kingdom," declaring that until Exclusion was enacted no taxes could be granted, and warning that anyone who lent money to the Crown upon the security of the Excise in order "to hinder the sitting of Parliament" would be held personally responsible to that august body.[117] The astute Winnington sought to cover his tracks by seconding a resolution, which had been inspired by rumors of Montagu's activities, that no member should be allowed to accept a place from the Crown.[118] The king, seeing that he could expect nothing but arguments from this parliament, prorogued it on January 10 and declared it dissolved ten days later.

In the third week of March, 1681 there assembled at Oxford a new parliament, one which was to witness the last brief round of the parliamentary struggle between Charles II and the Whigs. The members had been summoned to the South Midlands university city in order to deprive the opposition of the moral support of their partisans in London. The

Whig members, however, were left in no doubt that they enjoyed a considerable measure of popular support. As the London representatives left the capital for Oxford, riding on horseback (except for Treby, who traveled in his coach), they were escorted as far as Hounslow by "several hundred eminent citizens," also mounted.[119] Both Treby and Williams were returned to the new parliament without the necessity of campaigning in their respective constituencies or even visiting them.[120] The same was probably true of many other Whigs.

Among those traveling to Oxford that week was Sir Robert Peyton, released on bail from the Tower at the end of January and now hurrying to make his peace with Williams.[121] The latter was again unanimously reelected as Speaker. In his acceptance speech he told the House that his reelection showed that the feeling of the country and of the House was just what it had been during the last parliament, and he urged the members to "speak little and act well." The next day he told the king that the Commons had elected him "with one voice," to show "to your majesty and the world that they [were] not inclinable to changes." It is recorded that Williams "had not the good fortune to please the king, on this occasion."[122] Charles, however, had perhaps from the beginning no intention of keeping the parliament in existence for long unless it proved unprecedentedly willing to come to terms with him, and he probably did not much care who the Speaker might be. At all events, Williams was accepted.

The House of Commons immediately turned its attention to unfinished business left over from the previous parliament. Angry inquiries were made as to why the bill repealing the Elizabethan act against Dissenters had never gone to the king for his signature.[123] New bills were ordered to be drafted for the better uniting of Protestant subjects and for the banishing of all "considerable Papists."[124] Jones and Winnington were appointed to a committee that, under the chairmanship of John Hampden, was to inquire into what progress, if any, had been made towards the impeachment of the unhappy Danby.[125]

But the issue uppermost in everyone's mind was Exclusion. The king, probably on the advice of Halifax, was prepared to compromise to the extent of offering "limitations" on the Duke of York's right to the succession. Thus, the duke would be banished from the kingdom during the remainder of Charles' lifetime. On Charles' death, the duke's daughter Mary and, if she died without heirs, then the other daughter, Anne, would become regent for their father. But if the duke ever had a Protestant son, that son would take over the regency on coming of age. Privy Councilors would be nominated by the regent, but subject to the approval of Parliament. And during the course of all this, it would be a capital offense for anyone to take up arms on James' behalf.[126] In sum, James would be altogether a *roi fainéant*. The majority of the Court hoped that the Commons could be induced to accept these concessions. To an impartial observer of today they must appear clumsy and unworkable, and that is precisely how they appeared to the Whigs in March, 1681. On the 26th Jones voiced the objections of the Whigs in general and the Whig lawyers in particular to the "limitations" proposals. Firstly, he objected that a son or daughter of the duke, if made regent, would be too likely to yield to the father's wishes; secondly and above all, he objected that:

if you do not exclude the duke's title by law, the duke is king still, and then learned lawyers will tell you, that by the 1st Henry vii all incapacity is done away by his being king . . . lawyers will tell you it cannot be done.[127]

Neither King nor Commons being prepared to give way any further, it was left to Louis XIV to tip the scales. The French monarch finally decided, in that same crucial month of March, that the interests of his country and his religion would now best be served by supporting Charles and the Duke of York. A secret subsidy was quickly arranged,[128] and the king, relieved of financial pressure and seeing that the House of Commons was "not inclinable to changes" and was bent on Exclusion and nothing but Exclusion, dissolved the parliament on Monday, March 28. More than four years would pass before another parliament would be summoned —summoned by the very prince whom the Whigs had sought to exclude, and whose exclusion the Whig lawyers had sought to justify.

4

Quo Warranto

DURING THE PERIOD OF THE SO-CALLED EXCLU-
sion parliaments the Whig lawyers had served Shaftesbury,
Russell, and the other opposition leaders as useful auxil-
iaries. Because of their courtroom experience, they were
usually the most persuasive and articulate of the Whig
spokesmen. Most important of all, they possessed the constitutional and legal knowledge and skills needed to conduct a
campaign of parliamentary opposition to the Crown. In the
period after the Oxford debacle the ordinary Whig politicians, the leaders and the led alike, were deprived of a forum
in which to express their views. The lawyers, however, still
had the courts—in which they alone were licensed to speak
—and so it was that the Whig lawyers became the only
legitimate spokesmen (before the king's justices and in the
hearing of juries of his subjects) against the policies and
actions of the Crown.

The renewal of subsidies by Louis XIV allowed King
Charles summarily to dissolve the determinedly Exclusionist
Oxford parliament, ridding him—as it turned out, for the
balance of his reign—of the only major obstacle to his desire
(and that of his father and grandfather before him, and

perhaps that of every English king) to conduct the affairs of his kingdom as he himself thought best, with the advice of only a few personally chosen advisers. But other, if lesser, hindrances to unfettered executive rule still remained: most notably, the independent liberties and franchises exercised by the many city and borough corporations of the realm, as well as by trading and other sorts of corporations. As that arch-apostle of strong government Thomas Hobbes had remarked, such corporations seemed "as it were many lesser common-wealths in the bowels of a greater, like worms in the entrails of a natural man."[1]

The cities and borough towns derived their privileges from charters that were, in most instances, medieval in origin and, despite frequent later revisions, still essentially medieval in form, as well. The municipal corporations existing by virtue of these charters were in many instances small, often corrupt oligarchies dominated by and run for the benefit of a small number of bourgeois families and sometimes of one or more local landed magnates. Some cases existed—for example, Old Sarum—where the privileges enjoyed by the corporation had outlived the very town that the corporation was supposed to govern. But in spite of their defects and even, in some cases, "rottenness," the Whig opposition fought fiercely to protect the status quo in these corporate towns and cities. They did so for the very same reason that the king sought to replace their charters of privileges with new ones modeled more to his own liking and convenience: because they sent the majority of the members to the House of Commons and within their limits certain stipulated immunities existed against the force of royal writ. And, whereas in Parliament the Whig lawyers, though playing an important part, had been just a few of the voices raised amongst many in the clamor of debate, the fight to save the corporation charters was by its nature a legal battle fought almost entirely by lawyers alone. "It is now come to a Civil War," noted a contemporary observer, "not with the sword, but law. . . ."[2]

Events in London—the metropolis of the realm and its greatest corporate city—in the months following the dissolution of the Oxford parliament demonstrated clearly to the king what a nuisance a powerful corporation dominated by opponents of the Court's policies could be. The situation was probably not so bad as was suggested by the informer who told Secretary of State Leoline Jenkins that Sir George Treby, recorder of London; Sir Frances Winnington; Sir Robert Clayton and Sir Thomas Player, who had been members for the City in the Exclusion parliaments; Sir Richard Cust; Mr. Stroud; and Mr. Thomas Pilkington—at a "grand cabal" in the King's Head Tavern in Fleet Street on April 7, 1681—had declared that they "were for a free state and no other government."[3] In fact the City leaders obviously realized in which direction the political wind was blowing, for just two days before the rumored "grand cabal" Treby and the lord mayor, Sir Patience Ward, had conferred with the judges of the King's Bench over the withdrawal of an indictment presented by the City against the Duke of York for recusancy.[4] Some three weeks later the lord mayor, Treby, and the other members of the City's Court of Aldermen rejected two petitions, one of them presented by such eminent citizen as Player, John Dubois, Sheriff Slingsby Bethell, and Thomas Papillon, calling for a meeting of the Common Council in order to petition the king for a new parliament.[5] But the Common Council did meet on May 13 and on that occasion received an identical petition presented by Player. The council, in response, prevailed upon the aldermen to approve an address to the king requesting an immediate parliament, and also to approve a motion of thanks to those who had presented the petition. Treby, Player, Clayton, Pilkington, Dubois, and some others were nominated to draft the address, and Treby was to head a delegation to present it to His Majesty on May 15.[6]

One gets the impression from the above that during this period Treby, Lord Mayor Ward, and the other official leaders of the City, while they certainly sympathized with the Whig opposition to the Court, for understandable reasons would rather not have been too conspicuous in any deliberate flouting of the king's known will, but they were under constant pressure to act from the more extreme Whigs, such as those who brought in the petitions. Apart from the story of the cabal, the only specific mention that we have of actual participation by the recorder in partisan activities at this time is the reported boast by one of the Earl of Shaftesbury's secretaries, Samuel Wilson, that Treby was one of the "honest and ingenious men" responsible for managing Whig party finances in the City.[7] Treby's services were constantly sought by the activists, of course, because they realized the necessity of keeping their acts of defiance within at least the letter of the law. And Treby, because he agreed with their basic position, would not refuse; nor could he refuse, presumably, if he wished to remain the City's recorder. Nevertheless, in spite of the pressure, Treby seems to have remained within the king's good graces, for when he waited on the king on October 15, 1681—with the two new sheriffs, Pilkington and Benjamin Shute, who had succeeded Bethel and Henry Cornish in that office only a month before—to invite him to dine at the guildhall on Lord Mayor's Day, he was not included when Charles took the opportunity to chide the sheriffs for being "such disrespectful persons."[8]

By his own lights the king had good cause to be displeased

with the sheriffs of London. It was they who empaneled the London and the Middlesex juries—an important privilege at a time when juries tended in making their decisions to pay at least as much attention to political considerations as to the evidence presented in court. The government had its first inkling of what was to come when the then London recorder George Jeffreys was conducting a prosecution on behalf of the City in September, 1680. The lord mayor and aldermen sought an indictment from the London grand jury against the publisher of a pamphlet, rumored to have been written by Slingsby Bethel, criticizing their handling of the City's financial affairs. The publisher confessed and five witnesses swore to his guilt, but the jury empaneled by Sheriff Bethel brought in a verdict of *Ignoramus*. Jeffreys, who can hardly have been regarded as impartial himself "when he had laid home to them the monstrous perjury of such a return," sent them out to try again, but again they found *Ignoramus*. "Such a thing was never heard of before," according to Secretary Jenkins.[9] The following year, with the City leaders united against the Court and with Pilkington and Shute picking the juries, Jenkins and his royal master were to see several instances of just that sort of thing.

Soon after the dissolution of Parliament Charles and his ministers began their counterattack by initiating judicial proceedings against members of the opposition. They began with a comparatively minor figure, one Stephen College—a London joiner who was charged with seditious words and acts during the Oxford session. The Middlesex grand jury failed to find a true bill indicting their fellow citizen, thereby forcing the government to move the prosecution to Oxford, a city whose officials were much more closely controlled by the Crown and where College was quickly tried, condemned, and put to death in August.[10]

In the second week of October the Middlesex justices of the peace, under the chairmanship of Jeffreys, clashed with the sheriffs over the composition of juries. On October 12 the justices summoned the sheriffs to appear before them in Hicks Hall but were informed by Treby, their colleague on the bench, that the Court of Aldermen had ordered the sheriffs not to appear.[11] A few days later a London grand jury, which the day before had indicted several "papists and Jesuits" on the evidence of Titus Oates,[12] failed to find a bill against one John Rowse, accused of treason, because they doubted the credibility of the Crown's witnesses. The jurymen were severely reprimanded for this by Chief Justice Francis Pemberton of the King's Bench.[13]

Charles, quite understandably, was incensed by these impediments to his judicial campaign. "It is a hard case," he complained, "that I am the last man to have law and justice in the whole nation."[14] At a meeting of the Privy Council on October 18, the day of the Rowse verdict, it was noted that the Common Council had passed a resolution backing the sheriffs against the Middlesex justices who had fined them £100 each in absentia. Thus the whole government of the City was obviously implicated in the factious opposition to Crown policies, and if the City could be convicted of any wrongdoing this might be grounds for declaring their charter forfeit. It was decided to consult the faithful Sir George Jeffreys as to the legal possibilities of such action.[15]

Five weeks later, on November 24, the City once more demonstrated its ability to thwart the royal will. A grand jury of some of the most eminent citizens, including such stout Whigs as Sir Samuel Barnardiston, Papillon, and Dubois, returned a verdict of *Ignoramus* on an attempted indictment of the Earl of Shaftesbury on charges of high treason.[16]

This was, however, to be the last major Whig triumph in the City for nearly seven years.

Under the Tudors in the sixteenth century the manipulations of boroughs had mostly consisted of creating new ones that might return to the House of Commons members favorably disposed toward the Crown. The Stuarts, though not averse to seeking to control the Commons by other means, created few new boroughs. The creation of Newark as a new borough with the right of parliamentary representation, in 1673, was the last occasion on which this prerogative was ever exercised by the Crown. However, the tendency of the existing boroughs to be controlled by Dissenters throughout the century had caused the Crown from the very beginning to bring pressure to bear on them, usually by the threat of removing their charters by a writ of Quo Warranto.[17] Reading's charter was proceeded against in this manner in 1618, and in the following year Maidstone was forced to obtain confirmation of her charter, at great expense.[18] In 1629 Attorney General Heath used a writ of Quo Warranto against the corporation of Yarmouth, using the excuse that "the head of the body consists of two bailiffs, which is monstrous in nature, and dangerous and inconvenient in government." The town seems to have put up no serious resistance to this assault on their corporate customs and liberties.[19] Under Charles I such proceedings became even more frequent, especially in the period of "personal rule" between 1629 and 1640.[20]

At the time of the Restoration a thorough purge of borough corporations was undertaken, for obvious reasons. A royal warrant of May 7, 1661 stated that in drawing up all future charters for borough corporations:

there be express reservation to the Crown of the first nomination of aldermen, recorders and town clerks; the filling up of places in the Common Council with persons nominated by the borough, &c; and the future nomination of all recorders and town clerks; also that there be a proviso for elections for parliament to be made by the Common Council only.[21]

This measure is a useful indication of what Charles hoped for from the very beginning of his reign. It would have given the Crown virtually outright control of all corporations and of the city and borough elections to Parliament. However, the measure was never generally carried out. When a new charter was granted to Norwich later that same month, May, 1661, the conditions that had been stipulated in the royal warrant were omitted because they had already got rid of the objectionable officials and because of protests that such provisions would be "injurious to the liberties or interests of the town."[22] An attempt by the House of Lords (influenced by the Duke of York) to include the conditions by an amendment in the Corporations Act of December, 1661[23] was defeated by the Commons.[24]

In the early years of Charles' reign most of the purgations of corporate cities and boroughs were carried out under the provisions of the Corporations Act, which sought to avoid nonconformist control of corporations by means of compulsory oaths and the receiving of the Anglican Sacrament by all officeholders. Commissions were set up under the act to carry out its provisions. Usually composed of local landowners presided over by the lord lieutenant of the county, these commissions were empowered to remove any suspect officials even if they had conformed with regard to the oaths and the Sacrament.[25] These bodies, whose authority remained valid until Lady Day, March 25, 1663,[26] did much to extend the control of the landed gentry over the towns.

Even after the commissions had expired the old weapon of Quo Warranto could still be used against the boroughs. One of the charges in the impeachment of the Earl of Clarendon in 1667 was that he had used the threat of Quo Warranto proceedings to extort money from corporations even after their charters had been confirmed by Parliament.[27] And even when Clarendon was gone, Gloucester was forced to surrender its charter by the same method in 1671 and Northampton, because the corporation had annoyed the Earl of Peterborough, in 1672. Thus legal action or the threat of it "to the end that the succession in . . . corporations may be most probably perpetuated in the hands of persons well-affected to his majesty and the established government"[28] was nothing new in the 1680's, but at that time, presumably because the parliamentary check was removed and because the political divisions were now more clearly drawn, it was embarked upon to an unprecedented extent and with devastating effect.

One of the first, if not the first, suggestions of Crown action against a corporate borough's charter in the 1680's came ironically from Henry Pollexfen, the future champion of London's charter, who at this time, as was shown by his acting as Danby's counselor the year before, was still politically neutral in his acceptance of clients. On June 1, 1680 the deputy lieutenants of Devonshire wrote to the Duke of Albermarle pleading for government intervention in the borough of Tiverton, explaining that they were "troubled at the increase of conventicles, factions and disorder" in the town. Reading between the lines it would seem that the borough's charter was sheltering a hotbed of lower middle-class religious and political antiestablishmentarianism. Affixed to the lieutenants' letter was an opinion by Pollexfen that since it seemed that there was an insufficient number of legitimate burgesses, under the provisions of the Corporations Act, to elect others, the charter might be treated as automatically dissolved.[29] This initiated a series of Quo Warranto actions in that county in the ensuing few years.[30]

It was barely a month after the abortive attempt to prosecute Shaftesbury that the government commenced its action against the charter of London, a charter that was not more than eighteen years old at the time, though it was basically the same charter that the City had had for centuries. In 1638 Charles I, in desperate need of money to repel the Scottish invasion, in return for a payment of £12,000 had issued the City a new charter confirming all of the ancient rights and privileges that had been called into question by the Crown in the course of its four-year feud with the city over the question of ship money.[31] Subsequently, on June 24, 1663, after the removal of four or five aldermen who were *personae non gratae* to the government, Charles II had granted another new charter confirming all the privileges confirmed by his father in 1638 plus some later concessions wrung out of that unhappy monarch.[32] This was the charter that was now under attack.

In the third week of December Sheriffs Pilkington and Shute were served with a writ of Quo Warranto requiring the lord mayor, the aldermen, and the City to show to the justices of the King's Bench at Westminster in the following Hilary Term "by what they had their Privileges, Imunities &c."[33] Specifically it was charged:

> That the mayor, and commonalty, and citizens of the city of London, by the space of a month then last past, and more, used, and yet do claim to have and use, without any lawful warrant, or regal grant . . . the liberties and privileges following, viz.
>
> I To be of themselves a Body Corporate and Politic, . . .

II . . . to name, elect, make, and constitute [sheriffs of London and Middlesex].

III That the Mayor and Aldermen of the said City should be justices of the Peace, and hold Sessions of the Peace. All which Liberties, Privileges, and Franchises, the said Mayor and Commonalty, and Citizens of London, upon the King did by the space aforesaid usurp, and yet do usurp.[34]

Two reasons were given for the City's having forfeited its liberties. The first was a bylaw of September 17, 1674 levying certain tolls on those who brought goods to sell in the City's markets, which was described as being "in oppression of the king's subjects" and "an extortion, and a forfeiture of the franchise of being a corporation." The second reason was a petition by the Common Council on January 13, 1681 calling for the reassembling of Parliament,[35] a petition characterized as being "scandalous and libellous" and "the making and publishing it a forfeiture."[36]

Roger Morrice commented in his diary that "suites of this nature are sometimes. 10. or. 20. or 40. yeares before any considerable Processe go out upon them."[37] The proceedings in the London Quo Warranto suit did not take quite that long, but they were lengthy. It was not until October, 1682 that the City's reply to the charges, signed by William Williams, Sir Francis Winnington, and six other lawyers, was presented. Described by a supporter of the government as being "more in the nature of a manifesto or one of the last Westminster Parliament addresses than a loyal instrument,"[38] it claimed that the arguments pleaded by the attorney general were insufficient to cause the mayor, commonalty, and citizens to cease being a corporation and that, furthermore, no act, deed, or bylaw of the mayor, aldermen or Common Council should be regarded as the act or deed of the whole corporation. Pointing out "that London is the metropolis of England, and very populous, *et celeberrimum emporium totius Europae*," it asserted the right of the City to control markets and levy tolls and "that these liberties and customs of the city were confirmed by Magna Charta, and other statutes." It recalled the details of the Popish Plot and claimed that the prorogation of Parliament on January 10, 1681 had, in fact, interrupted justice "by reason whereof the citizens and inhabitants of the said city, being faithful subjects to the king, were much disquieted with the sense of apprehensions of the danger threatening the person of the king, his government and realm, by reason of the conspiracies aforesaid."[39] This brought a surrejoinder from the attorney general, to which the City replied with a brief rebutter. Finally, both sides joined in a demurrer so that the suit would be tried, on questions of law, by the judges only, rather than on questions of fact by a jury.[40] On December 19, 1682 the City's lawyers assured the lord mayor and Court of Aldermen that there was nothing in the attorney general's information against them by which they stood to forfeit their charter.[41]

The suit was argued in three separate hearings before the justices of the King's Bench. On February 7, 1683 the solicitor general, Heneage Finch, argued for the Crown and Treby replied on behalf of the City.[42] The attorney general, Sir Robert Sawyer, replied for the Crown on April 30, 1683, and Pollexfen presented the final argument for the City the following day.[43] Judgment against the City was pronounced by Justice Jones on June 12, 1683.[44]

Barring some considerable, unexpected change in the political situation the outcome was a foregone conclusion from the very start. It seems likely that the lawyers for the City may have chosen the demurrer procedure because by 1683 the sheriffs who would select the jury were no longer Whigs. But just as sheriffs could pack juries, so the Crown could equally easily pack the bench. Since 1668 Charles had always appointed judges *durante bene placito* rather than *quam diu se bene gesserit,* as had usually been the custom up till then.[45] And ever since the resignation of the great Sir Matthew Hale in February, 1676 from the chief justiceship of the King's Bench, judicial appointments had been influenced far more by political considerations than by either merit or deserts.[46] The death of Lord Chancellor Nottingham in December, 1682 opened the way for the moderate Tory Sir Francis North to be promoted from chief justice of the Court of Common Pleas to Lord Keeper of the Great Seal. The vacant chief justiceship was then filled by another moderate, Sir Francis Pemberton, who was appointed to it from the chief justiceship of the King's Bench. A hitherto comparatively obscure barrister, Edmund Saunders, who had been employed by the Crown for the past year in preparing the case against London, replaced Pemberton as chief justice. Just before the final hearings the moderate Sir William Dolben was moved from the King's Bench to the Common Pleas and was replaced by Francis Wythens, who had appeared in the previous year as junior counsel for the Crown against Shaftesbury.[47] Of the four justices who decided the case, then, two of them, Thomas Raymond and Sir Thomas Jones, were old and faithful supporters of any cause the Crown chose to espouse, another had been actively engaged in legal battles with the London Whigs in the preceding months, and the fourth, the chief justice, had been the principal author of the arguments on one side of the dispute over which he was now called upon to preside and judge.

This writer is far from being qualified to judge the validity of the legal arguments on either side of the case. One twentieth-century Whig historian has confidently described the Crown's arguments as "in all respects weak and in some frivolous,"[48] while a contemporary supporter of the Court wrote with equal confidence that Sawyer's arguments had completely outdone those of Treby and Pollexfen and had "confounded" the opposition altogether.[49]

Briefly the legal arguments were these: Finch, pointing out that all franchises and liberties originated from the king, maintained that "there is no rule in law more certain than that the misuser of a franchise is a forfeiture of that franchise." The fact that no city had ever lost its charter owing to an adverse judgment in a Quo Warranto suit was simply because, as was the case with several after the Restoration, they had always surrendered first. Noting that the City claimed special immunity because of clause nine of Magna Carta: "Civitas London' habeat omnes libertates suas antiquas, et consuetudines suas," and by virtue of acts of 1 Edward III and 7 Richard II guaranteeing their liberties from royal seizure, he rejected these precedents on the grounds that the Magna Carta clause referred not only to London but to all other cities as well, many of which had since had their charters revoked, and that the acts referred to were not bona fide Acts of Parliament. The mayor, aldermen, and Common Council, he argued, spoke for the whole corporation and, therefore, the whole corporation must pay the penalty of their wrongdoing. The levying of tolls on noncitizens was illegal unless specifically granted by the king in the corporation's charter, which it was not; and even if such tolls had been levied "time out of mind" the City had no right to increase them. Finally, the City's having said in the Common Council's petition of January, 1681 that the king, by exercising his prerogative privilege of proroguing Parliament, was causing "an interruption of justice" would have been criminal in an individual. For their misuse of power, they eminently deserved to forfeit their charter.[50]

Treby replied with three main arguments. He maintained, first of all, that a corporation was more than a franchise; it was a legal being and an immortal being that might be regulated by the government, might even forfeit individual privileges, but could never be dissolved except by an Act of Parliament. It was ridiculous, he pointed out, to charge that the City had lost its corporate entity months before and then to sue it in court as a corporate entity. He argued, secondly, that with regard to the tolls London was a special case, being the principal trading center of the kingdom, and had always been recognized as having special privileges. The new tolls had been necessary to meet expenses incurred because of the Great Fire; repairs were necessary if London was to continue to provide services for traders from all over the country. And even if the tolls were oppressive, which they were not, then they must be so declared in the proper courts, not just arbitrarily described as such, thus causing the charter to be forfeit. Finally, he reminded the bench that the king himself, in the Speech from the Throne at the beginning of the last Westminster parliament, had testified to the genuine dangers of the Popish Plot and had urged its rigorous investigation and prosecution. To say that the prorogation was "an interruption of justice" was to make a simple statement of fact and did not imply criticism of the king; the attorney general was not entitled to read meanings into the City's words.[51]

Sawyer and Pollexfen, in the final hearings some twelve weeks later, for the most part merely amplified and commented on the arguments of Finch and Treby. Sawyer, speaking for some five or six hours,[52] cited several past instances in which, he maintained, municipal corporations had forfeited all their privileges. He claimed that the government, not the City, bore the cost of the markets, and that for the City to seek to tax foreigners (noncitizens) was to misuse a privilege to the oppression of the king's subjects and, therefore, automatically made that privilege forfeit. With regard to the petition he asserted that the City had no jurisdiction to debate parliamentary prorogations or any other function of the prerogative. To say that the king had interrupted justice was indeed to be guilty of a criminal libel.[53]

Pollexfen, the next day argued that, while it was true that writs of Quo Warranto had been used against municipal corporations, yet it had always been for claiming privileges that did not legally exist, not just for claiming to be a corporate body politic. The precedents that Sawyer had cited for corporations losing all their privileges were taken from ancient medieval records "of uncertain and doubtful sense," whereas he could show the attorney general that the medieval acts of Parliament guaranteeing London's liberties were genuine, for they were among the records in the Tower. And even though Plantagenet kings had on occasion displaced the lord mayor and placed a royal *"custos"* over the City, was it known that such de facto acts were done de jure? He denied that the government paid for the London market facilities and repeated that London had always been recognized as having the right to levy market tolls. He repeated that the reference to "interruption of justice" was merely a simple statement of fact and no criticism of the king. Finally, he argued that only certain rights were delegated to the Common Council by the citizens, and among those rights there was none authorizing the Council to forfeit the charter. If individuals erred, individuals could be punished, but the City legally could not be.[54]

When the judges delivered their judgment six weeks later, Chief Justice Saunders was on his deathbed and Raymond was absent, but Sir Thomas Jones, who acted as spokesman, informed the court that Saunders and Raymond concurred with Wythens and himself in their decision: that when the Corporations Act stated that no corporation should be voided for any wrong done in the preceding years,[55] it obviously implied that a corporation charter could be voided for wrongdoing; that the petition was scandalous and libelous and making it and publishing it was a forfeiture; that the act of the Common Council was the act of the whole corporation; that none of the arguments offered were sufficient to excuse or avoid the forfeitures, and that the Crown's charge was well founded. The charter, they directed, should be seized into the king's hands, but official action on the matter should be postponed till the king's pleasure be known. Meanwhile, the attorney general entered a nolle prosequi, signifying the Crown's intention of taking no further action with regard to the now purely academic matter of the City's allegedly illegal claim to appoint sheriffs and to have its chief magistrates function as ex-officio justices of the peace.[56]

Probably the letter of the law was on the side of the Crown. And yet certainly, but for the prevailing political crisis, the Crown would never have sought to invalidate London's charter over a slight increase in market tolls or because of a petition concerning a matter of state. It is quite clear from the speeches of the lawyers on both sides what the trial was really about. Treby at one stage in his speech clearly expressed the essentially conservative nature of the Whig lawyers' theory of the constitution, which argued that only by preserving all the old impedimenta intact could royal usurpation of the liberty of the subject be checked.

> My Lord [he said], all innovations (as this must certainly be a very great one) are dangerous; this frame of government has lasted and been preserved for many hundreds of years, and I hope will be so as long as the world endures.[57]

Pollexfen, claiming "that I argue in this case for the old and known laws, as they have been ever practised through all ages,"[58] argued that if a corporation charter could be forfeited in a court of law then "I think it to be as great in consequence as ever any at this bar, as if Magna Charta were at stake." For if the charter of London could be seized and the corporation of the City dissolved then much of the established political and social framework of England was threatened: all ecclesiastical corporations, including universities, colleges, and hospitals, all the cities and larger towns would be compromised and vulnerable. "The very frame" of the government was threatened because the majority of members of the House of Commons were chosen by corporations, or at least their election was influenced by them. Were not peerages also a sort of corporation?[59] Like Treby, he insisted on the importance of preserving the status quo, which he portrayed as a healthy system of checks and balances:

> Perhaps the world itself, at least this little world, will no longer be able to subsist in health than the due order and just temperament of the several parts and powers therein are preserved, and contain themselves within their own bounds. The taking away or infeebling any principal part brings a lameness and deformity, pain and disorder upon, and at length confounds the whole. The laws answer their ends, whereof the principal is the preservation of the government, which preserves the laws, they cannot subsist one without the other; therefore whatsoever it is that tends to the subversion, or leaving at will and pleasure,

that which is so considerable in our government as corporations are, ought to be thoroughly considered.[60]

The law officers of the Crown, on the other hand, stressed the need to remove any obstruction that enabled a privileged few to oppress the many or behind which those few could shelter their factious designs to overthrow Crown and Commonwealth. "How many oppressions and offences would be daily committed," Finch asked, "if every corporation were a franchise and jurisdiction independent upon the Crown?"[61] Sawyer, noting that "this case between the king and the city must be acknowledged to be a case of importance, both as it refers to the general government of the kingdom, and that of the city . . . ," argued that

> this Quo Warranto is not brought to destroy, but to reform and amend the government of the city, by running of those excesses and exorbitances of power, which some men (contrary to their duty, and the known laws of the land) have assumed to themselves under colour of their corporate capacity, to the reviling of their prince, the oppression of their fellow subjects, and to the infinite disquiet of their fellow citizens.

Rejecting Treby's contention that corporations were immortal or indissoluble, "that no treasons or seditions against their prince . . . [no] murders, felonies [or] opressions of their fellow subjects" could be punished, he concluded: "If such notions as these could be true, . . . it would be unsafe for the king or any of his subjects, to live in or near a corporation."[62]

King Charles and his ministers did not hasten to take advantage of the judgment in their favor, presumably because they had already won effectual control over London several months before the Quo Warranto suit was tried.

The Whigs had suffered their first setback in September, 1681 in the election of the new lord mayor to succeed Ward. Sir John Moore, as senior alderman, would normally have been elected unopposed in accordance with the usual custom.[63] He was an openly professed adherent of the Court, however, and so two Whig aldermen, Sir John Shorter and Sir Thomas Gold, were put in nomination against him. This development may have incurred some unfavorable comment from Whitehall, for Treby addressed the Common Council before the poll was opened, telling them "that his majesty had graciously assured them that they should have a free choice according to their charter," but reminding them also that the words of the charter were that "they should choose and (one?) [sic] that was grateful to the King and fit for the government of the city."[64] As it happened, Moore was duly elected, but he received only a little over a third of the nearly five thousand votes cast.[65]

Meanwhile, probably in the hope that a new parliament must soon be called (for they can have had at most only the slightest inkling of Charles' new financial arrangements with Louis XIV), several of the Whig lawyers appear to have been working at the grass roots level of City politics—among the livery companies in whose hands lay the nomination of London parliamentary representatives. One of Secretary Jenkins' informers told him in November, 1681 that Sir William Jones, Sir Francis Winnington, and William Williams were using their influence with the Coopers company to get them to appoint as their clerk "one Browne," who, the informer went on to explain, had a record of misdemeanors against the government.[66] But no parliament was called, and in the following summer of 1682 the fatal consequences of Moore's election as lord mayor became apparent.

The Whigs had at first discounted Moore as a timid man

who could be easily influenced, and as long as the sheriffs were of their party they felt secure.[67] But at a City banquet in May, Moore, in accordance with an old but oft-disputed City custom,[68] by drinking to him, nominated Dudley North to be one of the sheriffs for the following year. North, a former Turkey merchant, was a brother of the soon-to-be Lord Keeper Sir Francis North and a Tory.[69] When the Common Hall was summoned by Moore to meet as usual at the Guildhall on Midsummer Day (June 24) to confirm North's nomination and to elect another sheriff to serve with him, an uproar ensued. Treby, as always scrupulously correct in the performance of his office as recorder, procured silence temporarily, but when he told the Hall "they ought to choose men loyal and firm to the Government," he was met with hissing and shouts of scorn. When he reminded them "that the Lord Mayor had drunk to Mr. North, they would not suffer him to go on."[70] Papillon and Dubois were put in nomination, and the outgoing sheriffs, Pilkington and Shute, despite the lord mayor's order to adjourn, continued taking a poll for several hours.[71] At a debate between both sides in the Guildhall on July 7, as to who had the right of adjourning the Common Hall, Williams and Pollexfen acted as advisors to Pilkington and Shute while Sir George Jeffreys and Saunders (not yet raised to the chief justiceship) advised the lord mayor. We know where Treby stood: he apparently had already given his opinion that the right of electing the sheriffs lay in the liverymen and that "the mode of taking the poll and of adjournment by the sheriffs was strictly consonant to ancient usage." On this occasion he merely stated that he had not adjourned the poll, not because the sheriffs had stopped him but because, the lord mayor having left, there was no one in the chair to authorize an adjournment.[72] The debate concluded with neither side having been satisfied.[73] At a poll conducted by the lord mayor a week later North and Ralph Box, a compromise candidate, were declared elected.

On July 27 Treby had the unpopular task of informing the Common Hall of the rejection by the lord mayor and the Court of Aldermen of a petition praying that Papillon and Dubois be recognized as the next sheriffs, an announcement that caused "much murmuring and discontent."[74] And two days after North and the Tory Peter Rich had been sworn in at the Guildhall on September 27 (Rich having been declared elected by Moore in place of Box, who had prudently declined to serve),[75] it was the Whig recorder, Treby, who had the task of presenting the two new officials to the Court of Exchequer Chamber—perhaps with a laudatory speech for appearance's sake.[76] But he did not attend the meeting at Shaftesbury's lodgings, on October 5, where some of the leading London Whigs, including Williams, Pollexfen, and several lesser lawyers, reportedly discussed the business of the sheriffs and the best means of taking legal action against Moore. Nor did he attend a similar meeting the following day at Pilkington's lodgings.[77] His official impartiality continued to be maintained—a factor that may have added to his influence in the councils of the City in the difficult year that lay ahead.

On June 14, 1683, two days after the King's Bench justices had delivered their judgment against the City, Treby officially reported it to the Court of Aldermen, but he declined to say what the consequences might be, except that the king would probably appoint a *custos* to administer the City. The aldermen thereupon resolved to petition His Majesty.[78] Four days later a petition of the lord mayor, aldermen, and commons of London, stating that they were:

> heartily and most unfeignedly sorry for the misgovern-
> ment of this your City, of late years, whereby the citizens
> have fallen under your majesty's displeasure; . . . [and]
> humbly begging your majesty's pardon for all our
> offences,

was received by Lord Keeper North on behalf of the king.[79]

In his reply the Lord Keeper again made it abundantly clear that market tolls and even petitions for a recall of Parliament were not what the king had really objected to in the City.

> It was not the seditious discourses of the coffee-houses, the
> treasonable pamphlets, and libels daily published and dis-
> persed thence into all parts of the kingdom; the outra-
> geous tumults in the streets; nor the affronts to his courts
> of justice could provoke him to it.

Rather it was that

> . . . the factious party were not content with the practice
> of these insolencies, but endeavoured to have them publicly
> countenenced by the magistrates: and for that end, in all
> elections they stickled to chuse the most disaffected into
> offices of the greatest trust in the government; and carried
> themselves with that heat and violence, that it was a terror
> to all sober and discreet citizens; and the city was so
> unhappily divided into parties, that there was no likelihood
> it could return to good order, so long as the factions
> retained any hope of procuring the election of magistrates
> of their own party for their impunity.[80]

It would have been as well, North suggested, had the City officials not waited until the judgment went against them in court before applying to the king. Even so, the king would not hold it against them if they would accept certain stipulations designed to prevent the aforementioned abuses: firstly, that no lord mayor, sheriff, recorder, common serjeant, or town clerk should be appointed without the king's approval, and if two consecutive unacceptable nominations were made then the king himself would fill the vacancy; secondly, the lord mayor and aldermen might dismiss any official, with the king's approval, and might reject any election to office of an alderman or other official, filling the vacancy themselves if dissatisfied twice; thirdly, the king should appoint all justices of the peace by commission, though he would undertake to appoint those City officials who customarily became justices ex officio unless it should prove necessary to do otherwise. If the City would accept these conditions, which were essentially those that Charles had sought to impose on all the cities and boroughs of England in 1661, His Majesty was, in fact, prepared to pardon their prosecution and confirm their charter with the necessary provisos added.[81]

Opinion in the City at this time appears to have been pretty evenly divided between the determined opponents of the Court and those whom Roger North described as being "of the church and loyal party," who were, in those weeks following the discovery of the Rye House Plot, determined "to stem that orage of faction" and so were "ready to have treated with the King."[82] The Common Council voted on June 20 to accept Charles' conditions.[83] That they never were in fact accepted seems to have been chiefly due to Treby's efforts.

When in September the Tory lord mayor, Sir William Prichard, announced the arrangements that he, Sawyer, and Finch had prepared, by which the City was to surrender its charter to the king and receive it back with the additional provisos added, the Common Council was quick to object that this went further than the king's declared intention of confirming their existing charter, merely adding the provisos on to it. On October 2 Treby pointed out to them that if the charter were taken away as a result of a judicial decision it could always be restored to them intact by a writ of error, but if it were once surrendered then there would never be any redress available to them: "Against Erroneous proceedings there may be Redress. But it will be unreasonable for the City to Expect redress agt their own Act."[84] He also warned them that, as he had explained to Sawyer a few days earlier,[85] for the aldermen to surrender the charter would be to contravene their oaths of office. His arguments succeeded in reversing the vote of the previous June: 103 voted against giving up the charter, only 85 voted to do it.[86]

Treby was surely wise in urging this firm stand. At the time it must have seemed the only chance the City had of ever regaining its old charter intact. And after the King's Bench judgment was put into effect the City was, it turned out, no worse off than it would have been had it surrendered and accepted the king's new charter; although the king made all appointments to office, as he would in effect have done under the new charter, yet the essential structure and functioning of the City government remained unaltered.[87] But Treby's efforts were to prove unnecessary. James II was to restore the old charter intact in October, 1688, and the Quo Warranto of June, 1683 was to be ultimately reversed—not by a writ of error but by an act of William's and Mary's first parliament.[88]

On October 4, 1683 the judgment against the London charter was entered and the charter became officially null and void. A commission was set up to supervise the affairs of the City, consisting of Lords Halifax, Rochester, and Worcester, and Sir George Jeffreys, who had just been appointed chief justice of the King's Bench and made a privy councilor. Treby and other office holders, both great and small, were turned out, Treby being replaced as recorder by "an obscure lawyer," Thomas Jenner.[89] In the frustration and disappointment of the moment many of the City leaders evidently sought to make a scapegoat out of Treby. By an ironic coincidence, considering what was to happen just five years later, it was James, Duke of York, who wrote gleefully the next day to tell William, Prince of Orange, the news of London's defeat. The duke reported that "many of those who voted against submitting to the proposal offered by his Majesty are very angry with themselves and their old Recorder Treby (who persuaded them to do it) for what they did."[90]

Now that London, later to be described by Charles James Fox as having stood in 1681 "like a strong fortress in a conquered country,"[91] was totally defeated, what corporation in England could hope to avoid purgation by the Crown?

Many provincial towns and cities had, in fact, already fallen or were about to fall. Between February, 1682 and October, 1683 thirteen municipal charters had fallen to the Crown and been replaced with new ones giving the Crown control over the election and appointment of municipal officials.[92] On October 27, 1683, three weeks after the fall of London, Quo Warranto writs were issued against the charters of the Cinque Ports. In all, before the end of the reign, more than sixty municipalities and some thirty craft and trading corporations were to be given new charters.[93]

Roger North tells us that in some cases "pickthank" courtiers, motivated by the desire to curry favor with the king, blackmailed corporations into surrendering their charters by the threat of legal action against them. In other cases there were enough good Tory citizens who took a delight in offering to surrender their charter to the king as a loyal compliment. Some corporations, being quite happy to leave matters of law and government to the Crown, took advantage of the king's known wishes to surrender their ancestral liberties in order that they might be "remunerated with considerable privileges, respecting their common profit and trade, which was commonly granted as they desired." According to Dr. Thomas Spratt it was a source of great satisfaction to King Charles

that so great a number of the cities and corporations of his kingdom have . . . so freely resigned their local immunities and charters into his . . . hands; lest the abuse of any of them should herinafter prove hazardous to the just prerogatives of the crown.[94]

Not all charters were "freely resigned," however. A few boroughs put up quite a struggle before they finally and inevitably succumbed. The leading Whig lawyers were called upon for assistance, of course, but their campaign against increased royal control over the corporations was destined to be completely unsuccessful in the end, mainly because they were always forced ultimately to appeal to a judicial bench that was packed against them. Parliament, to which they might have successfully appealed against the decisions of the courts, never sat during the crucial period—thanks to Louis XIV's munificence toward King Charles.

One may wonder, then, why the lawyers kept up the futile struggle on behalf of the corporation charters for so long—in fact, right down to the eve of James II's accession. For one thing, though none of the lawyers appear to have been in the least way implicated in the Rye House Plot, they were close enough to the inner councils of Shaftesbury and Monmouth in 1682–1683 to realize that some sort of coup was being contemplated by the opposition leaders. Up to June, 1683, then, the lawyers may have hoped for salvation from that direction. Again, there was always the hope that a change of circumstances might one day in the not too distant future compel Charles (as had happened to his father in 1640) to call a parliament that would vindicate their stand. Meanwhile, the Whigs must try to retain control of as many boroughs as possible.

Whatever their motives were, this campaign of the Whig lawyers on behalf of the charters of several of the provincial towns and cities was of obvious importance. The lawyers had no hope of immediate victory, but these local struggles provided them with favorable opportunities for agitation and propaganda. During this period of no parliaments and therefore of no elections (with their accompanying spirited debates between opposing partisans) the lawyers were able in the course of various local hearings, discussions, and trials to expound the Whig philosophy and to keep the Whig movement alive in at least some areas of the country. Even as the Crown steadily tightened its control over the nation at all levels, the Whigs were provided with forums from which to urge the preservation of local liberties and the desirability of limited government.

As early as the latter part of 1681 we find some of the lawyers at work in Oxford, paradoxically urging the citizens to demand a new charter from the Crown in place of their existing one. The explanation lies in the fact that Oxford was one of those cities that had had its liberties confirmed in 1661 with the provisos giving the king control over the election of the senior municipal officials. Perhaps stirred to action by the use made of the city by the Crown in the prosecution of Stephen College, and probably making use of contacts established during the Oxford parliament, we find the lawyers urging the citizens to seek a new charter with the objectionable provisos removed. Humphrey Prideaux wrote from Oxford to his friend John Ellis in October, 1681 :

if Oxford should carry it against the King, you shall find none else will allow it for him; which will be as great a dimunition to the King's prerogative as hath hapned in any King's time, except the last, when ye Crown itself was taken away. Jones and Winnington and Williams, with some other of that gang, have made them soe confident of their cause that they already proclaim victory, and talke of nothing else but of burning their last charter . . .[95]

The mayor and citizens soon after commenced an action in the courts, by a writ of mandamus,[96] to have the charter replaced, and in January, 1682 petitioned the king to the same effect.[97] However, they were acting in direct opposition to the prevailing political tide. The king rebuffed the petition, and by June, 1682 a Quo Warranto action against Oxford's charter, and hence its liberties and privileges, was initiated by Dr. Fell, Dean of Christ Church.[98]

The increased power exercised by the University of Oxford after the charter had been taken away led early in 1684 to a riot in which stones were thrown at the vice-chancellor and proctors amid cries of "a Monmouth, a Monmouth."[99] At the assizes in March of that year all the rioters but one put themselves on the mercy of the court. The one exception was defended by Williams and Winnington who, according to one of the Oxford dons, "both talked after their usual manner very scandalously and impudently, not to say very ignorantly and maliciously, to the apprehension of all bystanders." Despite this last claim the writer goes on to tell how the jury, packed by a sympathetic undersheriff "or his substitute," and ignoring the judge's instructions, found the accused "not guilty," whereupon a noisy demonstration broke out that ended with the acquitted citizen being carried home on the shoulders of some of his fellows "with shoutings and huzzahs."[100] A new charter, giving increased powers to the Crown and the University, was imposed on Oxford in September, 1684.[101]

In April, 1684 Williams unsuccessfully defended the charter of the town of Leominster against a Quo Warranto.[102] And in December, 1684 the "Dissenters" in the corporation of Berwick-on-Tweed consulted Pollexfen, John Holt, and other lawyers with regard to the Quo Warranto issued against their charter. They were urged not to surrender but to contest it in court, presumably for the same reason that Treby had given London similar advice and, perhaps, also because a new parliamentary election might be held before the courts could settle the contest. However, according to the Tory account, the "loyal party" in Berwick, by a majority of six votes, compelled acquiescence with the Crown's wishes.[103]

Because they were opposition politicians as well as opposition jurists, the Whig lawyers themselves were inevitably personally affected by this remorseless extension of royal control over the corporations. Particularly affected, of course, were those of them who held municipal recorderships. We have seen Treby ousted from the recordership of London in October, 1683. At the end of March, 1684 Maynard lost the recordership of Plymouth when that town, despite Maynard's warning that their charter was "as it were a trust that could not be surrendered, and if they did [surrender it] the surrender was void," were persuaded to yield by the Earl of Bath.[104] Williams was to lose the recordership of Chester later the same year.

Sir Robert Atkyns, eighteen months earlier, had been forced out of the recordership of Bristol, a post he had held since 1661, despite his claim that he had never taken sides but had always done "all I could, when I came amongst [the citizens of Bristol] to join them together and unite them; for ever since they grew rich and full of trade and knighthood, too much sail and too little ballast, they have been miserably divided."[105] He had certainly departed from such a policy in January, 1681 when he precipitated a crisis in the city's politics by contesting the by-election held to replace Sir Robert Cann, who had been expelled from the House of Commons for "abhorring," against Mr. Thomas Earl, a Tory merchant and former sheriff of Wiltshire. The recorder was defeated by just twenty votes,[106] so that the two political camps in Bristol at this time seem to have been fairly evenly matched.

Atkyns was defeated again in the election for the Oxford parliament in March, 1681. The campaign was a hard-fought one, but his opponents—Earl, and the new mayor of Bristol, Richard Hart—this time triumphed with a majority of 329.[107] The recorder and his fellow candidate, Sir John Knight, were determined to dispute this result, and their followers were confident that the Commons Committee on Elections and Privileges would quickly seat them in place of their opponents.[108] But the Oxford parliament did not sit long enough even to begin consideration of the dispute. From this time on Atkyns' political fortunes declined steadily.

The following September Earl was elected mayor of Bristol, and Mr. Richard Lane and Mr. John Knight (cousin of Atkyns' ally, but a staunch Tory) were elected sheriffs. One of their first official acts was to order "no respect to be shewn unto Sir Robert Atkins, at present their recorder, they intending to turn him out."[109] Shortly thereafter Atkyns and several other Bristol aldermen were indicted for having, during the election campaign for the Oxford parliament, "most riotously" taken it on themselves "to create an alderman without the consent of the then Mayor to strengthen the factious party."[110]

Atkyns was found guilty on this charge at the Bristol

assizes a few months later. But the Bristol recorder and onetime judge still had powerful friends in the government. In November he appealed the conviction to the King's Bench, where he was very courteously treated by Pemberton and the other judges. They allowed him to plead his own case, sitting in his cloak on a chair in front of the court, and eventually they overturned the conviction.[111] In December his younger brother, Edward Atkyns, one of the barons of the Exchequer, told Chief Justice North that Sir Robert was grateful to Secretary Jenkins and Attorney General Sawyer for warning him of a move by the Bristol Tories to have him indicted on another charge, and that he was perfectly willing, if the king or the Bristol corporation desired it, to give up his "troublesome" recordership. The only conditions that he stipulated were that his arrears of salary should be paid up and that the king and the attorney general should inform Bristol that all attempts to prosecute him further were to be dropped.[112]

Shortly thereafter Jenkins wrote to the new mayor of Bristol, Thomas Easton, informing him of Atkyns' conditions, stating that the king was willing to see the prosecution attempts terminated and saying that he hoped Bristol would satisfy Sir Robert as to the salary. The mayor replied that the city was willing to accept their recorder's surrender on those terms and suggested that Sir John Churchill, attorney general to the Duke of York,[113] would be a desirable successor. On December 14 Jenkins sent the mayor Atkyns' written "surrender," together with one further request from him —that all charges pending against his old friend Sir John Knight, Sr., be dropped also. The mayor must himself decide what to do about that, Jenkins advised, adding that he was very pleased by this suggestion with regard to Churchill but must refer it to the king.[114]

Less than a week later, immediately after Atkyns' resignation had been formally recorded, Churchill was in fact elected to the recordership. Reporting this to Jenkins, Mayor Easton claimed that he and the other city officials had no quarrel with the elder Sir John Knight or any of Atkyns' other associates except insofar as they had "disserviced his Majesty and his government here." It would be necessary for the peace of the city, he continued, to get rid of Knight and the majority of the aldermen, who were of the opposition party, as well as the next seven in line of succession to the mayoralty who would otherwise eventually become aldermen. He went on to imply that Quo Warranto proceedings were the obvious remedy and that the king should "direct our now Recorder to advise and join with us herein."[115] On January 10, 1683 the mayor's information was passed on to Churchill with a request for his own views on the subject.[116]

Judging from the above correspondence it would appear that Atkyns and his associates had had the support of the majority of the corporation's senior officials, many of whom, despite the Corporations Act, seem to have been Dissenters or at least sympathetic to Dissenters.[117] It is probable that they even had the support of the majority of Bristol's total population. They did not, however, apparently have the support of the more substantial citizens voting in the Common Council and in the parliamentary election of March, 1681. Atkyns alleged at the time that Hart had created four hundred new citizens immediately before the election.[118] If he had, that would largely account for the political revolution in Bristol. The new citizens would certainly have been Tories; probably most of them were local gentry and their retainers from the surrounding countryside. It certainly seems significant that Atkyns and Knight lost the election by 329 votes whereas Atkyns had lost by only twenty votes two months earlier. With the balance of power thus tilted in their favor the Tories were able, without the aid of a Quo Warranto, to elect their partisans to the key offices of mayor and sheriffs and so to gain effective control of the corporation. A Quo Warranto was only needed at the end to remove the last remaining traces of Whig power in the city.

On March 29, 1683 Atkyns wrote to Jenkins that he had completely retired from public affairs and was resolved to have nothing further to do with Bristol, but he complained indignantly that at a recent gaol-delivery in the city the grand jury had "unworthily reflected" on him by thanking the mayor and aldermen "for their late prosecution against me for several miscarriages as Recorder, whereby I was, as they falsely say, forced to surrender my place." This statement had been read in court before a large crowd, Sir John Churchill had publicly thanked the grand jury for it from the bench, and it had since been printed. As he had been cleared of the charges in the King's Bench, the secretary was asked to quietly but firmly suppress the printed address.

Although Atkyns must have been well aware of the government's policy with regard to corporations, he went on to suggest that such a policy was something that Jenkins should have no part in:

> It will be no commendation, I take it, to the justice and honour of the government, had it been true that I was prosecuted merely to make me weary of my office and force me to resign. That would look too like a design to some further end, wherein I am sure you would not have a hand.[119]

Jenkins could afford to be kind to the discredited ex-recorder. He expressed his hearty sorrow and regret at the happenings in Bristol, of which he claimed to have no knowledge. He would do his best, he promised, to suppress any attempt to raise the matter of Atkyns' recordership. Although he himself had referred to Atkyns' "surrender" in his correspondence with the mayor of Bristol, he now said that Sir Robert's "resignation" had of course been "voluntary."[120]

Despite the change in their city's power structure, the citizens of Bristol seem to have remained "miserably divided." In January, 1684 Jenkins received a report that "the loyal inhabitants" of Bristol—"old suffering cavaliers with their children, who influenced many more good men lately in the worst of times to turn the scale against Fanaticism and prevent the expectation of the late House of Commons to have Sir Robert Atkyns to assist them"—were being divided among themselves by the political ambitions of Sir John Knight, Jr.[121] Meanwhile, in response to a writ of Quo Warranto issued in November, 1683, the mayor and corporation had surrendered their charter to the king.[122] In May, 1684 a new charter was issued which, it may be presumed, excluded Atkyns and all of his associates from holding municipal office.[123]

Chester, where William Williams had been recorder since 1667, first drew unfavorable royal attention to itself by its enthusiastic reception of the Duke of Monmouth on his tour of several of the northwestern counties late in the summer of 1682. Greeted everywhere with shouts of "God save the Protestant Duke," he was entertained in Staffordshire by various Whig lords, including the Earl of Macclesfield, who had been one of the leading champions of Exclusion in the House of Lords and who had been expelled in 1681 from a position in the royal household.

Plans for Monmouth's visit to Chester had probably been laid early in the previous July when Chester's mayor, George Mainwaring, had entertained several leading London Whigs at a "venison feast."[124] The Duke arrived at about six in the evening on Saturday, September 9, accompanied by the Earl of Macclesfield and his son Lord Brandon; Lord Delamere's son and heir, Henry Booth, who had sat for Cheshire in the Exclusion parliaments; Sir John Mainwaring, a kinsman of the mayor; and Colonel Roger Whitley, who had sat with Williams for Chester City in the Oxford parliament. The ducal party was met outside the gates by the mayor and corporation, and they all then proceeded to a banquet at the "Plume and Feathers," where citizens paid five shillings to sit at the duke's table or half-a-crown to sit at the others. On Sunday morning Williams was one of the hosts at a reception at the mayor's home, and later both he and the mayor accompanied the duke to a service at the cathedral, where Monmouth stood as godfather at the christening of the mayor's infant daughter, Henrietta.[125]

On Sunday afternoon the duke and his suite moved on to the races at Wallasey. That evening rioting broke out in Chester, aimed at both the houses of the customs officers and at the churches.[126] Several of the churches were badly pillaged and damaged by the rioters, who were presumably Dissenters. James Taylor wrote the next day to the Countess of Yarmouth that the "fanaticks" had stored "great banks of money, powder and all sorts of ammunition," that they "openly [drank] the Duke of Monmouth's health, and pray[ed] in private conventicles for his prosperity," and that the lord lieutenant of Cheshire, the Earl of Derby, openly sided with them.[127] The time had obviously come for the government and its loyal supporters to take strong action.

Sir Geoffrey Shakerley, governor of Chester Castle and a deputy lieutenant of Cheshire, wrote to Secretary Jenkins the following week that he was afraid the mayor and the recorder would treat the rioters leniently.[128] A day later another citizen reported that Williams and Colonel Whitley had been the very first to congratulate one Birkenhead after he had been acquitted by a city jury on a charge of publishing treasonous literature, and that Williams and the mayor had released on bail two men charged with having broken into St. Peter's Church. This writer concluded: "I expect not to have them punished here according to their crime . . . tis certain the rabble take courage from their opinion of the Mayor's and Recorder's inclination."[129]

On September 25 Mayor Mainwaring and Williams presided over a city quarter sessions at which a bill was presented charging the rioters, but the jury declined to find it *billa vera*.[130] Three days later a hastily convened special Commission of Oyer and Terminer, headed by Sir George Jeffreys in his capacity as chief justice of Cheshire, sat to inquire into the riots.

Writing to Jenkins on the 25th Jeffreys had said that he expected Williams and the mayor to oppose the commission, "they being very unwilling that any stranger should intermeddle in their late disorders to which they themselves so much contributed."[131] Before the session opened, according to Thomas Cholmondeley (a cousin of Shakerley), Williams circulated among the jurymen empaneled from the entire county for the oyer and terminer proceedings, "letting them know he should be Recorder, when the Commission was over, and that he must look to defend the rights of the city."[132]

Williams and Alderman William Street, who had been mayor at the time Williams was chosen for recorder, and who was one of the most extreme Whigs in Chester, represented the city on the commission. No sooner had it been called to order than Williams rose to object that by the city's charter the corporation had the exclusive right to try all charges less than treason. When Jeffreys and Justice Warren replied that the provision in the charter was only permissive and did not rule out intervention by the Crown any more than did a similar provision in the charter of London (where such commissions often sat) Williams turned to the jury:

> He minded the citizens of their oaths as freemen, by which they were bound to defend their just liberties, and hoped no such vipers were bred within themselves as would suck the blood out of their own veins. He showed how dangerous it was to invade ancient rights, enlarging in as popular expressions as ever [were] heard.

Shouts of approval from the spectators followed this speech, but were quickly suppressed by the chief justice. Nor was the jury apparently impressed, for they found a true bill and brought in an indictment against the rioters.[133]

But Williams had not yet exhausted his resources. When the commission met on the following afternoon to act on the indictment, it could do nothing because the bill had not yet been endorsed for prosecution by the sheriffs. This accidental happening benefited Williams, for at four o'clock the commission expired and he was able to dismiss the court.[134] On October 9 the city quarter sessions, which had been adjourned till then by Williams on September 25, again assembled. Since it was known that the government intended to continue the proceedings against the rioters by moving the indictment made before the commission by a writ of certiorari to the King's Bench in London, the recorder sought to have the rioters (who once they had been tried for their offense and punished or acquitted in one court, could never be tried for it in another) indicted, tried, and, if necessary, punished at the quarter sessions, where the penalties could be made far less severe. The grand jury, however, perhaps because they did not fully comprehend their recorder's subtle scheme, were uncooperative and found true bills against only two of the accused. Peter Shakerley, a son of Sir Geoffrey, who acted as his father's deputy at the castle, did not have to use the writ he had brought to the sessions in his pocket, all ready to produce immediately if a general indictment were found.[135]

After the failure of this scheme the fortunes of Williams and his associates in Chester began gradually but definitely to decline. Although according to one report Jeffreys, on leaving Chester after the expiry of the commission, was accompanied out of the city by "an Innumerable Company of women who called out still a Monmouth a monmouth much to sr Geo: discontent,"[136] the Shakerleys' cousin, Thomas Cholmondeley, reported to Jenkins on September 30 that many who had welcomed Monmouth at the beginning of the month, alarmed by what had happened to him (he had been arrested at Stafford on September 23 and carried to London to answer to his father and the Privy Council for his activities in the North), were now wavering.[137] Cholmondeley and the dean of Chester, James Aderne, succeeded in prevailing upon a grand jury of the county to draft a loyal address to the king, condemning the recent disorders, that only one member, John Mainwaring, refused to sign. Dean Aderne wrote to Captain John Clarke that if Quo Warranto proceedings against Chester were contemplated by the government he and Peter Shakerley could probably supply them with the necessary information. "A great part," he concluded, "but not the greater part of the corporation deserve well of the King."[138] So it seems that here again, as apparently was the case at Bristol, we have a group of local gentry in the county, with the support of a minority of the citizens, acting in opposition to the majority of the citizens and seeking to discredit them in order to gain control of the city government.

However, their task was harder in Chester because they did not have the mayor as an ally, as was the case in Bristol and, as the Crown had had in slightly different circumstances, in London.

The assault on the Whig forces controlling Chester was led by Peter Shakerley from the castle. On October 2, he wrote to Jenkins describing the strong campaign then underway to have Colonel Whitley elected mayor on October 13, to succeed Mainwaring. The loyal party's only chance of success, he suggested, was for a government messenger to arrive with a summons calling Williams and Alderman Street to London before the election was held.[139] Left, however, to his own resources, Shakerley proved equal to the crisis. Although the Common Council put two Whigs, Whitley and Alderman Edwards, into nomination, Shakerley, entertaining the aldermen at a wine party immediately before they polled, prevailed upon a majority of them to vote for Edwards, who was by far the more docile of the two candidates.[140] The following April Jenkins wrote to tell Shakerley that the king was very pleased by his handling of affairs in Chester. The secretary also said that the government agreed that a Quo Warranto would be the best method of purging the city and promised Shakerley all reasonable assistance in carrying out his designs.[141]

On July 22, 1683 the Privy Council gave the official order for Quo Warranto proceedings against Chester's charter to begin.[142] On the following day, because the Rye House Plot, revealed just a month before, had had some Cheshire ramifications, it was ordered that all arms in Chester should be moved to the castle.[143] A house-to-house search carried out in the city at the same time uncovered fifty muskets in Colonel Whitley's house and as many at that of his son Thomas Whitley. Father and son claimed to have bought the weapons with the intention of one day forming a militia company for the king's service in Flintshire. Peter Shakerley's officers were not impressed by this excuse and confiscated the weapons.[144]

Understandably anxious to improve their image with the king, in August, 1683 the mayor and citizens of Chester entrusted Williams with a loyal address to Charles, which the recorder sent on to Jenkins, together with a request that he arrange for the bearer to have an opportunity to present it at Court. He added that the mayor and citizens were very anxious to wait upon the Duke of York in order to congratulate him on his recent fortunate escape from a shipwreck.[145] A week later Jenkins replied, telling Williams that the king had declined to receive the city's official address. His Majesty had preferred to receive an unofficial one sent him by the militia, clergy, and gentry of Chester, in which the citizens who subscribed to it "took notice of the Quo Warranto with all due submission," and had ordered it to be printed.[146]

Meanwhile, Mayor Edwards does not seem to have proved as docile as Peter Shakerley had hoped. At the ceremony of the setting of the Mayor's Watch on Christmas Eve, 1683 Williams praised the, by then, ex-mayor for his steadfast loyalty to the city. The recorder went on to remind the Chester citizens that theirs was a city "ancienter than records, and the head of the most ancient and noblest county palatine." He reminded them of their many charters and liberties, first granted by Ranulf, fourth Earl of Chester, and since confirmed by many kings and by Queen Elizabeth. In 1523 a Quo Warranto had been issued against the city, but their charters had prevailed. Should the city now, having more charters and laws on their side and with the precedent from Henry VIII's reign in their favor, "be afraid to meet the King in his own court and defend its just right?" He reminded them of the clause in Magna Carta guaranteeing the franchises and privileges of all the cities of the kingdom and then went on to praise Magna Carta itself as "the bulwark of English liberties." Like Treby in London and Maynard in Plymouth, he warned of the disadvantages of a surrender of their charter, which would be "self homicide." For once the charter was gone "they must submit to the perhaps [sic] of a doubtful commission reversible at will and pleasure." Finally,

> he repeated the oaths of a freeman leaving out, 'obedient and profitable to the King,' and with particular emphasis the part concerning maintaining the privileges and liberties of the city. Though there were of the body some homespun dissenters of frantic and fanatic brain, who conspired the betraying the charter by surrender or default, for his part he could not, durst not, consent to it. He amplified the fatal consequences of surrender. When the King and city called him to it, he would surrender what he had amongst them, but to the city.[147]

His speech seems to have had some effect. On January 5, 1684 a city grand jury called on William Street, who was once again mayor (having been elected to succeed Edwards), and all their fellow citizens to oppose the Quo Warranto "by all lawful means."[148] Six hundred of the freemen organized themselves into an "Association" to stand by the charter. On February 28, however, a majority of the aldermen refused to join Mayor Street in an appeal to the courts and voted to let the charter become forfeit. Prevented from using the city's seal for the purpose, the mayor sent to London a notice of appeal bearing his mayoral seal, but the courts apparently refused to accept it. Judgment was entered against the Chester charter by default in Trinity Term, 1684.[149]

The new charter, received on February 4, 1685, was the last new charter issued during Charles II's reign, which ended with his death two days later. It cost £251 4s. 6d. to procure. Colonel Werden, Williams' opponent in the 1673 election, and Sir Thomas Grosvenor, a Tory baronet who had sat with Williams for the city in the first two Exclusion parliaments, each paid part of this sum out of their own pockets. The remainder was raised by selling a portion of the city's silver plate and by mortgaging a part of the city's future revenues.[150] The charter named Grosvenor as mayor of the city and also named the other new officials. These men alone were given the right to elect their successors, subject to the approval of the king. Specifically excluded from the new corporation were the Whitleys, father and son; John and George Mainwaring; William Street; George Booth, formerly city prothonotary and presumably a kinsman of his namesake the first Lord Delamere; Michael Johnson, a freeman soap manufacturer of the city; and William Williams, "lately Recorder."[151]

Williams in Chester, Treby in London, Maynard in Plymouth, and Atkyns in Bristol had, it is true, fought in defense of their own careers and political interests. But, though their motives may have been to a certain extent selfish ones, in the new reign that began just after Chester received her new charter their Tory opponents were to discover that the Quo Warranto process which had been so useful in taking control of corporations out of the hands of "factious dissenters" and putting it into the hands of "loyal churchmen" could be just as easily used to oust factious churchmen and replace them with Dissenters or Catholics. Then Englishmen who had so "freely resigned local immunities and charters" or had forced others to do so would come to realize that the Whig lawyers had been essentially correct in their contention that the preservation of "the due order and just temperament of the several parts and powers" of government and the containment of them "within their own bounds" was extremely important because the surrender or loss of old liberties could so easily open up the way for new oppressions.

5

The Whigs on Trial

IN ADDITION TO DEFENDING CORPORATION charters against Quo Warranto suits, other kinds of opportunities presented themselves to the Whig lawyers between 1681 and 1685 for expressing opposition to the growing absolutism of the government and for urging the retention of a balance of power between King, Lords, and Commons. Simultaneously with its campaign to gain control of the corporations Whitehall also conducted a campaign against the Whig Party itself, a campaign designed to defeat its aims, to eliminate its leaders, and to convert or at least discourage its rank and file. But, as with the seizing of the charters, the government, no matter how arbitrary its intentions, had to pay lip service, at least, to the supremacy of the law by showing a willingness to defend its actions in court. As we have seen, the bench was packed in its favor, and the government always emerged triumphant in the political trials of the period. Even so, the trials gave the Whig lawyers yet another chance to proclaim publicly the Whig philosophy and the Whig interpretation of events.

The first great political trial of the period, that of Edward Fitzharris, arose out of some unfinished business of the

Oxford parliament. On March 25, 1681 Sir Robert Clayton and Sir George Treby had reported to the House of Commons details of a confession that Fitzharris, an Irish Catholic, had allegedly made to them in their capacity of justices of the peace, two weeks before, on March 10. Fitzharris had supplied them with many details that confirmed the Whig version of the Popish Plot; of a design to murder the king; of the complicity in the Plot of the Duke of York, the Earl of Danby, and the queen. Most important of all, Fitzharris claimed to have been hired by the papists to distribute a libel against the king, accusing him of popish and tyrannous ambitions—a libel that was to have been represented as the work of the Whigs.[1]

News of this new discovery, so reminiscent of the Dangerfield Plot of the year before, caused great excitement. A motion was made to print the text of the confession, and it was seconded by Sir William Jones, who remarked that "since Lord Stafford's Trial, people have been prevailed upon to believe the plot not true." Sir Francis Winnington, crying out "All is now at stake; therefore how long or short a time we are to sit here, . . . let not our courage lessen . . . let us go to the bottom of this business," moved for Fitzharris' impeachment as the best method of getting at the full truth, and his impeachment was accordingly resolved.[2]

The next day Attorney General Sawyer informed the House of Lords that on March 9 he had been ordered by the king to proceed at law against the Irishman (who had been interrogated by the Earl of Clarendon and Secretary Jenkins before being handed over to Clayton and Treby)[3] and that he had accordingly prepared an indictment against him. After a long debate it was finally resolved, with Shaftesbury and the other Whig peers dissenting, that Fitzharris should be proceeded against according to the Common Law. The excuse for turning down the Commons' request for impeachment proceedings was provided by Lord Chancellor Nottingham, who cited a declaration by the Lords in Edward III's reign —made when they were called upon to try those accused of the murder of Edward II—that it was not proper for the peers to try commoners.[4]

When news of the Upper House's decision and the grounds for it reached the Commons that same afternoon it caused considerable consternation. The danger was very apparent. If such a principle were once accepted, the Crown could, by employing only commoners in the more important government posts, neutralize the Commons' most effective weapon against it.[5] Jones immediately reminded them that during the previous parliament at Westminster the Lords accepted the impeachment of Chief Justice Scroggs, who was a commoner. He next raised the objection that the decision was reportedly that of the "lords spiritual and temporal," which raised the question as to whether the bishops (who of course would tend to be loyal supporters of the Crown) could have any say concerning an impeachment for a capital offense. Finally, he urged the immediate preparation of arguments for presentation to the Lords that would "assert and declare our right of impeaching in capital causes, and that the lords have denied us justice."[6]

Winnington's reaction was even more explosive. "I take this to be," he declared, "a new plot against the Protestant religion." He reminded the House that the justices of the King's Bench had recently dismissed a grand jury even though a recusancy indictment was pending against the Duke of York. Now the Lords were refusing to impeach Fitzharris. He too urged his fellow members to vote an assertion of their rights.[7] On a motion by Sir Thomas Player it was resolved that the Commons had the right to impeach commoners "for treason or any other crime or misdemeanour," that the Lords' refusal was "an obstruction to the further discovery of the Popish Plot, and of great danger to his majesty's person, and the Protestant Religion," and that "for any inferior court to proceed against . . . Fitzharris or any other person lying under an Impeachment in parliament for the same crimes for which he or they stood impeached [was] an high breach of the privilege of parliament."[8] No further progress was made in the matter, however, before the parliament was dissolved two days later.

The full truth concerning Fitzharris' case will probably never be known. It seems likely, however, that he knew more than was good for him because, while the Whigs in Parliament were anxious to see him impeached on a capital charge, King Charles reportedly wanted him hanged as quickly and as quietly as possible.[9] It seems probable that he had been used in some way by the government as an *agent provocateur*. On April 27, 1681 Chief Justice Pemberton, who had replaced Scroggs three weeks before,[10] and the other justices of the King's Bench assured a nervous grand jury that they might lawfully bring in an indictment against Fitzharris, which they did shortly thereafter.[11]

On April 29 the Irishman was brought before the court, by a writ of habeas corpus, to answer inquiries into the murder of Sir Edmond Bury Godfrey. On the advice of his wife, who was present in court, he tried to submit a written plea to the jurisdiction of the court and asked that Jones, Williams, Winnington, Treby, Pollexfen, Wallop, and a Mr. Smith be appointed as his attorneys. After some discussion and argument Williams, Winnington, Pollexfen, and Wallop were declared appointed by Pemberton, who described them as "gentlemen of fair credit and reputation in the world." Against Attorney General Sawyer's objections, Pemberton also ordered that Fitzharris be permitted to consult alone with them in the Tower.[12]

On May 2 the four appointed counsel appeared before the court to request more time to prepare a plea on Fitzharris' behalf against the jurisdiction of the court or else to be released from representing him. It would appear, reading the report of the proceedings, to have been genuinely true that they had not had prior knowledge of the contents of Fitzharris' plea submitted three days earlier, though Sawyer hinted that they had themselves written it. The fact that Mrs. Fitzharris, who had originally produced the document in court, kept urging the justices to appoint Jones and Smith also to assist her husband would suggest that perhaps they had been the authors of it.[13] Nevertheless, the events of the next few days suggest that the Whig lawyers were hoping to delay proceedings until the Michaelmas Term, probably in the hope that a new parliament would be called in the autumn.[14]

Pemberton was finally persuaded to allow an additional day of grace, so that the case came up for trial on May 4. The Crown was represented by Sawyer, Solicitor General Finch, George Jeffreys, Francis Wythens, Edmund Saunders, and, surprisingly, Serjeant Maynard, who had said in the House of Commons of the Lords' refusal to accept Fitzharris' impeachment: "this is a strange breach of the privilege of parliament, and tends to the danger of the king's person, and the destruction of the Protestant Religion, and I hope you will vote it so."[15] Although they had voted as he had hoped and forbidden any inferior court to proceed against Fitzharris, Maynard was now actively participating in such proceedings. He must have decided that this was a time to "trim."

The four counsel now made on Fitzharris' behalf a plea to the jurisdiction of the court that was precisely the same plea, word for word, as the one he had himself submitted a week earlier. Sawyer immediately demurred on the grounds that the plea was too general in that, although it stated that Fitzharris had been impeached by the House of Commons for high treason, it did not state under which particular treason statute, so that there was no evidence that the impeachment and the present indictment were concerned with the same treason. Williams immediately joined in demurrer, in order, as he explained, to show that the defense did not seek to delay matters in any way. He then asked for a remission till the following term in order that the defense might have time to prepare an answer to the demurrer. Meanwhile, he refused to allow Fitzharris to plead to the indictment until the question of jurisdiction had been settled. Despite the objections of counsel for the Crown, and with Justice Thomas Jones dissenting, Pemberton granted a further remission—but only until May 7.[16]

When the court assembled at eight o'clock in the morning on Saturday the 7th for the final hearing on Fitzharris' plea[17] a distinguished body of spectators was present. Shaftesbury was in the audience with Lord Cavendish, Lord Russell, Lord Grey of Werk, the Earl of Essex, the Earl of Macclesfield, and other Whig leaders as well as a good many Tory lords.[18] Opening for Fitzharris, Williams stated the basis of his case: that the defendant was being impeached, for "high treason, by the Commons of England in parliament assembled," and that the lower courts had no right to intervene. An impeachment, Williams maintained, was an appeal by "the people" through their parliamentary representatives and so, like any appeal by a private subject, it took precedence over a royal indictment. The king could pardon a man found guilty as the result of a Crown indictment, but he did not by law have the authority to pardon a man found guilty as the result of an appeal by a subject.[19] Parliament, the Welsh lawyer argued, was without doubt the highest court in the kingdom. The Commons were the greatest grand jury; the Lords were the greatest judges. How could such a court hand a case over to a lower court? "I do think it does not stand my lord," he said, "with the wisdom of the government." The present trial was "an impudent thing, if not an illegal proceeding." He reminded the bench that the next parliament might take exception to this interference in its affairs by an inferior court and that, being the superior court, Parliament would be the judge between itself and the King's Bench. He ended by recalling examples of judges in the past "some whereof fled, others were fined and others hanged for unjust judgments."[20]

Chief Justice Pemberton intervened, after Williams had spoken, to assert that the question at issue was not "whether an impeachment for treason, by the House of Commons, and still pending, be a sufficient matter to oust the Court from proceeding upon an indictment for the same offence," but rather "whether you have pleaded sufficient matter here to oust us of our jurisdiction."[21] Winnington, speaking next, attacked Sawyer's objection, stated three days before, that the defendant's plea was too vague concerning the precise offense for which he was allegedly being impeached. It was not, the ex-solicitor general claimed, "secundum legem et consuetudinem parliamenti" to impeach in the first instance for anything more specific than "High treason." Traditionally the judges had always declined to give judgment on the law and custom of parliaments; and even though the parliament in which Fitzharris had been impeached had been dissolved, yet Parliament as an institution, and as a court, might be presumed always to exist—various statutes called for its being summoned frequently.

The present trial, Winnington implied, was both illogical

and unlawful. It was ridiculous, he said, for a grand jury to indict Fitzharris when they, together with all other commoners of the realm, had already accused him in Parliament. No petty jury could justly decide as to his guilt, for they also were included among his accusers by virtue of the actions of the Commons at Oxford. If Fitzharris were acquitted by this lower court, Winnington demanded to know, should the High Court of Parliament be held to be bound by its verdict? Obviously not; but, if it were not, his life would be placed in double jeopardy, which would be unlawful.[22]

Wallop and Pollexfen concluded the case for the prisoner. Wallop reminded the court that in the case of the five "Popish lords" the judges had all agreed that they could not be indicted in an inferior court after they had been impeached in Parliament, although no specific accusations had yet been made against them and Parliament was at the time dissolved. Pollexfen contended that the defendant's plea was based on the record as it stood and averred clearly that the same treason was meant both by the impeachment and the indictment. What more, he asked, could be expected?[23]

Replying for the Crown, Sawyer stuck to his original objection. An impeachment, he said, was not an impeachment until the detailed articles of action were produced; any proceedings by the Commons up to that time merely constituted notice of intention to impeach. Yet the defendant's plea referred to an "impeachment"—an impeachment for an offense that was only vaguely described as "high treason." The court could take no notice of it.[24]

Sawyer was seconded by Solicitor General Sir Heneage Finch who, in what was described by one Whig spectator as "a jingling speech,"[25] contested the defense's argument that an impeachment by the Commons was an action by the entire English people. He pointed out that articles of impeachment always described the accused's offense as being "contra ligeantiae suae debitem et coronam et dignitatem domini regis," a formula that was not used in a private appeal by one citizen against another. The king, then, and not the subject, was the one allegedly offended by an impeached person; it was up to the king, therefore, to decide how he would secure satisfaction. As for the case of the five "Popish lords," the Upper House had used a writ of certiorari to have their trial removed from the King's Bench. Obviously, therefore, they had not considered that they had an automatic right to remove it.[26] Jeffreys later added that in that particular case the Commons had, in fact, despite what Wallop had said, already presented detailed articles against the accused.[27]

Three days later, on May 10, Fitzharris again appeared briefly at the bar to be told by Chief Justice Pemberton that the court, with Justices Jones and Raymond concurring, though with Justice Dolben doubting but not resolved, was of the opinion that his plea was not sufficient to justify their abandoning proceedings against him in accordance with the grand jury's indictment. Then he was returned to the Tower to await trial the following term.[28]

The decision could not have been an easy one for Pemberton and his colleagues from either the legal or the political point of view in this bizarre trial, in which the defendant's lawyers wished to prevent the court from trying him and condemning him to death only so that they could have him tried and condemned elsewhere. Legally they were at a disadvantage because, as Skinner's case and other incidents in this period showed, the "lex et consuetudo parliamenti," based as it was on a number of imperfectly reported late-medieval precedents, was still very vague. Despite the chief justice's disavowal, the basic legal issues at stake were the Commons' right to impeach Fitzharris, a fellow commoner, before the

House of Lords, and whether the initial steps taken against him by the Commons at Oxford constituted impeachment.

With regard to the first of these questions Blackstone, in the following century, was to state it as his opinion that, though a commoner could be tried by the Lords for a misdemeanor, he could not be tried by them for a capital offense. To back his opinion he cited the same precedent that Nottingham had appealed to in regard to Fitzharris' case: the Lords' disavowal, under Edward III, of their right to try commoners accused of the murder of Edward II.[29] Hales, apparently, had been of the same opinion.[30] But, as Jones had pointed out to the Commons at Oxford, there was a difference between impeachment by the Commons and an indictment by the Crown, and Edward II's assassins had been indicted by the Crown. Furthermore, the fact could not be denied that the Lords had a few months earlier accepted without the least scruple the impeachments of Scroggs and other commoners for capital crimes. Because the judges gave no explanation of their judgment with regard to Fitzharris' plea neither issue was settled definitely, for the abandonment by the Commons in the eighteenth century of the use of impeachment as a political weapon made such questions of purely academic interest.

Taking politics into consideration the justices knew what the king wanted: that Fitzharris' plea be thrown out. But they also realized that Williams' threats of future parliamentary action against them if they did anything to weaken the Commons' precious weapon of impeachment would not prove to be empty if a new parliament, with a Whig majority in the Lower House, were ever assembled in the near future. Representatives of the Court were said to be active at this time in several of the boroughs seeking to win the voters over to the king's side, which would seem to indicate that Charles foresaw the possibility of having to summon another parliament soon. However, the king reportedly told the judges, while they were considering Fitzharris' plea, that he would not have any more parliaments.[31] If he really did say that, it must have made their decision a great deal easier.

Maynard appeared again for the Crown in Fitzharris' actual trial for treason on June 9. The Irishman was quickly found guilty and died a traitor's death at Tyburn on July 1.[32]

Shortly after Fitzharris' execution Dr. Hawkins, the chaplain at the Tower, who was shortly afterwards elevated to the deanery of Chichester, issued what purported to be the final confession of Fitzharris, in which he stated that anything that he had said reflecting on the loyalty of the Duke of York or the Duchess he had been browbeaten into saying by Clayton and Treby, who had put words into his mouth when they interrogated him. The two city magistrates were soon exonerated, however, in a counterpamphlet entitled *Truth Vindicated,* which reminded readers that it was a matter of record that everything that the Irishman had allegedly testified before Clayton and Treby he had earlier testified to before the Council.[33]

When Mrs. Fitzharris asked that Sir William Jones be among the counsel appointed to assist her husband she was told by Chief Justice Pemberton that Jones was no longer practicing in Westminster Hall;[34] and, indeed, the ex-attorney general apparently never appeared at the bar again after the dissolution of the Oxford parliament. Perhaps he was already suffering from ill health; or perhaps, having enjoyed, as attorney general, preaudience at the bar, he did not wish to return to the scene of earlier glories in an inferior capacity.

He continued, however, to practice the law in an advisory capacity. In October, 1681, for example, he was one of two lawyers advising John Evelyn and the other executors of the will of the deceased Viscountess Mordaunt.[35] He also continued, as we have seen, to be active in politics in the City.[36] According to a newsletter of January, 1682 he had even expressed his intention to "put on a gown again" to help defend the City's charter.[37]

There is some evidence to indicate that Jones took part in the inner councils of the opposition at this time. Late in July, 1681 when William of Orange came to England hoping to effect a reconciliation between the anti-French Whigs and the king, it is reported that while in London he consulted with Lord Russell, the Earl of Essex, and Jones.[38] It was while attending a gathering of opposition leaders at John Hampden's house, Salton Court, Buckinghamshire, that Jones died, on the night of May 2, 1682. As a result of sleeping between damp sheets, he had developed a "fever" (presumably pneumonia), which quickly resulted in his death.[39]

It is fairly certain that by May, 1682 the Whig leaders, frustrated in their efforts to gain a parliamentary victory over their opponents at Court and faced with the growing counterattack in the law courts, were contemplating desperate and extralegal means of gaining their desired ends. Lord Trevor, a friend of Jones and a kinsman of Hampden, many years later told Arthur Onslow:

> that it was thought a great felicity to Sir William Jones, by his nearest friends that he died at this time, for as he was privy to the consultations and designs of the Lord Russell and the others of his set, and having made himself as obnoxious to the court as any of them and because of his superior abilities more dangerous, it was very likely he would have fallen under the suspicion at least of being engaged in the plot . . . and have been treated with a particular severity, which his timid nature could not have

borne, and might have drawn confessions from him, injurious to his friends and his own character.[40]

Roger North, a Tory, portrays Jones as becoming more and more disillusioned with the Whig leadership in his last two years. Being himself a man whose "personal Gravity and Virtue was [sic] great," Jones, according to North, came to hate Shaftesbury for his "unscrupulous character" and preferred not to remain in the same room with him.[41] Because Jones "was for doing his Work the formal Way, and hated Violence," North suggests that, after hearing what his fellow guests were planning, Jones' conscience was so stricken with guilt that it prevented him from fighting off the aftereffects of sleeping between unaired sheets.[42] Against this explanation must be set the undoubted facts that Jones had been active in political agitation in London and Oxford in 1681 and that, although over a year had elapsed since the dissolution of the Oxford parliament, he had apparently continued to work in close cooperation with the Whig leaders right up to the time of his death. A possible explanation would be that it was at this very meeting in Buckinghamshire that the possibility of using extreme, extralegal methods was first discussed, that Jones was shocked, and that had he lived, he would have felt constrained to sever all connections with the other Whig leaders for the sake of his principles and his personal safety, both. If this were true, it could also account for Lord Trevor's story that Jones knew of the Whig plot, though we have no accounts of any meeting to plan details of the plot earlier than the autumn of 1682.[43]

At all events, Jones' death was evidently a blow to the Whigs of London, who seem to have been depending heavily on him to defend their charter. The Whig Lord Fauconberg described his passing as "a loss to the city that can only be exceeded by that of their charter, which probably will follow."[44] The government, on the other hand, appears to have been greatly relieved by the removal of such a skilled and prestigious lawyer from the ranks of their opponents. "The peace newly made with the Algerians . . . and the peace made here with the Morocco ambassador, are of great importance," wrote Secretary of State Lord Conway, "and yet none more than the death of Sir William Jones."[45]

With Jones dead, William Williams appears to have taken his place as the principal legal adviser to the Whig leaders. Unlike Jones, Williams appears always to have cooperated closely with Shaftesbury, who consulted him and Wallop in preparing his defense against the indictment for high treason unsuccessfully sought against him by the Crown in October, 1681, and with him and Pollexfen in March, 1682 with regard to several actions for conspiracy that he wished to prosecute against various persons who had testified against him before the grand jury on that occasion.[46] Another time, Shaftesbury dispatched Williams down to Lancashire to secure testimony concerning a man who claimed to have been an eyewitness of King Charles' marriage, during his exile on the Continent, to Lucy Walter, the mother of the Duke of Monmouth.[47]

James Scott, Duke of Monmouth and Buccleuch, was the man chosen by Shaftesbury and his lieutenants as a popular figurehead around whose banner, despite the bar sinister it bore, they sought to rally the majority of Englishmen. The king's son (though undoubtedly illegitimate, despite all attempts to prove him otherwise) and a Protestant, Monmouth was chosen over William of Orange, the other possible Protestant alternative to the Duke of York as heir to the throne, because he was the more tractable. He also had the gift, a very desirable one in royalty and one that William lacked, of being able to appeal to crowds, as he showed on his various mock-royal tours of the country.

Williams' position as legal advisor to the Shaftesbury/ Monmouth group occasionally involved him in trials that had very little if any connection with politics. When Thomas Thynne, a leading Whig politician, was assassinated while riding in his coach in Pall Mall by three henchmen of the Swedish Count Konigsmarck in February, 1682, it was regarded at first as an attempt on the life of Monmouth, who had left the coach just a few minutes before the attack. The actual motivation for the killing was the fact that the count was a rejected suitor of Thynne's young wife. Williams led the prosecution and succeeded in procuring the conviction of the three actual assassins, but Konigsmarck himself, charged with being an accessory, was acquitted.[48] The following November Williams defended Lord Grey of Werk, one of Monmouth's closest friends and associates, who was charged with the abduction and debauchery of his young sister-in-law, Lady Henrietta Berkeley. Quite rightly, judging from the evidence, Grey was found guilty.[49]

The Whig peers were not the only ones who required the assistance of the Whig lawyers at that time; their assistance was also sought by the leading Whigs in the City who found themselves the targets of a campaign by the government to exact legal retribution for the political agitation accompanying the election of the new sheriffs in the summer of 1682. In November, 1682 Pilkington was fined £100,000 on an action of *scandalum magnatum* for some indiscreet remarks he had been heard to make about the Duke of York.[50] In May, 1683 Pilkington, Shute, Lord Grey of Werk, Bethel Cornish, and several others were tried in a nisi-prius court in the Guildhall, presided over by Chief Justice Saunders of the King's Bench, on a charge of inciting a riot at the polling for sheriffs on the previous Midsummer's Day.[51] Williams, Winnington, Wallop, Holt, Thompson, and a Mr. Freke appeared for the defense, Attorney General Sawyer, Solicitor General Finch, and George Jeffreys appeared for the Crown. An attempt by the defense to challenge the jury on the grounds that it had been empaneled by an interested party (sheriff Dudley North) was unsuccessful, whereupon the main argument turned on whether the sheriffs or the lord mayor had the right to adjourn the poll. The defense contended that this was merely a question of right between the mayor and the sheriffs and that it should be settled in a civil court. With regard to the rioting the defense maintained that the mere presence of the accused in the Hall did not automatically make them guilty. There was a certain amount of booing and hissing from the gallery during the present trial. Did that, Williams asked, make the officials of the court guilty of riot? None of the Crown witnesses, when challenged by Williams, could testify that they had actually seen any of the accused behaving improperly. Nevertheless, the jury found that all the accused did "in a tumultuary way, make a riot to set up a magistracy by the power of the people."

During this same month Williams aided Treby in the defense of Sir Patience Ward, the former Whig lord mayor, who was charged with perjury in the earlier trial of Pilkington for libeling the Duke of York,[52] in which Ward had testified that Pilkington had not been present during the conversation about the duke. Ward was found guilty as charged and shortly afterwards, hearing that he was to be placed in the pillory, fled the country.

The last major judicial manifestation of the political revolution in London occurred in November, 1684 when Williams assisted Serjeant Maynard in the defense of Papillon, who was charged with unlawfully procuring the arrest of the lord mayor, Sir William Pritchard, in April of the previous year.[53] Pritchard was demanding damages of £10,000. It had been a rather high-handed action and there was little that the defense could say. Jeffreys, now elevated to the position of Lord Chief Justice of the King's Bench, was presiding over the trial, and roundly castigated the Whigs for disturbing the peace of the City. The decision inevitably went against Papillon, who followed Ward's example and fled the country.

Ogg says of these trials: "Thus was England habituated to methods of justice savouring more of Edinburgh than of Westminster."[54] Leaving aside the question of justice in Scotland at this period, it must be remembered that injustice in Westminster Hall did not begin with the election of Tory sheriffs in 1682. There had been little justice in most of the Popish Plot trials. Green, Berry, and Hill were found guilty of the murder of Sir Edmund Bury Godfrey on obviously trumped-up charges. Nor must it be forgotten that even if Pilkington and Shute did not deliberately incite the riot on Midsummer's Day, 1682, they certainly did nothing to try to stop it. Pilkington probably did slander the Duke of York, and Ward probably did lie to cover up for him. It is easy to sympathize with men whose aim was to win the right to representative government—although representative of only one class, their own—against the pretensions of despotism, and one may well consider the evidence that convicted them as having been insufficient. But the fact remains that their trials were not particularly unfair for the age.

After Shaftesbury's flight into exile, in the autumn of 1682, the leadership of the Whigs passed into the hands of the "Council of Six": Monmouth, Russell, Algernon Sidney, Essex, Howard, and John Hampden. The discovery of the so-called Rye House Plot in June, 1683, as a result of which these six were arrested and accused of conspiracy to murder the king and raise a general insurrection, gave rise to a new series of trials that inevitably involved the Whig lawyers.

The first of these was the trial of William, Lord Russell, on a charge of high treason before a Special Commission of Gaol Delivery presided over by Chief Justice Pemberton of the Court of Common Pleas in London's Old Bailey on July 13, 1683.[55] Like Fitzharris, Russell suffered from the rule prevailing at the time by which anyone accused of a felony was denied legal counsel in any matter concerned with the facts of his alleged crime, though he was entitled to counsel in matters of law. A legal question came up at the commencement of the trial when Russell questioned the validity of the jury empaneled to try his case on the grounds that few of them were forty-shilling freeholders as the law required them to be. When the court replied that the rule was not customarily applied in London because most of the land in the City belonged either to one of the great corporations or else to a peer, Russell requested the services of Pollexfen, Holt, and a barrister named Ward to argue the matter on his behalf, and this was allowed by the court. The three counsel had come well prepared to debate the issue, Russell having been in consultation with them for some time prior to the trial. In fact, the Russell family appear to have spared no effort to obtain all possible legal assistance for their unfortunate relative.[56]

Among the lawyers consulted was Sir Robert Atkyns, who was living quietly in retirement at his home Lower Swell, in the Gloucestershire countryside near Stow-in-the-Wold, but who was evidently still a figure of some suspicion to the government, despite the fact that his Tory son was a deputy lieutenant of the county. Shortly after the discovery of the Whig plot his house was searched by local officials and every weapon removed, including the sword with which he had been knighted at the Restoration.[57] He communicated with Lady Russell through Hugh Speke, a student at Lincoln's Inn and a family friend whose father, George, and elder brother, John, had been among the members from Somerset in the Exclusion parliaments.[58] "I am not without apprehensions," Atkyns wrote:

> of danger that may arise by advising in, or so much as discoursing of public affairs; yet no fear of danger shall hinder me from performing that duty we owe to another, to counsel those that need our advice, how to make their just defence when they are called in question for their lives; especially if they are persons that have by their general carriage and conversation appeared to be men of worth, and lovers of their king and country and of the religion established among us.[59]

Nevertheless, he urged caution upon Speke and asked him to make immediate copies of his letters and then return them to him in order that nothing in his handwriting might be left lying about where it could fall into the wrong hands.[60]

Pollexfen and his colleagues were unsuccessful in challenging the composition of the jury that was to try Russell. They cited a statute of Henry V's reign, which stated that no man should serve as a juror to try a capital offense who was not a freeholder, and several other medieval statutes to the same effect. Attorney General Sawyer's reply cited a statute of Queen Mary's reign, which stated that all treason trials were to be conducted in accordance with the Common Law, and pointed out that the customs of London were part of the Common Law and that it was not customary to apply the freehold qualification to London jurors. This line of argument was upheld by the court. With the matter of the jury settled, Russell once again was left to defend himself. By the following afternoon, the evidence against him had been heard, the jury had found him guilty, and the court had condemned him to death. Two days later George Treby, acting in his capacity as recorder of London and faithfully performing his duty as always, signed the warrant for Russell's execution by hanging, drawing, and quartering. King Charles later remitted the sentence to death by a simple beheading, which was carried out on July 21—in Lincoln's Inn Fields so as to allow the largest possible crowd to see justice done.[61]

Speke, or someone else, sent a transcript of the trial to Atkyns, who immediately commenced mustering arguments for an appeal. In a letter written, ironically, on the very day that Russell perished, Atkyns cited Dyer's *Reports* (folio 99) as authority that jurors in a trial for felony must be possessed of forty shillings in freehold property or £100 in goods, and pointed out several miscarriages of justice in the trial. Russell, meanwhile, just a few minutes before he laid his head on the block, had handed to one of the sheriffs a paper in which he argued that meeting and consulting with others to raise an insurrection and to seize the king's guards to forward that end was not an act of treason as treason was defined within the statute of Edward III under which he had been charged, and arguing further that his having been present at several consultations of that nature might have constituted "misprision of treason" but was definitely not treason itself.[62] This latter argument Russell presumably derived from Atkyns' letter to Speke before the trial, in which the Lawyer had pointed out that being present while others "consult and conspire to do some treasonable act" does not make one guilty of treason, although concealing one's knowledge of it does make one guilty of "misprision."[63]

Russell's case was retried, with the general public acting as both judge and jury, in the altered political climate of 1689. In that year the Tory lawyer Sir Bartholomew Shower published a pamphlet, entitled *An Antidote against Poison,* in refutation of Russell's last message, which had been published as part of an effort by the Whig leader's family and friends to have the verdict of six years before reversed. Shower reminded his readers that a witness at Russel's trial, Colonel Rumsey, had testified that when he came to the house of one Shepherd, a wine merchant, in September, 1682, bringing a message from the Earl of Shaftesbury (who was in hiding in Wapping), Russell had been there with the Duke of Monmouth, Lord Grey, Sir Thomas Armstrong, and other plotters. They were discussing the necessity of postponing a planned uprising because their allies in the West Country were not yet ready. And Shepherd himself had testified that Russell and the others had often met at his house and had plotted there to seize the king's guards at Whitehall. Finally, Lord Howard, who in order to save his own life had turned king's evidence against his coconspirators, had testified that there had been a plan for a general uprising the previous October directed by Shaftesbury from his hideout in Wapping; that after Shaftesbury's departure Russell had been one of the six who had assumed leadership of the plotters; and that Russell had joined in their discussion and consented to everything that was done by them.[64]

Did the law recognize different degrees of clandestine action against the Crown? The Tory lawyer maintained that it did not, in an argument that by implication denied the justifiability of the "Glorious Revolution."

The meeting and consulting to make an insurrection against the King, or raise a rebellion with the kingdom be the end thereof never so specious for public good, though the rebellion be not actually raised, is high-treason by the laws of this land.[65]

The clause in the statute of 2 Edward III c. 2 "against conspiring and imagining the death of the King," he argued, "extends as well to civil death as natural." To plan the King's deposition, in fact, was as much high treason as to plan his assassination.

With regard to Russell's claim to be guilty of, at the most, the lesser offense of misprision of treason, Shower argued that "misprision of high-treason is the concealment thereof by a person who had a bare knowledge of the treason, without any mixture of his consent." But if one continually attended meetings at which treason was plotted, and did not object or reveal it at once to the proper authorities, then one was oneself "a principal traitor." He instanced the case of George Brook, who had been told of the plot to depose James I and place Lady Arabella Stuart on the throne, and had given his consent to it, and who on those grounds alone had been convicted of treason.[66]

Soon after *An Antidote* had appeared, Atkyns published a reply entitled *A Defence of the Late Lord Russell's Innocency,* a tract that had been drafted, its author said, at the request of Russell's family shortly after his execution and had since aided several laymen on trial for their lives for treason.[67] This published version was preceded by copies of two of the letters to Hugh Speke, one written before and one after Russell's trial. The best that Atkyns could do for Russell, however, was to seek to have him acquitted posthumously on technicalities, a resort to which the Whig lawyers were often forced in their attempts to defend the more extreme actions of some of their party.

The key point, Atkyns argued, was that Russell was

charged with treason under the statute of Edward III—specifically, under the clauses stating it to be treason "when a man doth compass or imagine the death of the King." Although an act of 13 Charles II, "for the safety and preservation of the king's person," did make it treason to compass or imagine deposing the king or levying war against the king in either speech or writing, it was totally irrelevant to Russell's case. Concluding and agreeing at a private meeting "to move and stir up insurrection and rebellion" and "to seize and destroy the guards" could hardly be construed as compassing and imagining the king's death. If, as Shower argued, the clause in Edward III's statute included planning merely to levy war against the king or to depose him, why was it felt necessary to pass the act of 13 Charles II? Levying war against the king was listed in the earlier statute as a separate treasonable offense from compassing or imagining his death, and yet Russell had been convicted of the latter offense by very dubious testimony that he had committed the former. Had the wording of the indictment been different, Atkyns was willing to concede, the evidence might have been sufficient to prove Russell guilty. Since one of the major accusations against Russell had been that he conspired with others to seize the king's guards and thereby threatened the king's life, Atkyns sought to invalidate the charge by an argument that expressed the traditional Whig objections to a standing army. The guards, he argued, had no legal existence, for they had not been voted upon by Parliament and the law recognized no military force except the militia unless it had been approved by Parliament. Therefore, a charge of conspiracy to seize the guards was legally meaningless.[68]

In a reply entitled *The Magistracy and Government of England Vindicated,* Shower repeated his former arguments, sought to demolish those of Atkyns, and pointed out that they claimed essentially that Russell was probably guilty but not as guilty as he had been made out to be.[69] Atkyns' answer was a second tract, *The Lord Russell's Innocency further defended,* in which he restated his essential argument that the treason statute under which Russell had been indicted defined two relevant forms of treason: compassing or imagining the death of the king and levying war against the king. In the first instance mere conspiracy and planning constituted treason; in the second, planning was not enough; an actual act of war had to occur. The statute plainly did not make a conspiracy to levy war an act of treason, yet the prosecution in Russell's case had sought to make evidence of just such a conspiracy into proof of a conspiracy to kill the king, thereby making nonsense of the fine distinctions evidently implied by the fourteenth-century statute. One new point that Atkyns brought up at this stage was that even before the statute of Henry V, which Pollexfen and his colleagues had cited as proof that Russell's jurors had to be forty-shilling freeholders, under the Common Law all jurors had to be freeholders, and the statute had merely set the amount at forty shillings. Therefore, the Marian statute, cited by the attorney general, putting all such trials on a Common Law basis had not removed the need for a jury of freeholders, but had merely done away with the forty-shilling qualifications.[70] The indefatigable Shower was soon ready with a further rejoinder,[71] but at this stage Parliament stepped in and declared in Atkyns' favor by passing an act to reverse the 1683 verdict against Russell on grounds exactly similar to those argued in his defense by Atkyns; that he had been

> by undue and illegal return of jurors, . . . refused his lawful challenge to the said jurors, for want of freehold,

and by partial and unjust constructions of law wrongfully convicted, attainted and executed for high treason.[72]

The other major trial arising out of the Rye House Plot was that of Sir Algernon Sidney,[73] which took place in November, 1683. Williams, Pollexfen, and three other lawyers were retained to assist Sidney, who was charged with treason not only for his complicity in the plot but also for having written a book, in answer to Sir Robert Filmer's *Patriarcha,* in which he had said that "the power originally in the people of England is delegated unto the Parliament."[74] Williams must have been glad of the opportunity to aid in the defense of such a principle. Because on a charge of treason Sidney could not have the direct aid of counsel in his trial, Williams compiled copious notes for his client's use in the courtroom. These notes are a useful primary source for the regulations and procedure in a treason trial at this time:[75]

> You may challenge 35 of the jury returned to try you without any cause.
> You may challenge as many more as you shall please shewing excuse for such challenge. Want of freehold in a juror returned in the county of Middlesex is a good cause . . .
> Consider of exceptions to witnesses. And when you make your exceptions pray they may be argued by counsel if the court shall reject them. Desire all evidence of hearsay from witnesses may not be given, but desire the Court to stopp that evidence.
> Watch the kings counsell in summing or argueing the evidence against you, (that) they do not offer anything that was not proved, and stop them if they do . . .

In his advice as to the defense to be made of the statement on Parliament, Williams expressed his own political philosophy:

. . . the substance of the words seems to tend to no more than to place the parliament to some purposes above the prerogative of the King, of which the King himself is one of the three states, and without whom there can be no parliament or act of parliament by the law, and it is no more, it may be then to the King having his lords and commons joined to him in parliament may do more than the king can do without them, . . .

Sydney was tried in Westminster Hall in November, 1683 before Jeffreys, who had been appointed Chief Justice of the King's Bench just two months earlier. The accused made much of the fact that some of his jurors were not freeholders, and a comparison of his defense with Williams' notes shows that he follows them very closely. In fact, while Russell's trial had lasted just two days, Sidney was able, by using "every delaying tactic he could squeeze out of the law," to extend his for two whole weeks.[76] But his case was hopeless from the start. The evidence of Howard, who had saved his own life by turning king's evidence against his coconspirators, convinced the Tory jury of Sidney's guilt, and he was beheaded on December 7.

Three months later Williams was able to appear in person before Jeffreys and the other justices of the King's Bench to defend John Hampden: because there was only one witness (Howard) to the fact, Hampden could not legally be charged with more than a misdemeanor.[77] Howard and Attorney General Sawyer's other witnesses could testify to no more than Hampden's having been present at several meetings of the Whig leaders that were held in his house and that had been followed by some rather suspicious actions on the part of some of those who had been at the meetings. Williams tried to discredit Howard by bringing in witnesses who testified that he had said during the previous summer that he knew nothing of the Rye House Plot. Jeffreys, quite reasonably, objected that one would not have expected Howard to go around proclaiming his guilt. And when Williams claimed that Howard was only making these accusations to save his own neck, Jeffreys pointed out that Howard already had his pardon and so could not possibly have such a motive. This was not such a valid objection, for Howard would have many good reasons not to change his story, even though he had been pardoned, for to be an apostate was one thing, to be a perjured apostate would be quite another. Williams finally fell back on the argument that presence did not necessarily imply consent:

> What is meant by consent when nothing was said, I must leave to the jury. I must agree the Lord Howard did swear that my client was in the company, but how far he did or did not consent, does not at all appear, and how far this will charge my client, I must leave to you gentlemen.

But Jeffreys instructed the jury to find Hampden guilty, which they did.

The very next day, February 7, Williams (assisted by Wallop) was engaged in defending Lawrence Braddon and Atkyns' friend Hugh Speke, who had been arrested the previous August for circulating a letter in which it was "not obscurely hinted" that the Earl of Essex, who had committed suicide in the Tower on the opening day of Russell's trial, July 13, had actually been murdered by partisans of the Duke of York.[78]

The letter, the original copy of which Speke admitted before the Council was in his handwriting, and which had been found in Speke's house, was addressed to Atkyns and must have caused the ex-judge to be regarded with even greater suspicion by the government than he had been before —especially when Speke's mother testified that Atkyns had recently been paying off her son's gambling debts. Bishop

Burnet, in fact, was moved to comment on Atkyns' behavior at this time that although he was "a very learned man," he was also "very hot and indiscreet."[79]

Tried on a charge of sedition, both men were found guilty. Speke was fined £1,000 and Braddon, who was also accused of having tried to suborn witnesses, was fined £2,000. In summing up the evidence in Hampden's trial, the day before, the chief justice had conceded magnanimously that Williams had argued "very ingeniously for the advantage of his client, as every man is bound to say what is best for his client." Jeffreys' evaluation of Williams' evidence in Braddon's and Speke's defense was far less tolerant:

> I know what use you would make of it, the use is just the same, as you make use of all sorts of ridiculous and shamming stories to set us together by the ears, and rake into all the dunghills that can be, to pick up matter to put us into confusion.[80]

Here the lord chief justice was expressing the indignation of every loyal Tory against the Whigs, whom they saw, perhaps with some justification, as querulous, scheming malcontents who for no good reason would stop at nothing to hinder quiet, peaceable government.

In the London Sheriffs and Rye House Plot trials, Williams and his fellow Whig lawyers—although the trials were political in origin and their political affiliations decided on which side they spoke—were engaged in a legal, not a political, struggle. With the exception of Williams' defense of Sidney's views on Parliament, the lawyers' arguments in these trials were concerned with points of law and justice and not with politics. Two main themes that they constantly stressed were that men should not be judged by the actions of their associates, and that proof rather than mere presumption of guilt should be necessary to convict. As Williams had said in the House of Commons, back in the autumn of 1675, "men are not to be imprisoned upon notions."

But in the case of the *East India Company* v. *Thomas Sandys,* which was tried before the Court of King's Bench in a series of hearings between Trinity Term, 1683 and Hilary Term, 1685, Williams was afforded an opportunity to express his political views. At this time, when neither of the two major political groups was yet a tightly controlled corporate entity with a single "party-line" opinion on every matter of public interest, the East India Company was bipartisan in its composition. Some of its highest offices had been held by such eminent Whigs as Sir Samuel Barnardiston, Papillon, and Dubois. But the majority of men who called themselves Whigs objected to the company for reasons that were both economic and political. In the economic sphere, the many merchants who were excluded from the company's activities were torn between their desire to be admitted to its exclusive ranks and resentment at the competition it gave both to older established companies (such as the Levant company) in the importation of oriental goods, and to English manufacturers (notably the silk weaving industry, which felt itself threatened by the increasing importation of silk cloth from India). In the political sphere, the Whigs saw the company as a closed monopoly run primarily for the benefit of certain favorite courtiers who held large shares of stock that they had received in return for their having supported the company's interest at Court. The basic issue was whether the king alone, assisted by his Privy Council, should control England's overseas trade and administer England's overseas possessions, or whether these things were subject to parliamentary legislation—whether, in fact, the legislative jurisdiction of Parliament extended beyond the shores of England.

The 1624 Statute of Monopolies had prohibited "all monopolies and all commissions, grants, licenses, charters, and letters patents . . . for the sole buying, selling, making, working, or using of anything within this realm or the dominion of Wales. . . ."[81] These Whigs felt that the prohibition ought now to be extended to overseas commercial operations.

In 1680 John Parkhurst had said in the House of Commons:

> By this company the birth-right of many thousands is prejudiced, and may well deserve a serious consideration . . . this company, by having the command of the treasure of the nation, cannot be controlled by any less than . . . a House of Commons.[82]

In their arguments on behalf of Sandys, who had had his ship and cargo confiscated by the East India Company and was now being sued by the company for interloping, Treby, Pollexfen, and Williams developed the same two themes. In the first set of hearings in Trinity Term, 1683, Holt, appearing for the company, stipulated the basic question at issue: did the company's charter entitle it to proceed against the defendant?[83] Behind this, he pointed out, was another question: could the king grant the company the right of sole trade to the Indies exclusive of all his other subjects? Holt sought to show that the grant was good by pointing out that the persons traded with in the East Indies were infidels. All Christian kingdoms were automatically in a state of perpetual warfare against all infidel kingdoms, he said, and no one could deny that the Crown had the sole right of controlling relations with enemy powers. All foreign trade, in fact, was inseparably involved with matters of diplomacy and of war and peace—all matters that lay indisputably within the jurisdiction of the royal prerogative. While it was true that clause thirty of Magna Carta guaranteed to merchants the right to travel freely, it also contained the conditions "unless beforehand publicly prohibited" and "except in time of war." The king could at any time prevent any merchant or other subject from leaving the country by a writ of ne exeat regnum—a fact that was legally incontestable. Also, Holt maintained, the king must have the right to control imports and exports in order to preserve the health of the national economy. The East India Company, operating under the charter, was not a monopoly as a monopoly was defined in Coke's *Third Institute*—that is, as being in possession of the sole right of trading in something to the restraint of privileges previously enjoyed by other corporations and persons—because no previous privilege to trade with the Indies had ever existed. Therefore, by its charter the Company was possessed of a valid franchise, one that certainly included the right to sue those who violated it.

Speaking in reply, Treby expressed the essential conservatism of the Whig lawyers when he claimed that there were three things that had "fair pretences" but were really "mischievous":

1. New Courts; 2. New Offices; 3. New Corporations trading into foreign parts or at home; which under the fair pretence of order and government, in conclusion tend to the hindrance of trade and traffic and in the end produce monopolies.[84]

He then went on to give one of the classic definitions of the Whig lawyers' attitude to the royal prerogative:

In this argument I am sensible I am to treat of a tender point, the King's prerogative but I shall treat it with that regard and deference that I ought, and as our books teach us. The prerogative is great; but it has this general and just limitation, that nothing is to be done thereby that is mischievous or injurious to the subject.

Englishmen, he argued, had long been trading freely with the East Indies, whereas the company's present charter had only been issued twenty-two years before. The company was, therefore, in fact, a monopoly according to Coke's definition. If the Scriptures decreed that all Englishmen were permanently at war with all infidels, he scoffed, then the grant of the charter was surely void for the king could not dispense with Scriptural law for the benefit of a few of his subjects or even all of them. Treby dismissed Holt's insistence on the king's right to control trade and foreign relations by observing that what was not harmful to the national welfare if done by a company could not be harmful if done by a private individual. If the king had given the company a license to do something that was not lawful for other subjects to do, then, Treby was prepared to concede, the king could proceed against Sandys for doing it without a license; but a license was not a specific hereditable right, as a franchise was, and therfore the company could not sue Sandys for infringement of a franchise. The king's prerogative, Treby concluded, was intended to establish and preserve the property and livelihood of his subjects. It could not be used to limit their right to property and their opportunities to earn a livelihood. Only the subjects themselves, through their representatives in Parliament, could act to restrain trade.

Shortly after these initial arguments, on August 9, 1683 King Charles granted a new charter to the East India Company[85] in which it was noted that although "by Virtue of Our Prerogative Royal, which We will not in that Behalf have argued, or brought into Question," all subjects not belonging to the East India Company had been forbidden by the previous charter to trade in the East Indies, some interlopers had ignored the prohibitions and the company was therefore given increased powers to deal with such intruders upon their preserves.[86] However, the prohibition was twice more "brought into question" by the Whig lawyers Pollexfen and Williams in the course of the next sixteen months. That the Crown attached great importance to Sandys' case is shown by the fact that the company was represented in these two latter hearings by the solicitor general and the attorney general, respectively.

Finch, speaking on April 19, 1684, reminded the court that Sandys had replied to the company's action against him by pleading a statute of 18 Edward III, which stated that the sea should be open and that all merchants should go with their merchandise where they pleased, to which the plaintiffs had demurred.[87] As to whether the company's charter was valid, Finch argued that since all infidels are aliens with whom it was forbidden to trade, no previous right of all subjects to trade with the Indies had ever existed and therefore the charter was not a monopoly in accordance with Coke's definition. It could better be compared to a patent granting the sole right to the profits from a new invention. As for the company's right to sue Sandys, Finch argued that any privilege that gave the grantee the right to earn money constituted a proprietory interest, and any attempt to infringe that interest was certainly actionable at law.

Pollexfen, replying two days later, conceded that the king could certainly restrain his subjects from leaving the kingdom and that he could certainly control trade in emergencies involving war or plague; but, the lawyer maintained, the king could not grant sole right to a trade to a single corporate body any more than he could prohibit all his subjects but one from leaving the country.[88] Emergency powers did not give the king the right to control all his subjects permanently with a license granted to just one. The granting of the sole control of an important trade to a single exclusive corporation was contrary to the law of the land, which forbade monopolies, and to the Common Law, which forbade anything that acted as a restraint on trade. Like all monopolies, single control of this important market, if allowed, would result in artificially high prices, would affect the livelihoods of those engaged in allied trades and services, and was bound to lead to every sort of oppressive abuse of power. The Turkey, Barbary, Muscovy, and similar companies were no precedent. They had been confederate unions of merchants in particular trades, each trading independently with his own stock, that anyone might join and enjoy the advantages of, but that did not pretend to any right to prosecute interlopers. The East India Company was something quite different—an exclusive joint-stock company, dominated by a small oligarchy of wealth. The excuse that the East India trade was different from all others because it involved dealing with infidels who were ipso-facto enemies, he rejected with the reminder that England had long had diplomatic and trading relations with the nations concerned, a state of affairs that hardly implied a state of war between them. Even if the company's charter were valid, it only entitled the company to half the value of Sandys' ship and to half of his goods, with the other half of each going to the Crown. By what right did the company now come into court to sue for more? "The antient laws, the antient ways," Pollexfen concluded, "is what I endeavour, and against new ways upon any pretense whatsoever."

Attorney General Sawyer, presenting the final argument for the company in the Michaelmas Term, 1684, claimed that the law differentiated between domestic trade and foreign trade and that what applied to the former did not necessarily apply to the latter.[89] The Common Law, he maintained, did not in fact apply at all to overseas trade, the control of which rested entirely with the Crown. As for the company's right to sue for damages in Sandys' case, Sawyer argued that the grant of the right to confiscate an interloper's ship and goods applied to only one clause of the charter and was concerned with only one offense. No specific penalty for offenders being stipulated in the clause that forbade subjects other than members of the company to enter East Indian waters, the company might reasonably sue the defendant for damages.

Williams, in his reply to Sawyer, questioned the legality of the grant of a trading monopoly to the company and the legality of the company's methods of enforcing that monopoly:

> This charter restrains the king in his prerogative, the kingdom in its trade, the subjects in their freedom to trade; the king is concerned in his revenues, the subject in his right in this question.[90]

With regard to the prerogative Williams claimed:

> We that argue for Mr. Sandys, argue for the king's prerogative . . . the king by his grant cannot exclude himself of his prerogative . . .

By the charter to the company the king had deprived himself and his successors of their prerogative of granting trading rights in the East Indies to any others of their subjects and even of the right to trade there themselves. The king was depriving the Crown of some of its rightful revenues. The subject was deprived of his right as an Englishman "of trading in any place upon the seas or beyond the seas." The liberty of the subject was infringed when a private company was given the right to dispose of his property and to imprison him. It could be argued that there was a need for some sort of body to regulate the trade with the East Indies, but Parliament alone could say what sort of a body it should be. "That the king hath the power to do this by the advice of his great council, the parliament is not doubted." If subjects were to be deprived of their traditional rights for the sake of well-regulated trade with the Indies, that deprivation must be ratified by their representatives in Parliament. A foreigner, Williams reminded the judges, could not be naturalized and thereby be granted the full rights of an English subject except with the consent of Parliament; conversely, a subject surely could not be deprived of those rights except by the same body. "This work is too heavy for the pen of an attorney or solicitor, to put into a bill for the great seal without the deliberation of a parliament."

In delivering his decision on January 31, 1685 Jeffreys maintained that it was the king's undoubted prerogative to decide when to call Parliament and what he should consult it about. Williams was urged "to save himself the trouble of advising the king" on these matters "until such time as he be thereunto called." "But," Jeffreys noted:

> it hath been too much practised at this and other Bars in Westminsterhall of late years, to captivate the Lay-Gens, by lessening the power of the king, and advancing, I had almost said the prerogative of the people . . .[91]

This was a distortion of the position held by Williams and his colleagues, which was the same in Westminster Hall as it had been in Parliament. They regarded the royal prerogative as sacred and inviolate and as not to be extended or diminished by anyone, including, as Williams said, the king himself; but in any action that went beyond the scope of the Crown's prerogative, the people had the right or "prerogative" to have their consent sought through their elected representatives. The judges and the law officers of the Crown were understandably willing, for the sake of efficiency and convenience in governing the country, to extend the royal prerogative to the uttermost limits for which they could find any sort of justification in law. Conversely, the Whig lawyers were concerned to confine it within the narrowest bounds that they could legally justify.

The judicial defeat of the Whigs between 1681 and 1685 was more absolute and decisive than their parliamentary defeat had been. The coming to the throne of James II, whom they had fought so hard to exclude from it, set the seal on the ruination of their hopes. For the next three and a half years, the limitations of the royal prerogative were to be determined by the new king himself, his ministers, and his mouthpieces on the judicial bench. Opposition lawyers were to be allowed little say in the matter.

6

The Reign of James II

NOT SURPRISINGLY, ONE OF THE VERY FIRST victims of James II's reign was the informer Titus Oates. Back in June, 1684 James, then Duke of York had sued Oates for *scandalum magnatum* in that he had described the duke, openly in a coffee house, as a "traitor." With damages of £100,000 assessed against him, Oates was of course unable to pay and so went to prison.[1] On May 8, 1685 Oates was brought back before the King's Bench to answer two charges of perjury in evidence concerning the Popish Plot, that he had given half a dozen years before.

He had evidently known for some time that these charges were pending and on January 30 had written to Treby asking for any of Coleman's letters that he might have retained from the days of his chairmanship of the House of Commons Committee of Secrecy. Four days later he wrote again, rather desperately, to "begg" the use of the letters and to "humbly beseech" Treby to accept the brief for his defense.[2]

In the first letter Oates had written: "I must interest you to show mee what favour you can. It is my right to be preserved by all and every of those whom I have faithfully served . . ." But the lawyers, who had felt it their duty to rally to the defense of Shaftesbury, the Council of Six, and the London magnates when they were in distress, evidently felt no obligation to soil their hands—and perhaps risk their own necks—by coming to the aid of the wretched tool whom they had once employed so effectively to discredit the Court and to send many Catholics to imprisonment and death. "I am certain noe man hath a better cause than I," Oates wrote in his second pleading letter to Treby, "but I expect to bee run doune." If he flattered himself in the first part of that statement, he showed a realistic appraisal of his chances in the second. By February 10 it was common knowledge in London that both Treby and William Williams had refused to represent the informer.[3]

Henry Pollexfen, Sir Francis Winnington, Williams, and Treby were all subpoenaed by Oates to give evidence on his behalf at his trial. Pollexfen and Winnington failed to put in an appearance. "They will not come," Oates complained to Chief Justice Jeffreys, "they are frighted away." Williams and Treby showed up but were of little assistance to the accused. When asked what credit had been given by the Commons to Oates' testimony in 1680, Williams referred the court to the votes of the House. "My lord," he concluded, "my memory is never very good, but especially in a case that is at such a distance of time, and which consists of so many particulars as this." Treby was only a little more informative. "There was a vote," he admitted, "all the kingdom knows of, that they were satisfied there was a plot, but whether that vote was grounded altogether upon his evidence, or how far upon his evidence, I cannot tell, nor what any man thought of it besides myself." He was not asked, and he did not volunteer, what he himself had thought. Richard Wallop, alone of the Whig lawyers, appears to have aided Oates professionally during his trial, and even he may have done so reluctantly.[4]

The Duke of Monmouth's desperate, ill-conceived, and ill-led rebellion of June, 1685 apparently received no active support from any of the leading lawyers, although after it was over Williams did act on behalf of Lord Brandon and Lord Delamere, who were accused of plotting to raise the Northwest for Monmouth. He secured their release from the Tower on bail and arranged a speedy trial for them.[5]

Henry Pollexfen played a rather extraordinary role, considering his record during the previous few years, in the "Bloody Assize" trials of those who had supported Monmouth, conducted so ruthlessly by Chief Justice Jeffreys in the West Country in the autumn of 1685. As senior member of the Western Circuit, Pollexfen functioned as the Crown's chief prosecutor in the judicial massacre. Roger North, who detested Pollexfen, suggests that he was chosen for the task by Jeffreys because the chief justice wished to make "friends with the anti-court party."[6] Just a few months before, at the trial of the leading Puritan divine Richard Baxter on a charge of sedition, Jeffreys had shouted Pollexfen down when he sought to speak for the defense, crying: "I know you well . . . You are a patron of the faction."[7] There seems to be no reason for Jeffreys to have wished to befriend Whigs at this time, when their fortunes were at their lowest ebb, and if he had so wished it is unlikely that he would have tried so hard to have Lord Delamere convicted a few months later.[8] The truth of the matter probably was that as leader of the circuit it would have been difficult for Pollexfen to refuse the commission without appearing to condone the rebellion, which with his political background would have been particularly dangerous. As a good constitutional lawyer who was connected with the landed gentry, he probably was not too sympathetic towards a rebellion on behalf of an illegitimate pretender to the throne, a rebellion supported chiefly by the laboring classes and very badly managed, besides.[9] We have seen that down to 1680 he had tended to be politically neutral in the exercise of his profession. The worst that he can be accused of, really, is condoning Jeffreys' excesses by his silence, for Jeffreys liked to examine the witnesses and the accused himself. In the most notorious of these trials, that of the unfortunate Lady Alice Lisle, the chief justice almost immediately took over from Pollexfen and conducted the entire trial himself.[10]

In May, 1685 Jeffreys had been raised to the peerage, as Baron Jeffreys of Wem. The death of Lord Keeper Guilford early in September made it possible for James to honor the chief justice when he arrived at Windsor on September 28, triumphant from his sanguinary work in the west, with a promotion to the highest legal office in the kingdom, the Lord Chancellorship. While Jeffreys' years of loyalty were thus being rewarded it is not surprising to find William Williams, who had always been the most outspoken of the Whig lawyers, facing a criminal charge by the government.

On June 18, 1684 it had been noted by Narcissus Luttrell that "the attorney generall has exhibited an information against Mr. Williams for publication of Dangerfield's narrative."[11] Thomas Dangerfield, a rogue with a long criminal record, had testified at the bar of the House of Commons, on October 26, 1680, that the Duke of York, the Earl of Peterborough, Lady Powis, and other Catholic leaders had employed him to fabricate a "sham" Presbyterian Plot that might divert attention from the Popish Plot, and had even suggested that he should assassinate the king and the Earl of Shaftesbury.[12] On November 9 the House had ordered Williams to have the narrative printed, with the profits from its sale to be paid to Dangerfield.[13] Now Williams was accused of having "maliciously" and "seditiously" published it on his own initiative and of having himself pocketed the proceeds.[14]

The sources differ as to just who was responsible for such action being taken against Williams at this time. Burnet explains that

> this was driven on purpose by the Duke's party to cut off the thoughts of another parliament; since it was not to be supposed that any house of commons could bear the punishing, the speaker for obeying their orders.[15]

For this very reason Roger North says his brother, Lord Keeper Guilford, was opposed to the prosecution, for

> to prosecute a speaker, in the vacation of parliament, for what he had done by the order of the House of Commons in the last sessions of parliament, was by no means gracious or like to be well taken in any succeeding parliament . . .[16]

In fact, King Charles, in March, 1684, had intimated to Barillon, the French ambassador, that despite the provisions of the Triennial Act he had no intention of summoning a parliament.[17] Perhaps the Duke of York and his friends were unaware of the king's intentions, but that seems unlikely. North goes on to place the blame on Jeffreys, to whom he attributes a purely personal motive.

> . . . Williams had been sharp upon Jeffreys when he was upon his knees at the bar of the house for abhorring; and they were both Welshmen: therefore Williams must be prosecuted.[18]

And this explanation has been generally accepted.[19]

However, Jeffreys' biographer, H. B. Irving, disputes the story that Jeffreys had been reproved on his knees at the bar of the House by Williams for opposing the petitions for a new parliament in 1680.[20] He points out that the only sources for it appear to be the statement by North, quoted above, and the taunt flung at Jeffreys by a witness in the College trial, in 1681, that he had been "on his knees" before Parliament. Irving contends that this is hardly to be taken as the literal truth and points out that no record of any such proceeding is to be found in the Commons *Journal*.[21]

Certainly North, writing many years after the event, could have been mistaken. The Commons *Journal* for November 13, 1680 reports that on that day Mr. Trenchard reported to the House that the committee to which the petition of the City of London against Jeffreys had been referred was resolved "that Sir George Jefferyes, Recorder of the City of London, by traducing and obstructing Petitioning for the Sitting of this Parliament, hath betrayed the rights of the Subject." After several members had spoken in support of the resolution, it was adopted by the House, which then ordered "that an Humble Address be made to his Majesty, to remove Sir George Jefferyes out of all publick Offices," and a committee was appointed to draw it up.[22] Three days later the address was presented to the House, adopted, and ordered to be carried to the king by those members who were Privy Councilors.[23] So, although Jeffreys may have been called to testify before the original committee, it does not seem that he ever appeared in person before the whole House, let alone that he was ever reproved on his knees by Williams. Even so, Jeffreys—along with the many other enemies that Williams must have had at the Court—probably enjoyed the prospect of seeing the Speaker of the Exclusion parliaments humbled by the law at last.

The Duke of York had as much if not more cause to dislike Williams than any one else, for the Dangerfield narrative had depicted the duke as plotting the assassination of his brother. Burton, a former Treasury official, told the House of Commons in 1691 that the duke had directed Williams' prosecution, together with those of Oates, Pilkington, and Ward, through his solicitor, Mr. Swift.[24] There is no need to seek a complicated political motive. The duke was no doubt motivated by a very understandable desire for revenge.

As might have been expected, Williams pleaded that "for what he did in Parliament he was not accountable to answer before the court of King's Bench."[25] In February, 1685 he was ordered to appear before that court to offer his plea.[26] It was evidently at this time that Sir Robert Atkyns prepared a formidable argument on Williams' behalf, *The Power, Jurisdiction and Privilege of Parliament,*[27] because it refers to only one parliament, "at Oxford," since that of 1680 and, therefore, must have been written before James' parliament, assembled in May, 1685. But if Williams appeared in court in 1685, and if Atkyns delivered his argument (which was finally published as a tract in 1689), there seems to be no record of the proceedings. Perhaps because of the complicated constitutional issues involved it was to be another year before the case was finally settled. Meanwhile, Mr. Swift and a Mr. Gwilliam were kept busy in "a long search in many of the *Journals* of the House of Commons and taking notes relating to the printing of votes in the cause against Williams."[28]

James' first and, as it turned out, only parliament assembled on May 19, 1685. Despite steps taken during the elections to ensure that supporters of the government were very much in the majority in the House of Commons,[29] Maynard was reelected for his old constituency of Beeralston and sided with the opposition minority in opposing the granting of additional taxes on the ground that they were obviously intended to finance a standing army that probably would be made up of papists. He also is reported to have opposed a bill for the preservation of the king's person, because of several derogatory references in it to the Duke of Monmouth.[30] Treby, however, failed to be returned for his former constituency of Plympton, Devonshire, and though he sent a petition to the House of Commons in June claiming that he had been defeated by unlawful means, it was referred to a probably unsympathetic Committee on Elections and Privileges, where apparently nothing ever came of it.[31]

Williams, who lost his seat for Chester, where he no longer exerted any authority, but was returned for Montgomery, fell a victim to the same committee, which in the first few weeks of the session made every effort to unseat as many of the opposition members as it could. After hearing the committee's report on June 10, the House resolved that because the burgesses of some of the small surrounding towns had not been given the opportunity to vote, ". . . William Williams Esquire is not duly elected a Burgess to serve in this present parliament for the Shire-Town of Montgomery."[32] The parliament dispersed on the following November 20 without the Commons having taken any action concerning the prosecution of their ex-Speaker for carrying out their orders.

It had been "reliably reported" that Williams' case would come to trial in the Michaelmas Term, 1685, but by the following January the exact date had yet to be set.[33] Finally, on May 8, 1686, on a motion of Attorney General Sawyer, the justices of the King's Bench scheduled the hearing for the following Thursday, May 11. Some of the judges had already let it be publicly known that they considered Williams' plea that the King's Bench had no jurisdiction over his actions as the Speaker of the House of Commons as "intollerable and of a very seditious and ill influence, and ordinarily used by very ill men in very ill cases, as by the very Regicides themselves that Murdered the King."[34] It is not surprising therefore that one observer commented at this time: "It lookes cloudly on Mr. Williams."[35]

The hearing on May 11 was presided over by Chief Justice Sir Edward Herbert, who had succeeded Jeffreys as chief justice of the King's Bench in October, 1685, just as two years earlier he had succeeded him as chief justice of Chester. Jeffreys had urged his successor "to execute the law to the utmost of its vengeance upon those that are now known, and we have reason to remember them, by the name of Whigs";[36] and, indeed, at the hearing Herbert would listen to no arguments from Pollexfen, who acted as Williams' counsel. The following terse account illustrates most vividly the arbitrariness of the proceedings:

> Defendant pleads that by the law and customs of England, the Speakers of the House of Commons have signed and published the Acts of the House, etc.
> Mr. Attorney-general demurs.
> Mr. Jones (for the prosecution) was beginning to argue, and took some exceptions, as that he doth not aver the libel in the information, and that in the plea to be the same.
> Lord Chief Justice—Court do you call it? Can the order of the House of Commons justify the scandalous, infamous, flagitious libel?
> Mr. Pollexfen then said, I have no more to say.
> Lord Chief Justice—Let judgement be for the King . . .[37]

Faced with this uncompromising attitude Williams, a week later, allowed a second plea, in bar (that is, that there was no case to answer), to lapse and submitted himself to the court, which imposed a fine of £10,000.[38] He then drew up a petition asking the king for mercy, in response to which

James declared that he would be satisfied with only £8,000.[39]

Referring to Williams' case in a speech before the court of Queen's Bench in the case of *Stockdale* v. *Hansard* in 1639, Baron John Campbell stated: "my Lords it is not impossible . . . that the prosecution really may have been collusive, although I do not by any means aver that it was so."[40] This charge is serious enough to require an examination of the facts. What aroused Campbell's suspicion was that:

> . . . Sir William Williams suddenly became a great favourite with the Duke of York, when James II,—was very much encouraged and petted by that sovereign after the fine had been paid and was employed by him as one of the counsel upon the prosecution of the seven bishops . . .[41]

He further suggested that the very rapidity of the trial indicated collusion.[42]

At first sight it is indeed strange that James should have so readily excused his old enemy of one-fifth of his fine and also that apparently the Crown law officers did not demand Williams' imprisonment until the fine was paid, as was usually done.[43] Part of the answer is to be found in a letter from Williams, written on July 11, 1686[44] to James' brother-in-law, Laurence Hyde, Earl of Rochester:

> My Lord,
> I owe my liberty, the benefit of my profession, the remains of my fortune and reputation to your Lordship. When the capias issued against me for my fine, your Lordship alone prevailed to have my bond accepted by the King, allowing me convenient time to raise and pay my money, and a present abatement of 2000 l.: this is the product of your Lordship's generous and frank mediation with his Majesty for me without the aid or concurrence of any person.[45]

The rest of the answer must be deduced from the situation within the government at this time. Early in 1686 Lord Treasurer Rochester found that his influence with King James was growing less and less.[46] The old Court Party by this time had become split into two groups. One of them, headed by Rochester and including Sir Leoline Jenkins and possibly Godolphin, was anxious to keep down the Whigs, but was also becoming more and more worried over James' attacks on the position of the Established Church. The other group, the so-called Jesuit cabal headed by the Earl of Sunderland and James' Jesuit confessor Father Petre, was gaining ever greater influence over the king.[47] At the same time James' government was suffering from a shortage of willing legal talent. The crisis had come in March over James' efforts to dispense with the penal laws against the Catholics. Attorney General Sawyer, upon being ordered to draw up warrants authorizing Catholic clerics to hold benefices in the Church of England, had refused to do so, saying:

> this is not merely to dispense with a statute; it is to annul the whole statute law from the accession of Elizabeth to this day. I dare not do it; . . .[48]

In the same month Sir Heneage Finch, the solicitor general, was dismissed for his refusal to defend the issuing of letters patent to the Catholic Sir Edward Hales, authorizing him to hold a commission in the army contrary to the provisions of the Test Act. He was replaced by Sir Thomas Powis, "an insignificant man, who had no qualifications for high employment except servility." Sawyer was retained, however, because it was essential that at least one of the law officers of the Crown should be a man of ability.[49] During the next twenty-one months, claims Macaulay, "when the government wished to enforce the law, recourse was had to Sawyer. When the government wished to break the law, recourse was had to Powis."[50]

It is possible, therefore, that sometime early in 1686 Rochester, fearing that Sawyer was about to be dismissed and anxious that he should not be replaced by a tool of Sunderland's cabal, had decided that Williams, being an Anglican and a Whig, would if appointed in Sawyer's place act as a restraint on James' extremist tendencies. And if he, Rochester, enabled Williams to escape fairly lightly from the Dangerfield Narrative prosecution, Williams, if he became attorney general, would presumably look to the treasurer as his patron and benefactor, and could, therefore, be persuaded to act in accordance with his wishes.

If this was so, sometime early in 1686 Rochester must have approached Williams with an offer to negotiate with the king on his behalf, and at the same time must have approached James with the suggestion that Williams would be a good replacement for Sawyer. Such a theory is borne out by the fact that at the time of Hales' case it was rumored that Williams was to replace Sawyer,[51] and in one contemporary source the replacement is reported as actually having taken place.[52] Williams's submission in May, therefore, may have been at Rochester's suggestion. Perhaps, too, the treasurer had suggested to Herbert that the case be settled as quickly as possible, and the less said the better. Williams' acquiescence in such a scheme would explain the otherwise rather inexplicable fact that Williams stood up for Chief Justice Herbert as a champion of Parliament in the debate on the indemnity bill in 1689.[53]

To that extent the final trial in 1686 may have been collusive. But to suggest that the original prosecution in

1684 was collusive would seem to be ridiculous. For a year after the information was first laid against him, Williams continued to plead vigorously in the courts in behalf of various Whig causes. It is unlikely, if he were cooperating with James, that he would have been turned out of the parliament of the king's supporters in June, 1685. Campbell hints that Williams never actually paid his fine,[54] but the records indicate that he did; the Treasury books show that on July 19, 1686 a royal warrant was issued authorizing the attorney general "to acknowledge satisfaction on record of the fine of 10,000 l. imposed . . . on William Williams, esq., the king being fully satisfied thereof by the receipt of 8,000 l. and the acquittal of 2,000 l. residue thereof."[55] Two weeks later the £20,000 bond into which Williams had entered for payment of his fine was ordered to be returned to him.[56] What is still more convincing, however, is that three large payments were made out, on July 12, August 11, and October 12, 1686 from "Mr. Williams' fine now paid into the Exchequer," to the ordnance for Hull, Plymouth, and Portsmouth.[57] If the money was never really paid in, it is difficult to see how it could have been paid out. But most convincing of all is the fact that in the years immediately following the revolution of 1688, when Williams was endeavoring to have the verdict against him reversed and to be recompensed for the fine he had paid, some of his enemies (including Sawyer until his death in 1692) tried unsuccessfully to discredit him by accusations that he had secretly been a tool of the Court while he was Speaker of the House of Commons in 1680 and 1681, but none of them suggested that the prosecution had been collusive. And Sawyer, as attorney general, surely would have known if it had been.

We have Williams' notes for a speech of self-vindication,

delivered in 1695, in which he cites the Dangerfield Narrative prosecution as evidence of his loyalty to the Commons:

> If I had betrayed all or some of ye Com'ons;
> If I had submitted to the information;
> If I had tamely yielded and confessed;
> It had been better with my estate,
> But worse with my reputac'ion.
> I value much more your rights and my own honor,
> than I do my estate. The money I may recover
> againe, or not want; The dishonor had been
> irrecoverable.[58]

Surely he would not have dared make such a speech if there were men (as, if it were true, there must have been) who could testify that his two years stand on behalf of the "rights of the Commons" had been a fraud.

Rochester continued to decline in favor with James, until he was eventually dismissed in December, 1686. Williams was forbidden by the king to reward him in any way for his services.[59] But though the king cooled towards the patron he continued to favor the client. Later in his letter to Rochester of July, 1686 Williams says:

> and what I value more, your lordship hath disposed his Majesty to a good opinion of me: this adds to his bounty and clemency some care of me by concerning himself in the suit of the Earl of Peterborough.[60]

In June, 1686 London had learned that "the Earl of Peterborough [had] brought his action of *scandalum magnatum* against Mr. Williams, late speaker, for licensing of Dangerfield's narrative; to which he hath given bail."[61] In view of the decision in the first prosecution Williams must have felt fairly certain that it would be hopeless to contend this second suit. A rumor went around that he had fled overseas.[62] What he did was to apply again to James, who, it appears from the letter, without any prompting from Rochester, interceded with Peterborough and persuaded him to be satisfied with £150 while a non prosequi was entered on the rolls. The maligned earl, however, continued his prosecution of the printers and publishers of the narrative and is said to have received £6,700 plus costs.[63]

There were probably two reasons for James' sudden favor towards Williams. One is that, as we have seen, to further his plans for absolutist rule and the undermining of the Established Church he needed in his government an able lawyer who did not share Sawyer's particular scruples. The other is that at about this time James, as he was breaking with so many of his old friends and supporters, "openly indulged and courted his ancient and professed Enemies; and in a particular Manner those People and Families in the *West,* which had been so severely treated at the Beginning of his Reign."[64] The Dissenters, who were particularly numerous in some areas of the west country (including Chester), would be attracted by the policy of indulgence exemplified in his first Declaration of Indulgence published in May, 1687, and the leading gentry could perhaps be charmed or bribed into coming over to his side. Williams had connections that perhaps were useful to the king in this regard. He owned a house in Wrexham that was rented by a group of Congregationalists for use as a manse. The wife of his friend George Mainwaring, together with her sister and probably several other friends and acquaintances of the former recorder, belonged to one of the three Dissenting Congregations that existed in Chester at this time.[65]

In pursuit of his plan James made a long tour of the West Country in August, 1687, traveling from Windsor to Portsmouth, Bath, Gloucester, Worcester, Ludlow, Shrewsbury, and Whitchurch, finally arriving at Chester on the 27th. In an obsequious speech of welcome the city's recorder, Sir Richard Lieving, said that "the Corporation was his Majestie's Creature, and depended upon the will of its creator," and that "the sole Intimation of his Majestie's Pleasure should have with them the force of a Fundamental Law."[66] However, the mayor, Sir Thomas Grosvenor, who had occupied one of the seats for Chester in the 1685 parliament, is said to have indignantly rejected the king's offer of a peerage and the colonelcy of a regiment in return for his support of a bill repealing the Test Acts and the penal laws against the Catholics in the next parliament. Other leading citizens also declined to promise the king any assistance in doing away with the Test Acts and other penal laws.[67] Greatly disappointed, James nevertheless ordered a new charter to be prepared for the city, which was ultimately issued on September 15, 1688 and which specifically stated that none of the new city officials need take the oaths of allegiance and supremacy or conform with the requirements of the 1662 Act of Uniformity. Leading Dissenters in Chester were named by the charter to most of the city's major offices, but every one of them declined to serve, and a month later, in desperation, James restored the old pre-1685 charter.[68]

It seems very likely, though there is no direct evidence of it, that it was during the king's visit to Chester that Williams finally agreed to enter his service. Certainly he was in the city and was in touch with some of the king's friends. The Bishop of Chester, Thomas Cartwright, was a staunch ally and confidant of James. He owed his elevation to the episcopacy to the king, he was one of the Ecclesiastical Commissioners, and just two months before he had played a prominent role in the proceedings whereby Magdalen College, Oxford, had been compelled to accept a Catholic president. On August 29 Williams and one of his sons dined with the bishop, who had just come from a political conference with the king.[69]

On September 6 Cartwright called on both Williams and Sir Richard Lieving.[70] Perhaps it was on this day that Williams first heard that he was soon to be restored to the coveted recordership (and he was restored the following month),[71] but it was not until December that the announcement was made that Sir Thomas Powis was to be appointed attorney general in place of Sawyer and that the new solicitor general was to be William Williams, who also would receive a knighthood.[72]

Barillon the French ambassador explained this surprising development by saying that "Williams wishes to atone for his past conduct," and observed, "there are people who think it is not a thing to be proud of." Indeed, one anonymous contemporary versifier had nothing but scorn for the onetime Speaker of the Exclusion House of Commons now turned apostate:

> *Williams,* this tame Submission suits thee more
> Than the mean Payment of thy Fine before.
> Poor Wretch, who after taking down thy Arms,
> Has a Court-smile such over-ruling Charms?
> Bankrupt in Honour, now art tumbled down
> Below the abjectest Creature of a Crown.[73]

Later commentators have been no kinder. One early nineteenth-century writer explained cynically that Williams, "finding his country politics . . . inconvenient, . . . abandoned them and adopted those of the court. . . ."[74] Irving considers that "there has seldom been in the history of political apostasy a case so glaring."[75] This view was evidently shared by Macaulay, who conceded that "Williams was driven to extremity," but felt that his way of escape

> was indeed, a way which to a man of strong principles or high spirit, would have been more dreadful than beggary, imprisonment or death. [To] sell himself to that government of which he had been the enemy and the victim. [To] expiate his Whiggism by performing services from which bigoted Tories, stained with the blood of Russel and Sidney shrank in horror.[76]

One biographer charitably explains that the Williams of 1687–1688 was a "trimmer,"[77] but his conduct does not really fit that of the trimmer, defined by Halifax as a man who, instead of throwing all his weight to one side or the other, perceives that it is best to stay in the middle, thus keeping the ship of state on an even keel and not endangering the passengers.[78] It would be more accurate to depict Williams as rushing from one side of the ship to the other. The champion of Parliament and "the people" became the champion of the royal prerogative. In February, 1678 he had said in the Commons: "Though I have not a gown on with tufts, . . . yet I am bound to preserve the prerogative of the crown, as if I had."[79] But, whereas at that time he had used his knowledge of the law to argue that the royal prerogative, though real enough, was strictly limited, now, ten years later, he was to use that same knowledge to argue that the prerogative was practically unlimited.

A careful examination of Williams' probable motives for becoming James' champion, when formerly he had been among his bitterest enemies, indicates that financial considerations and ambition, particularly the latter, were the two most important factors. The libel suit begun by the Earl of Peterborough in June, 1686 presented a real financial threat. The medieval statute *De Scandalis Magnatum* had first been revived in 1676 by Shaftesbury, who successfully sued Lord John Digby under it for £1,000, for casting reflections on his loyalty. The cost of damages quickly became inflated. Only a few months later, a Dr. Hughes was forced to pay Lord Townshend £4,000 for reflections he had made on his character and behavior. But these were moderate sums compared to the £100,000 assessed in 1684 against Titus Oates for *scandalum magnatum* against the Duke of York.[80] Just how wealthy Williams was is difficult to estimate. His epitaph states that he was generous to his family,[81] and certainly he owned three estates—Caeau Gwynion, Glasgoed, and Llanforda—which presumably gave him a fair income from rents. The £8,000 for his fine was probably raised by a mortgage on one of these. The fact that he entered into a £20,000 bond that he would pay his fines in 1686 shows that he was considered to be worth at least that much. But probably he was not worth much more, on which case a verdict in Peterborough's favor—and the decision in the earlier prosecution made such a verdict almost certain—would very probably have ruined Williams financially.

Macaulay seemed to feel, as we have seen, that Williams should have welcomed such an opportunity to become a martyr for the Whig cause. But no other political figure of the day made such a sacrifice voluntarily. Besides, Williams was a family man with a wife and children to consider. And it is quite unlikely that anything useful would have been achieved by such a heroic gesture.

It is to be noted, however, that eighteen months elapsed between James' rescue of Williams from Peterborough and Williams' appointment as solicitor general. During this period Williams may well have "trimmed." He certainly neither said nor did anything against the government (for James could always hold the threat of another libel suit over his head), but neither, so far as we know, did he aid the government in any way. Presumably, he could have pursued such a course of action indefinitely. The question remains as to why he accepted the solicitor generalship. Perhaps James, with his desperate need for an able and cooperative lawyer, brought pressure to bear and recruited Williams by means of a combination of threats and promises. The office was a lucrative one and would give Williams a chance to regain the money he had had to pay out to meet his fine.[82] Another factor influencing his decision may well have been that he was now fifty-three years of age and therefore unlikely in those times to live more than another decade at the very most. He must, therefore, while there was still time, move out of the professional doldrums in which the winds of political chance had left him, if ever he was to reach the top of his profession.

His feelings may well have been similar to those ascribed by Irving to Jeffreys in 1680:

> He has already plunged deeply into the politics of his day; he has seen a political party put to death innocent Papists on the evidence of villains; he has seen the courts of law used as the instruments of faction, the judges swayed by passion and prejudice on the one side and the other; he has felt the pains of defeat and the merciless accompaniments of political victory; he has witnessed the unscrupulousness of statesmen, the brutality of the mob. One day he hopes to grasp power and authority in his own person.[83]

Indeed, a further incentive to Williams may have been provided by the consideration that the solicitorship would put him in a strong position to compete with Jeffreys for the king's regard and, possibly, to replace him eventually as Chancellor.

One of the reasons given by North for Jeffreys' having

allegedly instigated the Dangerfield prosecution was that Williams was a Welshman. Jeffreys quarreled at one time or another with all his fellow Welsh lawyers in London: his cousin Trevor Williams, Sir Thomas Jones, and William Williams. Irving claims that the three of them were jealous of Jeffreys because he was the most successful Welshman in the legal profession.[84] Williams and Jeffreys had crossed swords in court on several occasions, of course, and it is more than likely that during the latter's term as chief justice of Chester the two often clashed over local issues. So strong were the feelings between the two men that when Williams was counsel for the Presbyterian leader Baxter in 1685 he made a point of not appearing in court personally, lest his appearance prejudice his client's chances.[85]

Jeffreys' position was not too secure. The dismissal of Rochester the year before had left the chancellor as the only strong adherent of the Church of England in the government, and there had been rumors at the time that he too would soon be dismissed.[86] He declined to sign the Declaration of Indulgence in April, 1687 and let it be widely known that he had done so. By the end of the year there was a strong rumor that Jeffreys was to be dismissed and replaced by James' recently appointed Catholic judge, Sir Richard Allibone. Williams knew full well, and so did everyone else including the king, that he was a far better lawyer than Allibone. "The appointment," says Irving, "filled Jeffreys with misgiving."[87]

The Common Law court of King's Bench was the scene of two trials of great constitutional significance during James' reign: that of the "Seven Bishops" in June, 1688 and that of the case of *Godden* v. *Hales* two years earlier. Hales, a convert to Catholicism, was appointed a colonel in one of

James' foot regiments in November, 1685. In defiance of the Test Act of 1673 he had not taken Communion according to the Anglican order, nor had he taken the oaths of allegiance and supremacy, nor had he subscribed to the declaration denouncing the doctrine of Transubstantiation within three months of being appointed. Godden, a servant of Hales, was the pawn in a collusive suit that was designed to establish James' right to dispense with the Test Act and thus to be free to place reliable Catholics in key positions in the army and navy, the government, and the schools.[88]

Godden made the first move early in 1686 when he reported Hales to the authorities at Rochester in Kent. On March 29, 1686 Hales was found guilty under the Test Act and fined £500. He refused to pay the fine, however, pleading that the king had granted him a dispensation from taking the oaths and fulfilling the other provisions of the act and from all pains and penalties ensuing from his not doing what the act enjoined. Godden, who under the act was entitled to receive the £500 fine, thereupon sued Hales for it in a suit of debt. It was this suit that came before the King's Bench, only to be settled finally by all the judges, sitting as a court of Exchequer Chamber, eleven to one in Hales' favor.[89]

In February, 1674 Solicitor General Sir William Jones, in advising a committee of the House of Lords who were considering changes in the sumptuary laws, had given it as his opinion that the king had the right to grant dispensation from a law to individuals, though he could not suspend an act of Parliament.[90] But whatever Jones may have said twelve years earlier, the Whig lawyers were not prepared in 1686 to defend James' right to grant Hales a dispensation from the Test Act. When ordered by the judges to appear on Hales' behalf (because no counsel would do so voluntarily), Treby "absolutely refused." And if Winnington, who received a similar order (together with Trinder and Wallop), ever spoke in court on the colonel's behalf no record of his doing so has come down to us.[91] Nor were some of the Tory lawyers very anxious to speak for Hales. As has been mentioned above,[92] Finch resigned the solicitor generalship rather than become involved in the case, and it finally fell upon his successor, Powis, to represent the colonel, while a minor Tory barrister, Edward Northey, argued on behalf of Godden.[93]

Speaking for the Crown, Powis insisted on the king's undoubted prerogative right to administer the affairs of the kingdom in whatever way seemed to him best and that that right included the free choice of any of his subjects to serve him in any capacity. Within certain obvious limitations any subject might be appointed by letters patent to any office and such letters patent might include a *non obstante* clause exempting the appointee from any statutory disability that might otherwise make him ineligible for the office. Certainly the use of *non obstante* clauses to dispense with statutory requirements had its origins in canon law, but it had become a recognized part of English law by the end of the fifteenth century. As his basic authority Powis cited the decision of the judges in the 1487 "Case of *Non Obstante*," as it was reported in Coke's *Twelfth Report*.[94] This important decision, which was also cited by Coke in presenting his argument as chief justice of the Court of Common Pleas in the case of the *Post Nati* in 1608, laid it down that "Every subject is by his natural ligeance bound to obey and serve his sovereign. . . ." and that, although the statute 23 Henry VI c. 8 stated that notwithstanding any *non obstante* clause to the contrary no one should every serve as sheriff of a county for more than one year, yet the king might "by a special *non obstante* dispense with that act, for that the act could not bar the king of the service of his subject, which the law of nature did give unto him."[95] It was true, as Coke and others had pointed out,[96] that the king could not grant a dispensation in a case where to do so would mean condoning an obvious wrong—for example, where a man acquired an office by simony, or in a case where the property rights or other lawful interests of other subjects would be prejudiced thereby. But, Powis argued, there was nothing in the Test Act that made it automatically wrong for a Roman Catholic to hold a commission in the royal forces. It did not say that Catholics could not be commissioned but only disqualified them if at the end of three months they had not satisfied the test requirements, and it followed that for a Catholic to hold a commission was not a *malum in se*. The tests must be regarded, then, as purely a matter of administrative policy, and so able to be dispensed with by the king at his discretion.

Chief Justice Herbert, in explaining why he and the overwhelming majority of his colleagues had decided in favor of the defendant Hales, gave as their *rationes decidendi* the precedent of the Case of *Non Obstante* and their acceptance of the particular interpretation of the Test Act suggested by Powis. Modern authorities, albeit in some cases reluctantly, generally agree that their decision was a just one.[97] Herbert further stated that because the kings of England were "sovereign princes" and the laws of England the "king's laws," not only could the king dispense with the penal laws in particular cases, and for particular, necessary reasons, but the king himself was the sole judge of these necessities and reasons, and his power in this regard was "not a trust invested in or granted to [him] by the people" but was rather grounded in "the sovereign power and prerogative of the kings of England."[98]

These dicta, so strongly reminiscent of those used by Charles I's judges in support of their decision in the Ship Money Case of 1637–1638, were alarming in their implications. Parliament's exclusive control over taxation was unchallenged after 1641, but if the king were to be allowed a virtually unlimited power of dispensation then Parliament's equally important control over legislation would be severely limited. Certainly it would not be able to protect the exclusive power and privileges of the Church of England. Sir Robert Atkyns expressed the Whig attitude toward the case sometime later in a pamphlet entitled *An Inquiry into the Power of Dispensing with penal statutes.*[99] Atkyns' pamphlet, after restating the details of Hales' appointment and the trials resulting from it, stressed the necessity of protecting "his Majesty's good subjects" from Catholic recusants who were "a great danger to them." The Test Act, passed by Parliament to provide just such protection, provided that any appointments to office that did not satisfy its requirements were thereby "adjudged void." Hence the illegality of all such appointments was in fact a judgment of Parliament. The pamphlet then went on to argue, as Williams had done in Fitzharris' case, that such a judgment, given by "the supremest Court of the Nation . . . must not be contradicted by any other Court, nor by all the courts of the Nation put together; this Supreme Court exercises its Legislative and Judicial Power both at once, and shall all be lost Labour?"

Going on to discuss the nature of law itself, the pamphlet cites Fleta, Bracton, Fortescue, and other medieval legal authorities to show that the laws were not the creations of monarchs but rather "the Articles of Agreement chosen and consented to by Prince and people, to be the Rule by which all are to square their Actions." Therefore, the Crown could not claim to be the sole author of the laws and, hence, to be possessed of the right to dispense with them at will. Turning to the question of dispensations themselves, Atkyns reminded his readers that dispensations had their origins in the papal curia and were, therefore, by the Protestant mind, presumably, to be regarded with suspicion. After citing William Chillingworth's warning in the third chapter of his *Religion of Protestants* that

> He that would usurp . . . an absolute Lordship over any People, need not put himself to the Trouble of abrogating or disanulling the Laws made to maintain the Common Liberty, for he may frustrate their Intent, and compass his Design as well if he can get the Power and Authority to interpret them as he pleases, and to have his Interpretations stand for Laws. If he can rule his people by his Laws, and his Laws by his lawyers . . .

Atkyns declared, "I hold there is no just or lawful Power of dispensing with any Act of Parliament in any other Hands than in those that are the Law-makers, that is, the King and Parliament in Conjunction."

Considering next the arguments used by Hales' lawyers, Atkyns noted that they had based their case on the contention "that an Act cannot bar the King of such Service of his Subjects, which the Law of Nature did give him." But, Atkyns asked, would such an argument be accepted as granting to the king the power to be the "sole Judge of the Persons fit to serve him in all cases" when the king and Parliament had disabled papists from entering the royal service? The king's sovereignty was not being questioned; but the title "sovereign" merely implied that the king had no other kings over him, not that he was absolute. The Test Act had been intended to protect the king's sovereignty from usurpation by a foreign power—by Rome. When the pope at Avignon had tried to use John's resignation of the kingdom of England to Innocent III as the basis for asserting his authority over Edward III, Edward's parliament had affirmed that John's surrender of sovereignty had been invalid both because he had made it without the consent of his Great Council and because it had been contrary to his coronation oath. The circumstances in Hales' case, Atkyns concluded, were essentially the same.

If these thoughts were in Atkyns' mind during James' reign, he did not express them openly at the time. His pamphlet was not published until the eve of the assembling of the Convention parliament in January, 1689.[100] He and the other Whig lawyers were effectively cowed into silence where political matters were concerned. An anonymous newsletter, dated June 1, 1686 and obviously written by a Tory, reported that the entire bar were "at present intimidated and deterred from meddling, till they see which be like to get and continue uppermost—the Prerogatives or the hitherto pretended Liberties of the Subject and limitation of Royal Power by Statutes and Acts of Parliament."[101] Meanwhile, they could busy themselves in the practice of their profession, confining themselves to purely private matters. In June, 1685 we find Atkyns representing himself as defendant in a civil suit over an estate in Hertfordshire against a plaintiff who was represented by William Williams. In another civil suit concerning an estate, in the same year, Williams and Holt appeared for the plaintiff, Charles Howard, against the defendant Duke of Norfolk, whose chief counsel was Henry Pollexfen. Throughout 1688 Pollexfen was kept busy representing Henry Hyde, Earl of Clarendon,[102] who was defendant in a scire facias suit brought against him by the queen dowager, Catharine, over some property that they both claimed. The earl had tried first to secure Williams' services in the case, but the king, his brother-in-law, had declined to give the permission that Williams, as solicitor general, would have needed before accepting a brief against a member of the royal family.[103]

But if all of our seven Whig lawyers practiced discretion rather than valor during this period, Williams alone yielded to the temptation to accept office under James. The only major event of his seventeen-month career as solicitor general was the Trial of the Seven Bishops in June, 1688 for publishing a libel against King James in that, in a petition presented to him the month before, they had claimed that his Declaration of Indulgence issued that same month, because it suspended the penal laws against the Catholics and Dissenters, was illegal. It is the only event connected with Williams' solicitor generalship reported by Macaulay and is presumably, therefore, what he meant when he referred to "services from which bigoted Tories shrank in horror." But would one have expected "bigoted Tories" to do otherwise? A Tory is, almost by definition, a staunch defender of the Church of England; and the position of the Church of England as the Established Church, as well as the authority of its rulers, the bishops, was threatened by the libel prosecution. But in addition to menacing the Church, the prosecution's assertion of the king's prerogative right to set aside parliamentary statutes (not just by a single dispensation as in Hales' case, but to the point of total suspension) also threatened to nullify altogether the legislative power of Parliament.

The Crown's claim to the prerogative power of suspension, unlike its claim to the dispensing power, was not based on any Common Law precedents. It was derived from the power exercised by the medieval popes of suspending, as well as dispensing with, ecclesiastical laws. This power, it was argued, together with other papal prerogatives as well, had been transferred to the English monarch by the Act of Supremacy. The question was: did the fact that the popes, as God's vicegerents on earth, had been regarded as being entitled to suspend God's laws, now mean that the king, as supreme governor of the Church of England, could suspend the laws of Parliament, particularly laws concerning religious worship?[104] Charles II, first in 1662–1663 and again in 1672, had twice failed to secure parliamentary acceptance of a Declaration of Indulgence. James had now issued two such declarations (the first in April 1687) without even consulting Parliament. With the legislative power of Parliament and the established Anglican settlement thus in danger, it is not difficult to account for the strange combination of lawyers— four Tories and three Whigs—who pleaded the bishops' cause. Even so, there is no quarreling with Ranke's comment that "parts were singularly changed."[105]

The four Tories were Sawyer, Finch, Sir Francis Pemberton, and Sir Creswell Levinz. Pemberton, the oldest and most experienced of all the lawyers taking part in the trial, had been lord chief justice of the King's Bench from 1681 until 1683, when he was, first, demoted to Common Pleas and then, finally, dismissed from the bench altogether—for having displayed, it is said, a lack of severity toward the Whig plotters.[106] Levinz had been dismissed from the King's Bench by James for opposition to the government's actions in Hales' case. The three Whigs were Treby, Pollexfen, and John Somers, who before the trial was still an almost unknown lawyer. Pollexfen had recruited this future Lord Chancellor for the defense because, he said, "no man in Westminster Hall was so qualified to treat an historical and constitutional question."[107]

Against this formidable team, comprising "almost all the

eminent forensic talents of the age,"[108] Williams, to all intents and purposes, stood alone. Officially, of course, he was acting as assistant to his superior, Sir Thomas Powis, but all contemporary sources agree that it was Williams who directed the prosecution.[109] It seems strange that Williams had been content with the junior appointment, but James may have been reluctant to deprive the faithful Powis of his job or to demote him, and it is likely that Williams had been promised rapid promotion to a far higher position—if his services proved to be satisfactory. The other Crown attorneys were the recorder of London, Sir Bartholomew Shower, a Serjeant Trinder, and a Serjeant Baldock, none of whom made any significant contribution to the prosecution.

Lord Chancellor Jeffreys, the only other competent lawyer (besides Williams) remaining in the king's employment, was apparently opposed to the trial. He told Lord Clarendon that it would be the downfall of all the king's plans.[110]

The judges, Lord Chief Justice Sir Robert Wright and his colleagues, Sir John Powell, Sir Richard Allibone, and Sir Richard Holloway, none of them outstanding lawyers, would probably not have been occupying their distinguished offices had there been more competition to sit on James' bench. They were in an uncomfortable position, torn between their loyalty to their royal master and their fear of the public gallery, where at the final hearing sat at least thirty of the leading peers of the realm, who might conceivably one day sit in judgment on them for their part in this trial. Wright is said to have regarded every peer as if he had a halter all ready in his pocket.[111] Powis, too, was apparently rather awed, and his opening speech for the prosecution has been described, not inaccurately, as "not so much the statement of an accusation as an apology for the prosecution."[112]

But not so Williams; throughout the trial he ignored the hostility of the crowd, which was often expressed by shouts and hissing, and pursued his arguments relentlessly. The author of "Horatius at the Bridge" could "scarce forbear to cheer," and whereas Macaulay had earlier condemned Williams for moral cowardice, when writing of the trial itself he was betrayed into referring to the Welsh lawyer's "dauntless courage,"[113] though it was a courage born, perhaps, of political desperation.

Williams has often been accused of unnecessarily rude and disrespectful conduct towards the bishops.[114] Though his father was a parson, Williams seems never to have shown any particular regard for the church. Nevertheless, except for three lapses from good manners his attitude toward the bishops throughout the hearings was what one would normally expect from a prosecutor towards the accused. He seems to have been in a particularly bad mood at the preliminary hearing on June 15. Perhaps, as Mackintosh suggested,[115] he was not too happy at the situation in which he found himself. When the Bishop of Peterborough, a name with unpleasant associations for Williams, tactlessly made a reference to the Dangerfield prosecution of two years before, the solicitor snapped back at him: ". . . you were one of them that prosecuted me, for aught I know; or if you did not prosecute me, you preached against me; or if you did not, some of your tribe did."[116] When the same bishop asked that the information against them be read in English, Williams replied sarcastically that the bishops were all well known to be learned men and ordered it read in Latin. Finally, a few minutes later, he advised Peterborough, who was whispering to Sawyer, to pay attention to what was going on in the court. Apart from these three lapses, all in the preliminary hearing, all directed at the one man, and all within a few minutes of each other, Williams always showed a proper respect for "my lords, the bishops."

It was against the defense attorneys that Williams really directed his barbs, particularly Sawyer and Finch, who were put at a disadvantage in having to argue against methods that they themselves had ruthlessly employed during a number of years. When Sawyer moved to present an objection to the information before it was read, Williams reminded him that he himself had often rejected such a motion as being irregular: "And I hope the case is not altered; however you may be, the court is the same." And later, he remarked that he was glad "that they have learned of me to tack about." In the final trial, Williams referred frequently to the trial of Sir Algernon Sidney. When the defense contested the validity of his evidence as to the identification of the bishops' handwriting, he retorted that much weaker evidence had been accepted as to Sidney's handwriting: "I conclude that this is good evidence, unless a lighter evidence will pass in this court to make a man guilty of treason than of misdemeanour."

All of the preliminary hearing and the first half of the final trial on June 29 were taken up with routine evidence, and by arguing over a multitude of minor technical objections that the defense, showing great ingenuity, raised at every conceivable opportunity. As Powis pathetically complained: ". . . as soon as ever we offer to speak, presently there are two or three upon us." Nevertheless, Williams fought back with all the great forensic skill at his command, handicapped though he was by lack of inspired support from the other Crown attorneys and the great reluctance of the terrified Crown witnesses to say anything definite against the bishops. The two really important issues were those debated in the final half-day of the trial: whether the bishops had the right to petition the king, and whether the king had the right, by his Declaration of Indulgence, to suspend the penal laws against the Catholics and the Dissenters.

The essence of the defense case was put by Sawyer. The bishops, he argued, were but doing their duty in opposing the declaration. The Elizabethan Act of Uniformity specifically charged the bishops with seeing that its provisions were maintained. It was, therefore, their duty to urge the king against any measure that would ruin the Established Church. It was also their duty, as peers of the realm, to advise the king when he was acting in any way contrary to the laws of the land. And for the king to suspend the laws without the consent of Parliament was illegal. As proof of this he cited: firstly, the Statute of Provisors in Richard II's reign, in which Parliament granted the king dispensing powers but only until the next parliament met; secondly, Charles II's Speech from the Throne in February, 1663 in which he had said, "I could heartily wish I had such a power of indulgence to use upon occasion . . ."; thirdly, the fact that an Act passed by the House of Lords in response to that speech, which gave the king a certain measure of dispensing power, was rejected by the Commons; and finally, the Commons' declaration of February, 1673 "that penal statutes in matters ecclesiastical, cannot be suspended but by act of parliament."

Pollexfen made the most impassioned speech for the defense. The penal laws, he claimed, were the foundations upon which rested the whole religious and political framework of the kingdom. James' Declaration of Indulgence was "not agreeable to the laws of the land; and . . . for this reason, because it does, at one blow, set aside all the law we have in England." "If so be the king's will be not consonant to the law," Pollexfen contended, "it is not obliging."

It was Somers who made the last speech for the defense— a short speech but one that demonstrated his legal and constitutional erudition. He cited the unanimous opinion of the judges of Exchequer Chamber in the case of *Thomas* v. *Sorrel* (1674) that "there never could be . . . suspension of an act of Parliament, but by the legislative power." The young barrister then emphasized the difference between the king's *dispensing* power of a law in the case of a few particular persons, an action the legality of which he considered to be rather dubious, and the king's *suspending* the action of a law altogether, which is what James had in fact sought to do by his declaration and which was certainly illegal. Even Powis, arguing on behalf of Hales two years earlier, had made no claim on behalf of the Crown for a suspending power even though he had argued strongly for the Crown's right to dispense.

Williams, replying for the Crown, argued that the place for petitions was Parliament. He dismissed the fourteenth-century Statute of Provisors on the grounds that the circumstances behind it were unknown and riposted with the Statute of Appeals, passed by Parliament in Henry IV's reign, which laid it down that the Lords should not proceed in any case except those brought before them in the form of impeachments by the Commons. "And this," Williams declared,

> is the course that should have been taken by my lords here, and they should have stayed till the complaint had come from the Commons in parliament, and then it had been regular for them to address the king; but they were too quick, too nimble.

As to the suspending power, Williams rejected the defense's examples. Declarations of the House of Commons, he argued, did not have the force of law. If you argued that they did then you must also argue that the Exclusion Bill was law, because the Commons had voted their approval of it in 1680. He explained away Charles II's surrender of the suspension principle in 1672 as a political maneuver to get money for the Dutch war. The basic issue, he concluded, is not whether the king has a suspending power but whether he has the right to issue ecclesiastical proclamations. The bishops say his proclamation of indulgence is illegal, the king says it is legal—who but Parliament can decide? The bishops should have waited until Parliament met rather than stirring up public disaffection by their overhasty methods.

Finally he reminded the court of the 1609 case *De Libellis Famosis,* recorded in Coke's *Fifth Report,* in which the judges of the King's Bench had decided that a publication,

> if slanderous to the king or government, it is a libel and to be punished: in that case the right or wrong is not to be examined, or if what was done by the government was legal or no; but whether the party have done such an act.

Certainly Williams scored a point with regard to the legal validity of resolutions voted by the Commons. But if the defense had not really proved that the king had no dispensing or suspending power, neither did Williams prove that he had. In fact, the solicitor, while rejecting the arguments of the defense, seems to have wished to avoid making a direct assertion of the prerogative right of dispensation or of suspension. Instead, he hedged by transferring the argument onto the less controversial ground of the royal right to issue ecclesiastical proclamations. And he based his demand for a verdict against the bishops on *De Libellis Famosis,* which conveniently made it possible to ignore as irrelevant the nature or validity of the libel. The points at issue between the king and the Church should be judged by Parliament: this was in conformity with general Whig principles. But the fact cannot be avoided that a verdict favorable to the Crown would have been generally interpreted as a vindication of dispensation and suspension. And it is interesting to speculate what Williams' stand would have been if the matter ever had come up in a future parliament called by James. Probably he would have continued to hedge. As it was, he was to declare in a parliament called by William III: "Is anything more pernicious than the dispensing power? There is an end of the legislative power, gone and lost."[117]

His disavowal of the bishops' right to petition outside Parliament seems strange coming from the man who, as Speaker in 1680, had roundly denounced Sir Francis Wythens and others for their opposition to popular petitions calling for a new parliament. His answer to such a charge might have been that it would have been useless to wait for a parliament if there was going to be no parliament.

In fact, some writers have suggested that at the time of the trial Williams and everybody else acted in the knowledge that James had no intention whatever of calling a parliament.[118] If this were true, then Williams was guilty of the most cynical equivocation. But the facts do not uphold the suggestion. All the indications are that James had every intention of complying with the Triennial Act by calling a parliament in the autumn of 1688. Bishop Cartwright's conference with James in Chester, referred to previously, was concerned with who should represent that city in the next parliament. The king, as we have seen, tried to bribe Sir Thomas Grosvenor to support his policies in Parliament. In August, 1688 Jeffreys told Clarendon that he hoped that the king had learned his lesson from the result of the bishops' trial, and that he would be moderate with Parliament.[119] On August 24 the king, in Council, actually ordered the Chancellor to issue writs for a parliamentary election on November 27;[120] and in September Lord President Sunderland wrote to Williams telling him to arrange for his own election either from a Welsh constituency or else from the borough of Wallingford in Berkshire.[121] In 1681 Charles II, having lost control of the House of Commons, had given up on Parliament and had turned to the law courts to achieve his political purposes. Now James, ironically, having lost control in the law courts, was planning to see what he could do with a parliament.

After the acquittal of the bishops, meanwhile, Williams had left Westminster Hall to the accompaniment of jeers and hissing from the mob; and Jeffreys, presiding over the court of Chancery in another part of the Hall, on being told the cause of the uproar, smiled, feeling that his hold on the Great Seal was safe—as indeed it was, for a little while.[122] Williams retreated to the country for a time but returned to London to perform one more official function for James in October, when he took part in the inquiry into the circumstances attending the birth of the Prince of Wales.[123] One night that same month the mob broke his windows in Gray's Inn and wrote rude inscriptions over his door.[124] Realizing finally that no parliament was going to be called immediately and that he was not going to replace Jeffreys as Chancellor, Williams retired from the public scene again till December.

King James, meanwhile, in a last minute effort to win back the loyalty and affection of the majority of his subjects, on October 5 abolished the hated Ecclesiastical Commission and restored the charter of the City of London. On October 17 charters were restored to all other corporations.[125] Both Treby and, after him, Somers refused the position of recorder of London when offered it by James, probably because they felt that the office could only be an embarrassment in such uncertain times.[126] On November 5 William of Orange landed in Devonshire, and during the following six weeks the overwhelming majority of England's men of influence went over to his side. Noting this trend away from James, Evelyn remarked in his diary on December 2 that "it lookes like a Revolution."[127]

7

The Lawyers' Triumph, 1688-1689

IT WAS TO BE EXPECTED THAT THE WHIG lawyers would eagerly greet William of Orange when he came as their deliverer in December, 1688. A formal welcome was extended to the prince on December 20, two days after his arrival in the capital, by George Treby, newly restored to his old office of recorder. Since the lord mayor was indisposed (perhaps diplomatically), Treby acted as spokesman for the City. After recalling the "late Danger" when "Church and State" had been "brought to the Point of Destruction, by the Conduct of Men . . . that broke the Sacred Fences of our Laws, and (which was worst) the very Constitution of our Legislature," Treby concluded:

Great Sir. . . . Your Highness, led by the Hand of Heaven, and called by the Voice of the People, has preserved our dearest Interests The Protestant Religion; which is primitive Christianity restor'd. Our Laws; which are our ancient Title to our Lives, Liberties, and Estates; and without which this World were a Wilderness. But, what Retribution can we make to your Highness. Our Thoughts are full charged with Gratitude . . . And late Posterity will celebrate your ever-glorious Name, till Time shall be no more.[1]

A pithier compliment was paid William by Serjeant Maynard when he went to court to pay his respects a few weeks later. On the Prince's remarking that he had heard that Maynard was the oldest lawyer in the country, the serjeant replied:

> Yes, and please Your Highness, I am so, I have outlived many great Lawyers and Judges; and indeed I was afraid, had not your Highness come just when you did, That I should have outlived the Law itself.[2]

William Williams, in the company of the veteran Whig leader Colonel Titus, sought an interview with Prince William at Hungerford on December 16 but could not gain admittance. However, two days later it was "creditably reported" in London that the solicitor general had been "received into favour" by the prince.[3] Meanwhile, Sir Robert Atkyns had terminated his six years of rural retirement and reappeared on the national scene to be introduced to Prince William by the Earl of Macclesfield.[4]

During these weeks of constitutional crisis in December, 1688 and January, 1689, advice was very naturally sought from those lawyers whose stand during the previous decade now seemed about to be so eminently justified. The Earl of Clarendon, on arriving in London on December 14, immediately sent for his lawyer Henry Pollexfen "to confer with him that [he] might better know how to govern [himself] in this wonderful exigence." Pollexfen told Clarendon that his royal one-time brother-in-law, by trying to flee out of the kingdom, had abandoned the government and forfeited all right to the Crown and "that his being now at Feversham, though he should come back to London, signified not a rush." The Prince of Orange, with his army behind him, Pollexfen advised, had only to declare himself king and send out writs for the election of a parliament. Pollexfen's next piece of advice—that the prince ought to call for an election in accordance with the system used during the Cromwellian Protectorate, which he described as "a far more equal way of election than the old constitution"—startled Clarendon. "Good God bless me!" he wrote later in his diary, "what a man is this? I confess, he astonished me; and so we quickly parted."[5] Pollexfen's reputation as a "republican"[6] may be derived from this incident, but he seems in fact only to have been advocating franchise reform.[7]

On or about December 22 the Lords, meeting as a "Council of the Realm" in their House at Westminster, summoned Maynard, Holt, Pollexfen, Atkyns, and George Bradbury to advise them on legal matters.[8] There seems to be no record of the advice they gave, but they probably approved the Lords' invitation to Prince William on Christmas Day to take over the direction of the kingdom's affairs until the convention called for the following January 22 could meet.[9]

In addition to the compliment of having their advice sought in this time of crisis, the Whig lawyers were also rewarded in the first few months of the new reign, which began on February 13, 1689, by appointments to those legal and judicial offices under the Crown from which they had been firmly excluded during their previous decade in opposition. On February 27 King William, as he had by then become, approved the appointment of Serjeant Maynard as one of the Lords Commissioners of the Great Seal, together with Anthony Keck and Serjeant William Rawlinson.[10] The three were sworn in before King and Council at Whitehall on March 5.

Towards the end of November, 1688 Lord Chancellor Jeffreys had been ordered by King James to move into quarters in Whitehall Palace and to bring the Great Seal with him. On November 28 the Seal was used to authorize writs ordering the election of a parliament to meet on January 15, 1689. Only fifteen of these writs were ever sent out to the counties, the remainder were burned as James came to realize the full seriousness of his position. At the beginning of December the king installed the Chancellor in Father Petre's old rooms right next to his own, so that he could have the Seal firmly under his control and close at hand. When James made his abortive attempt to flee the country on December 11 he took the Seal away with him and dropped it into the Thames, hoping thereby to "create difficulties and incidents" that would embarrass William. Jeffreys, trying to escape to the continent himself on the same day, was recognized (in spite of his disguise as a seaman) and arrested at Wapping, and brought back under heavy guard to the Tower, where he would die on April 4, 1689 before Parliament could get around to impeaching or attainting him.[11]

The office of Chancellor having fallen into some disrepute during Jeffreys' tenure of it, the appointment of the three commissioners was apparently an attempt to sever the Chancery court from politics by appointing three skilled and knowledgeable men who would have nothing to distract them from their judicial duties (though, as we shall see, Maynard continued very active in Parliament during his entire period of office). Another theory, that the Great Seal was put into commission in order to multiply the number of offices in the gift of the Crown, seems disproved by the fact that both Rawlinson and Keck were men entirely "without political claims or influence." Precedents for such an appointment can be found in the Protectorate period when the practice had been adopted of having the Chancery court presided over by several of the judges sitting coordinately. An order of the Privy Council, dated as early as February 18, 1689, had ordered one of the Chancery clerks to make copies "of all commissions that were granted by Oliver the Protector for custody of the Great Seal, and send them to Sir Robert Atkyns for his perusal." So it may have been Atkyns who suggested the three-man commission.[12]

On March 1, 1689 warrants were issued appointing Pollexfen attorney general in succession to Sir Thomas Powys, and Treby solicitor general in succession to Williams. Pollexfen was knighted at Whitehall, together with Keck and Rawlinson on March 5.[13]

On April 12 William approved a provisional list of new judicial appointments which named John Holt as chief justice of the King's Bench, Pollexfen as chief justice of the Common Pleas and Atkyns as chief baron of the Exchequer (replacing his brother Edward).[14] Pollexfen and Edward Ward, who was named on the provisional list as a puisne justice of the Common Pleas, both told Lord Clarendon on April that they had refused to go on to the bench.[15] Ward's refusal was accepted, but on April 24 the formality was observed of appointing Pollexfen a serjeant-at-law, and on May 6 he received his patent as chief justice.[16] Holt and Atkyns had already received their respective patents on April 17.[17]

Macaulay claimed that it was because of Pollexfen's association with Jeffreys and the "Bloody Assize" that he "could not with propriety be put at the head of the first criminal court in the realm" (the King's Bench) despite his "professional attainments and Whig principles."[18] It is hard to see, however, why Pollexfen's largely passive role in the sanguinary proceedings in the West Country in 1685 should have been held against him any more than Holt's brief period in office as James' personally appointed recorder of London. While it is true that Holt was younger than Pollexfen, he had an equally distinguished career and had not been so consistently opposed to the Crown as had the Devonshire lawyer; and William, just as much as any of his predecessors, favored as wide an interpretation of the royal prerogative as possible.

Treby was promoted to attorney general to replace Pollexfen, and his place as solicitor general was filled by John Somers, who thus took the first step on the ladder that was to lead him in less than four years to the position of Lord Keeper of the Great Seal and, ultimately, to the chancellorship.[19]

Sir Francis Winnington's motives and actions at this time are shrouded in mystery. His name was on the provisional list of judges of April 12 as a puisne justice of the King's Bench,[20] but he evidently either refused the position or was rejected at the last moment, for the elderly William Gregory, Speaker of the first Exclusion parliament and a baron of the Exchequer from 1679 to 1686, was appointed in his place.[21] The most likely explanation probably would be that Winnington, in whose heart ambition always warred with caution, did not wish to identify himself with the new regime for fear that a second "Restoration" might be imminent.

William Williams, who had not been able to wait long enough for his reward, could not hope for much from the new government. In May, 1689, however, he was appointed a King's Counsel along with Roger North and two others,[22] and in the following September he was awarded the office of *Custos Rotulorum* of Merionethshire in his native Wales.[23] Even though he was a political *persona non grata,* his reputation as a barrister evidently remained high, and his services continued to be sought in a variety of notable causes.[24] Early in 1692, for example, he appeared with former Attorney General Sir Thomas Powis before the House of Lords to plead the cause of Lady Elizabeth Mordaunt, daughter of the Earl of Peterborough who had threatened Williams with ruin six years before. She was being sued for divorce by her husband, the Duke of Norfolk, on the grounds of her adultery with Sir John Germaine.[25] Although Williams was not successful in defending her, he was rewarded in May by being appointed Solicitor General to the Queen, to whose household Lady Elizabeth belonged.[26] This was the highest office Williams was ever to achieve after the Revolution.

When the convention assembled at Westminster on January 22, 1689 to tackle the problem of providing England with a new and settled government, the services of the "Gentlemen of the Long Robe" were naturally much in demand. The House of Lords summoned to their assistance Atkyns, Holt, Sir Cresswell Levinz, Pollexfen, Bradbury, and William Petyt, a qualified barrister who was employed as Keeper of the Records in the Tower of London.[27] The House of Commons included among its members Williams, Maynard, Treby, Pollexfen, Holt, and Somers, as well as Sir Robert Sawyer and Sir Heneage Finch.

Maynard, Treby, Pollexfen, and Holt were all returned by constituencies in Devonshire, which had been the first county to welcome the Prince of Orange officially.[28] Pollexfen sat for the city of Exeter and Treby for his old constituency of Plympton, which had reinstated him as its recorder. Maynard was again elected for both Plymouth and Beeralston. When he finally decided to represent the former, Holt, at his suggestion, was returned as his replacement by the electors of Beeralston.[29] Three weeks after the trial of the bishops, Williams, in addition to being raised to the rank of baronet, had been appointed by James to the office of "Steward and Keeper of the Courts Leet and Views of Frankpledge of

Menai in Anglesey."[30] Probably it was that position, in which Williams was confirmed in June, 1689 and which he held for the remainder of his life,[31] that enabled him to procure his return for the Anglesey borough of Beaumaris.[32] Somers was returned for his native city of Worcester.[33]

The Commons, after choosing Henry Powle as their Speaker and joining with the Lords in a formal invitation to William to continue administering the affairs of the kingdom,[34] turned on January 28 to the consideration of recent events and formed themselves "into a Committee of the Whole House under the chairmanship of John Hampden to consider the state of the nation."[35] Sir Christopher Musgrave, a Tory, voiced the question in everyone's mind when he said: "I would be clear whether the intention is to depose the King; and, if he had forfeited his inheritance to the Crown, I would know from the Long Robe, whether you can depose the King or no."[36]

Maynard, perhaps exercising the privilege of seniority. was the first to reply:

> The Question, is not, whether we can depose the King; but whether the King has not deposed himself. Tis no new project; our Government is mixed, not monarchical and tyrannous, but has had its beginning from the people. There may be such a transgression in the Prince, that the People will be no more governed by him . . .

Maynard's position was endorsed by Treby, who declared himself "in conscience satisfied" that "the King has lost his legal Government, and is fallen from it." The king that could not or would not govern, he continued, was no longer king; and this king neither could nor would govern. James, he reminded the members, had assumed "an inherent indispensable Authority to vacate all your Laws, dispense with the Act of Uniformity, and set up the Ecclesiastical Commissions." Parliament, as a result, had been in danger of atrophying to the stage where the *Parlement* of Paris now found itself under Louis XIV—"a body of Registers, only to record the King's Will and Pleasure by his Dragoons." He recalled how James I had said to one of his parliaments that "when a King breaks in upon his Laws, he ceases to be a King."[37] A king who would break the laws, Treby reminded them, was the type of king that the Whigs had warned against during the Exclusion controversy, and this was precisely the type of king that James II had in fact turned out to be. He moved the question: "Whether King James II has not made an Abdication of the Government, and that the throne is void." William Williams, not to be outdone, moved for a resolution that "James 2, by withdrawing himself from England, has deprived the kingdom of England, of the exercise of Kingly dignity."

Somers suggested that a precedent would be necessary if the kingdoms of Europe were to be persuaded of England's right to depose her delinquent king. He suggested that the case of King Sigismund of Sweden, who had made attempts to establish Roman Catholicism in the country and been turned out by the Swedish people in 1599 in favor of Charles IX, provided ample justification for the English people to treat James in a similar manner. Maynard rejected the example, however, remarking that no English king could be said to have rendered himself incapable of the Crown just because he was a papist.

Pollexfen, opposing a motion by former Justice William Dolben, "that King James . . . having voluntarily forsaken the government, . . . it is a voluntary Demise in him," pointed out to the House that a *voluntary* desertion or demise on the part of the king would leave the Crown to descend in accordance with the normal line of succession, in which case there was nothing for them to discuss. In fact, he reminded them, James had not departed voluntarily, but had been driven out of the country, in fear of his life, amidst "the noise of Arms."

This reminder that the king, to whom they had nearly all at one time or another sworn allegiance, had in fact been expelled as the result of an armed rebellion, even if little or no blood had been shed, touched the consciences of the Tory members on a tender spot. They were somewhat uncomfortable at finding themselves playing an active role in what could from some points of view be regarded as a treasonous assembly. There must have been a fear in the hearts of many of them that with the principal pillar forcibly removed, the whole edifice of the state might very quickly crumble away, leaving the country open to anarchy and social upheaval.

Sir Thomas Clarges expressed this Tory fear when he remarked that if the Crown were vacant and the convention had the power to fill it, the constitution would be altered from a hereditary to an elective monarchy. Sawyer stressed the danger of regarding the government as dissolved by James' departure. The government consisted of King, Lords, and Commons, and if it were dissolved then none of the three would have any legitimacy; the country would be without a government because no one and no group could claim to exercise legal authority. "All men," said Finch, summing up the Tory position, "can agree that there is no security in [James'] return. But whether his administration does so cease as to lose his Titles, every man must swear to his Vote, [in order] that he whom you shall place on the Throne is lawful and rightful King."

When the debate was ended the House passed its resolution:

that King James the second, having endeavoured to subvert the Constitution of the Kingdom, by breaking the Original Contract between King and People; and, by the Advice of Jesuits, and other wicked Persons, having violated the fundamental Laws; and having withdrawn himself out of this Kingdom; has abdicated the Government; and that the Throne is thereby vacant.

John Hampden was ordered to "carry up the said Resolve to the Lords, for their Concurrence."[38]

The House of Lords, while engaged in debating the Commons' resolution during the next few days,[39] relied heavily on the opinions of their legal advisors. The Earl of Nottingham[40] argued in favor of a regency as being "the best remedy" and coming "nearest the law." The regent, ruling in King James' name, would be endowed with full royal powers including the power to exclude King James by force of arms if necessary. But when the question was put to Atkyns as to "how the word 'Regency' is consistent or fitted with our laws?" he made that same objection that Sir William Jones had made to a similar proposal during the debate over Exclusion.[41] A regent as such was a subject, but if he were allowed royal powers then he would be king in all but name. Nottingham's proposal was rejected by the narrow margin of fifty-one votes to forty-eight. When the Lords came to consider the Commons' assertion that James had forfeited the throne by breaking the original contract, they appealed to the lawyers for "an account of what the original contract is, and whether there be any such or not?" Atkyns replied that he believed "none of us have it in our books or cases, not anything that touches on it," and that he thought "it must refer to the first original of government." The very fact that the constitution of England was a limited monarchy argued that an agreement must have been reached between monarch and people at some stage. The monarch himself would not have limited his own power. He cited the Elizabethan theologian Richard Hooker as saying that "all public government is by agreement" and referred, as Treby had done in the Commons, to James I's acknowledgment that the king was bound by the laws. And that he concluded was what the contract was—"the laws of the kingdom." The other lawyers substantially agreed. "The body of the Common law," said Bradbury, "Must be taken to be that original contract."

When asked by the Lords on January 31 for their opinion on the Commons' assertion "that the throne is thereby vacant," the lawyers generally concurred with Atkyns' refusal to give an opinion on the grounds that that was a question not of common law but of *lex et consuetudo parliamenti*. He cited as precedent the refusal on the same grounds by the judges to give an opinion in 1455 on the validity of the Duke of York's claim to the throne. Bradbury went so far as to say that he thought there was "a possibility" that what the Commons asserted was true, but even he concluded that "the posture of affairs is now only fit for Parliaments."[42] The politicians, then, would simply have to solve the constitutional conundrum for themselves; the lawyers, as lawyers, disqualified themselves from doing so. When the members of both houses came to tackle the matter, however, they left the matter primarily to the lawyers among their number.

Battle was joined on February 2 when the Lords sent down their proposed amendments to the Commons' resolution. They suggested that the word *abdicated* should be replaced by the word *deserted,* and that the words *and that the throne is thereby vacant* should be omitted.[43] On February 6 committees from both houses met in a free conference to try to settle the disagreement between them. The committee of the Commons, led by John Hampden, comprised Pollexfen, Maynard, Treby, Somers, Holt, and eighteen other members, including Sacheverell and other leading Whigs. The committee representing the Lords was led by the Earl of Nottingham and included the Earls of Clare and Pembroke, the Bishop of Ely, and others.[44]

Somers and Holt began the debate by presenting arguments to prove that the Commons' use of the word *abdicated* was not only valid but even preferable to the Lords' suggested use of the word *deserted*. Somers argued that both words were of classical origin and clearly determined meaning. He cited Grotius and other commonly accepted legal authorities to show that "abdication" of an office could be effected by the officeholder either by express words, orally or in writing, or by the commission of acts inconsistent with holding that office. That was how the Commons meant the word to be interpreted. As Holt put it:

> the doing an act inconsistant with the being and end of a thing, or that shall not answer the end of that thing, but quite the contrary, that shall be construed an *Abdication* and formal *Renunciation* of that thing.

Somers cited examples from civil law to show that "deserted" could indicate a state of affairs that was "temporary and relievable." If the Lords really intended to secure against James' return, he warned, they should adopt the Commons' wording.

Nottingham then suggested that before any decision was reached between *abdicated* and *deserted* the conference should discuss the matter which was the crux of the Lords' objection to the Commons' resolution: just what was meant by the conclusion that the throne was "thereby vacant"? Did it imply that the entire line of succession was thereby cut off?

If so, then the Lords felt that that was tantamount to making the monarchy elective. Maynard responded by arguing that the two questions were inseparably linked:

> the constitution, notwithstanding the vacancy, is the same, the laws that are the foundations and ruler of that constitution are the same. But, if there be, in any particular instance, a breach of that constitution, that will be an *Abdication,* and that Abdication will infer a vacancy.

Clarendon disagreed. Abdication, he reminded the conference, implied express renunciation of the office concerned. Somers had argued that it could be done by actions that were a breach of the "original contract." But "this breaking the original contract," he argued, "is a language that hath not been long used in this place, nor known in any of our law books, or publick records. It is sprung up, but as taken from some late authors, and those none of the best received." (He was presumably thinking of Thomas Hobbes.) The coronation oath, he went on, was certainly not the "original contract," for the king was bound by the laws and was owed allegiance from the very moment that he succeeded to the Crown. Maynard had said that Parliament could step in once, in an emergency, to fill a vacancy on the throne; but once done it would provide a precedent for evermore. The Crown would never again be really stable. Nor had the Commons yet proved that the throne was vacant. Somers was using *abdicate* according to its meaning in civil law, but the English constitution was grounded on the Common Law. "I hope," he concluded, "I shall never see our old laws altered; or if they be, God forbid we should be the voluntary agents in such an alteration."

How ironic, in the light of the legal and constitutional history of the preceding seven years, Clarendon's last remark is! Since 1681 the Crown had sought to twist and shape the law, especially in regard to the Quo Warranto actions against the city and borough charters, in order to use it towards the desired end of an absolutist monarchy and a possible Roman Catholic restoration. The Tories had supported it in its efforts almost to the end, while the Whigs had cried out in vain for a continued adherence to the "old laws." Now the Tories were rallying to the defense of those laws, while the Whigs were trying, as they had done during the Exclusion crisis of 1678–1681, to bend them in such a way as to permit Parliament to place upon the throne a ruler who would not seek to deny them those rights and liberties that they felt were their birthright. In a decade the political-constitutional wheel had turned full circle.

It was Treby who answered Clarendon on behalf of the Commons. They could not decide whether the throne were vacant, he argued, unless it were first clearly established exactly what James had done. The concept of an original contract, he went on, had antecedents that no good Englishman would impugn, for it was Bishop Hooker who first mentioned the idea in his *Ecclesiastical Polity,* in which he wrote that "government originally did begin by compact and agreements." As for abdication, Treby was willing to concede that it implied an act of will on the part of the abdicator, but were not James' actions during his reign proof of a will to renounce the government?

> He hath by these acts . . . manifestly declared that he will not govern according to the laws made; nay he cannot do so, for he is under a strict obligation, (yes, the strictest) and superior to that of the original compact between king and people, to act contrary to the laws, or to suspend them.

King James might have left because he was compelled to by force, but he had definitely left in a state of unwillingness to keep the compact; therefore, surely the word *abdicated* best described the intention.

But, if the king could renounce the throne by his acts, Nottingham asked Treby, what happened to the old established principle that the king could do no wrong? There was great difference, Treby replied, between an occasional breach of the law—for which the king's ministers could be held responsible—and an all-out attack on the constitution itself, for the constitution provided the only means whereby the subject might secure redress for occasional breaches of the law.

After this last exchange the conference once again turned to the question of whether the throne was in fact *vacant*. Sacheverell began the discussion by reminding the Lords of what they were already, perhaps guiltily, aware—that if King James were still on the throne then nearly everyone in the whole kingdom was guilty of mass treason. Pollexfen then commented that if the Lords thought that James had ever "deserted" the government, then they must agree that the throne was vacant, for the throne and the government were one and the same thing; and, if they said that James had only ceased to exercise it, then he still had the right to it and might return at any time. In fact, if the Crown still lawfully belonged to James, he could not lawfully be kept from it. Even to impose a regency on an unwilling monarch "would be setting up a commonwealth instead of our ancient regulated government by a limited monarchy."

Perhaps discomfited by the weight of so much legal sophistry, Clarendon could only repeat the Lords' basic objection: if the throne were vacant, did not that make the monarchy elective? And Maynard once again made his common sense point that this was an extraordinary circumstance that made it necessary to supply a particular defect. The Commons, he claimed, were of no mind to alter the constitution any more than the Lords were. He then went on to insist that, if there were a lawful heir, the Lords name him. This they refused to do. Nottingham's only reply was to insist again that the Commons could not say that the throne was vacant and yet pose as upholders of the principle of hereditary monarchy.

It was at this point that Somers appealed to the powerful authority of legal precedent. The word *vacant* as applied to the throne was, he claimed, a part of the Common Law. For in 1399 the Lords and Commons, after hearing Richard II's formal resignation of the Crown and government read, had resolved that the throne *fuit vacua,* and there were several other references to the "vacancy" of the throne in the record of the proceedings. Lord Rochester replied that in view of the troubled history of the Lancastrian dynasty, the proceedings that had resulted in their mounting the throne hardly constituted a happy precedent. His brother Lord Clarendon agreed and went on to refute Somers' precedent by pointing out that the parliamentary proceedings that had placed Henry IV on the throne had been repealed by the first parliament of Edward IV because they had set aside the rightful heir to the throne. Treby came to Somers' rescue, however, pointing out that proceedings of Edward IV's first parliament had been repealed by Henry VII's first parliament, with the result that the precedent still stood. Lord Pembroke retorted that Henry VII had been a usurper and went on to insist that the throne could only pass by lawful hereditary right. Treby's reply was that if only those statutes were accepted as valid that had been passed under kings who had inherited the throne lawfully, lawyers would find themselves in a state of considerable confusion.

The Lords were still not convinced, however, and the

conference ended without the two sides' having reached any agreement. Lord Bolingbroke was later to describe its deliberations as having been of the sort that "might have been expected in some assembly of pedants, where young students exercised themselves in disputation, but not in such an august assembly of the Lords and Commons in solemn conference upon the most important occasion."[45] Yet it is important to remember the political background to the discussion and to bear in mind that neither side could come right out and express its innermost feelings. Both sides suffered from two unbanishable fears, fears largely inspired by the events of 1642–1660. First, there was the fear of a possible future restoration of James, at which time they might all be called to account for what they were now doing by courts and a parliament packed with James' supporters. Second, there was the fear of a possible breakdown of the nation's whole social and constitutional system, a breakdown that could ultimately lead to one or the other of the twin evils of anarchy and democracy. Nottingham and the other representatives of the Lords—Tories who because of their great political power and high social and economic position were naturally most concerned to preserve the legal, constitutional, social and economic status quo—were anxious to put a legal face on their actions both to prevent any disruption of the political and constitutional establishment and to protect themselves from reprisals in the case of any future political upset.

The Whig lawyers, who did nearly all the talking for the Commons in the conference, were probably almost as anxious as the Lords to preserve the status quo,[46] but above all they were as lawyers anxious to preserve the law and the constitution. Though forced perhaps to resort to some twisting and manipulation of the law, they wanted to proceed in such a manner that they also could, in the event of a future restoration, with a fairly clear conscience defend their actions in a court of law. To this extent, then, the spokesmen for the Commons were essentially in agreement with the spokesmen for the Lords. The essential difference between the two groups and the reason that no agreement was reached in the conference was that whereas the lawyers representing the Commons wished to force the Lords to acquiesce in proceeding in such a manner as would legally and constitutionally bar James from the throne entirely and forever, the spokesmen for the Lords were undoubtedly anxious to leave a legal and constitutional loophole that would permit James to be restored if ever that seemed to be the most desirable course —if, for example, the "revolution" ever seemed to be getting out of their control. The fact that Clarendon and Rochester were also probably motivated by a desire to see their niece Mary placed on the throne, perhaps with William as regent, must be considered as another unspoken factor underlying the debate.

Though later historians have tended to make much of Somers' role,[47] it was really Treby who won the debate in its superficial aspects between the representatives of the two houses. It was Treby who finally upheld the validity of Somers' 1400 precedent for the use of the word *abdicate* by pointing out that, though the statute in which it occurred had been repealed in 1461, the repeal had itself been repealed in 1485. And it was Treby who provided a respectable antecedent for the "original contract" theory—after Somers' view of it had been impugned by Clarendon—by pointing out a reference to it in Bishop Hooker's famous work.

However, for the reasons given above, it was force of circumstances (particularly Mary's refusal to occupy the throne without her husband as an equal partner and William's own threat to return to Holland if he were not given full regal power) rather than any learned arguments by either Somers or Treby that finally caused the Lords to inform the Commons on the following day, February 7, that they had "agreed to the Vote sent them up of the 28th of January last . . . without any alterations."[48] The Whig lawyers' interpretation of the events of October to December, 1688 was to be the officially accepted one.

In a second debate on the state of the nation, on January 22, William Williams had been one of the first to support Lord Falkland's suggestion, originally put forward by Halifax, that the throne having been declared vacant, means for the "preservation of the laws of England for the future" should be considered before steps were taken to place someone else on it.[49]

When in the first week of February the House of Commons came to appoint the committee that was to draft the "Declaration of Rights," it was George Treby and not, as some secondary sources claim, John Somers who was elected chairman of the committee.[50] Just as Treby's leading role in the conference with the Lords has been obscured, so has his position as chief member of this key committee, whose members were the architects of the famous document that was to be the first major achievement of the "Glorious Revolution," remained unrecognized, obscured by Somers' reputation as the leading constitutional lawyer of the day. Actually, there does not appear to be any evidence in the primary sources to support such claims as that "Somers doubtless had the principal share in [the Declaration's] composition,"[51] or that Somers was "the leading member" of the committee.[52] In addition to Treby, the committee included such outstanding lawyers as Williams, Pollexfen, Sawyer, and Holt, none of whom were likely to have allowed themselves to be completely dominated by one who was a comparative youngster.

The preamble to the Declaration of Rights[53] listed the various abuses of the constitution and breaches of the law that had occurred "of late years" and, particularly, during the reign of "the said late King James." Abuses against which the Whig lawyers had raised their voices in Parliament between 1678 and 1681 and in the law courts between 1681 and 1688. In those latter years they had protested in vain, usually, because, except for James' subservient one in the spring of 1685, there had been no parliament to back their protests. Now, however, the Declaration stated that "the pretended power of suspending of laws" and "the pretended power of dispensing with laws" were "illegal," and thus Atkyns' argument with regard to Hales' case and the stand taken by Treby, Pollexfen, and Somers in the Trial of the Seven Bishops were declared to have been correct.[54] In stating that "it is the right of the subjects to petition the king, and all commitments and prosecutions for such petitioning are illegal," the Declaration upheld the stand of the Whig "Petitioners" against the Tory "Abhorrers" in the autumn of 1680 and also, again, the position taken by the defenders of the bishops. In stating that "the subjects which are Protestants may have arms for their defence suitable to their conditions and as allowed by law," the Declaration guaranteed Atkyns in the undisturbed possession of the sword which he treasured because King Charles had knighted him with it at the Restoration and which King Charles' officers had confiscated from him during the Rye House Plot scare.

The Declaration's statement that "freedom of speech and debates or proceedings in parliament ought not to be impeached or questioned in any court or place out of parliament" particularly upheld Williams' position in the Dangerfield Narrative Case and that of Atkyns and Pollexfen, who had sought to defend him. The Declaration's statement that "jurors ought to be duly impanelled and returned, and jurors which pass upon men in trials for high treason ought to be freeholders" echoed the arguments that Lord Russell and Sir Algernon Sidney had used, at the prompting of the Whig lawyers, to object against the juries that condemned them to death for their implication in the Rye House Plot. The Declaration's final statement, that "for redress of all grievances and for the amending, strengthening, and preserving of the laws, parliaments ought to be held frequently," expressed the desire of the lawyers never again to have to go through long years without a parliament behind them, supporting their efforts to have the government of the kingdom of England run, as the new coronation oath would state: "according to the statutes in parliament agreed on and the laws and customs of the same."

William and Mary accepted the Declaration on February 13, 1689 and on that very day were proclaimed king and queen. The Revolution was an accomplished fact. The lawyers had triumphed in their effort to maintain their proparliamentary interpretation of the Common Law.

Conclusion

IN ANALYZING THE POLITICAL CAREERS AND actions of the Whig lawyers from 1678 to 1689 one is constantly struck by the way in which, because they were lawyers, they were always influenced by two conflicting considerations: that of a proper regard for the undoubted, lawful rights of the Crown and that of a proper regard for the rights that they were convinced the law guaranteed to the subjects. It is surely true that the two essential conditions for a good governmental system and a healthy state are, first, that there be a strong and effective system of law that is respected and adhered to by both the governors and the governed, and second, that all citizens be permitted the maximum of individual liberty within the limits of the law. The problem is to determine the extent of those limits. What powers should the governors have? What rights should be possessed by the governed? In the period from 1642 to 1660 Englishmen had learned through bitter experience the unpleasantnesses and the dangers that could result from overthrowing established institutions and upsetting the balance of the constitution. But the Restoration, when it came, left many of them—and particularly many members of the landed,

business, and professional upper-middle class—still dissatisfied with the status quo. Through their representatives in
Parliament, they wished to have more influence than their
fathers had had on the domestic and foreign policies of the
royal government. At the same time, they wanted a minimum
of royal interference in their own local governments and
their economic activities. The Whig lawyers, because they
came from this class and were politically and professionally
associated with it, nearly always emphasized, and sought to
use the law in support of, the rights of the subjects of the
Crown.

Their concern was the preservation, always by lawful
means, of the privileges and power of Parliament (especially
the House of Commons), local liberties, franchises, and
immunities, and the rights and liberties of individuals. It is
true that for reasons of partisan advantage they acted in a
manner prejudicial to individual rights and liberties between
1678 and 1681 with regard to the unhappy victims of the
Popish Plot scare, and on some other occasions besides; but
they only did so because, owing to deficiencies in the laws
and the judicial system of their day, they could do so legally.
The Common Law and the statute book were their conscience. Their first loyalty was to the law and, under the law,
to the political institutions established by it.

One such institution was the monarchy, and the political
constitution implicit in England's laws made the monarch
powerful, irremovable, and unable to do any wrong. This
legal inviolability of the royal office was the basis of the
Whig lawyers' dilemma when, because they felt that his rule
would greatly imperil the Common Law or at least their
interpretation of it, they sought to bar James Stuart from the
throne in 1679–1681, and later they sought to justify having
driven him off it in 1689.

Most of the intellectuals of the day saw the monarchy as deriving its authority from some primal "social contract." For the lawyers, however, as Atkyns and his colleagues told the House of Lords in February, 1689, the "original contract" meant "the laws of the kingdom" handed down from the remotest English ancestors. The usual Whig concept of the social contract, and the concept that became an essential part of the Whig tradition, was that set forth by John Locke in his *Second Treatise on Civil Government* (1690), a work which, as Peter Laslett has shown,[1] Locke originally drafted in 1679–1680 in support of the Whig campaign for Exclusion. An important part of that concept is the recognition of the right of revolution as it was expounded by Locke at the beginning of his thirteenth chapter:

> There remains still in the people a supreme power to remove or alter the legislative when they find the legislative act contrary to the trust reposed in them; for all power given with trust for the attaining an end, being limited by that end, whenever that end is manifestly neglected or opposed, the trust must necessarily be forfeited, and the power devolve into the hands of those that gave it, who may place it anew where they shall think best for their safety and security.

Precisely the same argument, of course, is set forth in the Preamble to the American Declaration of Independence.

The right of revolution, applicable when the ruler breaks his contract with the ruled, like so many other rights claimed by seventeenth-century Englishmen, had a feudal precedent. It is an abstraction of the recognized right of a feudal vassal whose lord had failed to keep his end of the feudal bargain to issue a *diffidatio,* or "defiance," renouncing all obligations to the Lord. Such a right was stipulated, in a modified form, in the Great Charter that the English barons had forced King

John to sign and set his seal to at Runnymede in 1215. The sixty-first clause of the Charter stated that if the king or his justiciar, on being informed of any grievance by at least four members of an elected committee of twenty-five barons, failed to provide redress within forty days, the twenty-five barons, "together with . . . the entire country," might "distress and injure [the king] in all ways possible—namely by capturing [his] castles, lands and possessions and in all ways that they [could]." Magna Carta was a basic and undoubted part of the law of England, and if it endorsed revolution then revolution was legal. However, the clause referred to included a reservation: the king could be harassed but nothing might be done against his person or the persons of his wife and children. So the right of revolution, insofar as it existed at all, was limited. And in all subsequent versions of the charter, those issued after John's death, the sixty-first clause was omitted. Therefore, though some vague notion of the right of revolution may have remained alive in the English folk-memory as part of a general tradition of resistance to any king who sought to become an absolute despot, it certainly had no existence in English law.

Locke's theory of the right of revolution, of course, was not based on feudal precedent but rather on logical deduction from first principles using the process of "reason." The lawyers, however, employed a different reasoning process from that of the philosophers. Their reason was the "reason of the Common Law";[2] their self-evident premises were the basic principles of law that were inherently perceivable by all thinking men, the "natural law"; and their logical developments were the legislated statutes and the judicially determined precedents promulgated down through centuries of English legal history. They agreed with Locke that the powers delegated to the state were limited, but they also shared Hobbes' belief that the state itself was indissoluble. Herein lay the difference between the Whig lawyers and most other adherents of what came to be known as the Whig philosophy.

It was the essence of their argument in 1681 that the constitution could contain no internal, self-destroying contradictions. Going back to one of the first principles of "natural justice," they pointed out that the supreme law was the public good; anything that was contrary to the public good must, therefore, be unconstitutional. "The King cannot pardon treason against the government," Winnington argued with regard to Danby's case in 1679, "for then the government cannot be safe from evil ministers. . . ." The public good obviously necessitated the preservation of the Crown and the kingdom, and a Roman Catholic monarch must ipso facto be destructive of both. The constitutional solution seemed obvious: a parliamentary statute of Exclusion. As Jones put it in November, 1680, "to doubt that the legislative power of the nation, king, lords and commons [could not pass an Exclusion Bill was] to suppose that there [was] such a weakness in the government as must infallibly occasion its ruin." But King and Lords declined to join the Commons in passing the desired statute. The lawyers were left at a loss, for no other solution was sanctioned by law. No lawyers of note were involved in the illegal conspiracy, to which some of the other Whig leaders finally resorted in desperation, to assassinate King Charles at the Rye House; nor were any of them involved in Monmouth's illegal last desperate resort to armed rebellion.

In the discussions ensuing from King James' flight to France in December, 1688 the Whig lawyers were faced with a tougher constitutional problem than the one they had faced during the Exclusion controversy: namely, how to justify having driven off the throne, with the aid of foreign arms, a lawfully annointed and crowned king. But though the problem was more complex, the changed political situation made it possible to apply a solution of rather dubious legal validity, a solution that relied on the force of precedent rather than on the use of a parliamentary statute. Treby, Somers, and the others were compelled to resort to the writings of the Dutchman Grotius to justify their argument that James had "abdicated," and to a 1399 resolution of the Lords and Commons to support their conclusion "that the throne was thereby vacant." By so doing, however, they steered the English constitution safely through one of its most tempestuous crises and preserved the appearance of continuity in the English monarchy. The lawyers did not make the Revolution. It can be argued that without them precisely the same course of events might have occurred. What they did do was make the Revolution *legal*. As their spiritual inheritor Edmund Burke remarked a century later: "They threw a politic, well-wrought veil over every circumstance tending to weaken the rights, which in the meliorated order of succession they meant to perpetuate; or which might furnish a precedent for any future departure from what they had then settled for ever."[3]

Any historical study is only really significant insofar as it has some relevance to contemporary situations and problems. It seems important, therefore, to point out that the political careers of the Whig lawyers between 1678 and 1689 exhibited three aspects that were to be of significance in the later development of politics in the Western world. For one thing, their actions, albeit unwittingly, provided a good example of the basic principles of what would come to be called "loyal opposition." Never were their attacks on the policies of the

Court directed against the Crown itself, nor even against the king who wore it, but always against "evil ministers." And even in their opposition to the ministers of the Crown the lawyers never resorted to any means that were unlawful. Thus they demonstrated that it was possible for a person to be determinedly opposed to the policies of a particular government of a nation while at the same time remaining devotedly loyal to the nation's constitution and laws. Only with the general recognition that such an attitude was possible could the ethics of government ever be lifted above the level of the law of the jungle. Today the principle of loyal opposition is an integral part of the governmental systems of the English-speaking nations and of some few others, and there are yet other nations that would perhaps be the better for adopting it.

Again, in an age when the political trend in Europe was toward despotic monarchies of the type exemplified by Louis XIV's government of France, the Whig lawyers expressed in their speeches in Parliament and in the law courts a continuous and firm opposition to the principles of absolutism. By doing so they played a considerable part in guiding England in such a way that by 1701 she presented Europe with an example of a solidly based and effective and yet limited monarchy—an example that most of the European nations sought to emulate in the period from 1789 to 1914. The principles of individual liberty and limited government that the Whig lawyers enunciated were taken up by the American patriots of 1776, echoed in the Declaration of Independence, and built into the Constitution of the United States in 1787. Later, during the crisis of 1861–1865, President Abraham Lincoln and the federal government of the United States followed the Whig lawyers' precept that one may never depart from the lawfully established constitution.

The leaders of the Confederacy, on the other hand, acted on the Lockeian–Whig notion that they had the right to withdraw from, or overthrow, a government that in their judgment failed to protect not only their lives and liberties but also their property—which included, so far as they were concerned, the right to proprietorship over fellow human beings (provided that they were of a particular color).

Also, it is to be noted that today there is a trend, both in the United States and in the world at large, towards more powerful and more centralized government. American opponents of this trend are continually appealing for a "return" to the principles of the Constitution and thus, indirectly, back to the principles enunciated by the Whig lawyers at a time when they were faced by a somewhat similar crisis. It is for this reason that so many of the speeches of Treby and Pollexfen, of Williams and Winnington, of Maynard, Atkyns, and Jones have a familiar ring to them, and are, in fact, directly relevant to the modern political situation.[4]

The Revolution Settlement, said Trevelyan, ". . . was the triumph of the Common Law and lawyers over the King, who had tried to put prerogative above the law." But the prerogative was in fact an integral part of the Common Law, and the triumph of the Common Law was an established fact by 1660, what the Revolution Settlement really meant was the triumph of the lawyers', and particularly the Whig lawyers', *interpretation* of the Common Law, as against the interpretation of Common Law favored by the first four Stuart kings and, therefore, usually asserted in the courts by those jurists who were their servants.

The Act of Settlement of 1701, which declared that thenceforth all judges should hold office for life during good behavior, meant that in reaching their decisions the justices of Westminster Hall no longer needed, as a de facto condition of retaining their places on the bench, to take into account the desires of the monarch. Various provisions in the Trials for Treason Act of 1696 concerning indictments, the presentation of witnesses, the selection of juries, and legal aid for the accused reflected the experience of the Whig lawyers in the various political trials of 1681–1686 when, even if their fellow partisans whom they defended were probably guilty as charged, the processes that served to convict them were certainly unjust.

The right to a fair trial by an impartial judge and a properly selected jury is generally regarded as basic to Anglo-American liberties today. But the Revolution Settlement is important above all because it established, beyond any further doubt, the supreme constitutional role of Parliament. Since 1660 no one had challenged that body's sole right to authorize the levying of new taxes; but except in regard to taxation its exact powers and status continued to be vague and subject to question. By defending the existing city charters in the Quo Warranto proceedings the Whig lawyers had sought to prevent the Crown from gaining decisive control over parliamentary elections. In Williams' case they had tried to maintain the principle that the Speaker of the House of Commons was responsible for his official actions only to the House. In Sandys' case they had maintained that Parliament must regulate the nation's overseas trade and the government of the colonies. By their passive resistance in Hales' case, and by their active opposition in the case of the Seven Bishops (together with their Tory colleagues), they had defended the legislative power of Parliament against the Crown's use of dispensations and suspensions. Historically it may well have been true, as the Stuart kings and their legal advisors sometimes argued, that Parliament was originally a creature of the Crown, an advisory body entitled to pass only on those matters specifically referred to it by the king. But the Whig lawyers, in their political speeches and in their legal arguments between 1678 and 1689, implied that the High Court of Parliament was both legally and politically omnicompetent and supreme. The Revolution Settlement certified that in the future it would indeed be so.

It is true, as several modern historians have pointed out, that the Revolution Settlement left King William possessed of essentially the same powers as those enjoyed by his immediate predecessors. But the Whig lawyers had never urged that the lawful powers of the Crown should be diminished, only that its powers should not be exceeded—particularly at the expense of Parliament. And this, the Settlement fairly effectively ensured. The development during the eighteenth century of the cabinet system of responsible government meant that by the early nineteenth century the execution of those royal powers had devolved upon the leaders of the majority in the House of Commons.

It is also true, of course, that the Revolution, though it undeniably had the support of the great majority of Englishmen of all classes, did nothing immediately to better the political, social, or economic lot of the English common man. But the working-class Englishman probably fared at least as well under the supremacy of Parliament, even if Parliament really represented only the upper and upper-middle classes, as he would have done if subjected solely to the paternalistic whims of a capricious absolute monarch and his favorites. And the extending of the franchise (by the various Reform bills of the nineteenth century) to the point that there was almost universal adult male suffrage in Great Britain would, by early in the twentieth century, place the supreme power of the ommicompetent Parliament under the control of the ordinary British citizen.

Thus the bloodless Revolution of 1688–1689 can be seen to have been the essential first step toward the establishment of parliamentary democracy in Great Britain. For that reason the Revolution, and the triumph of the lawyers that it represented, surely may be labeled "Glorious."

Notes

N.B.: The following abbreviations have been used through-out:

CJ:	*The Journal of the House of Commons*
CSPD:	*The Calendars of State Papers Domestic*
CTB:	*The Calendars of the Treasury Books*
DNB:	*The Dictionary of National Biography*
HMCR:	*The Historical Manuscripts Commission Reports*
LJ:	*The Journal of the House of Lords*
ST:	*A Complete Collection of State Trials* . . . (ed. by Cobbett)

Chapter 1

1. Sir Wm. Dugdale, *History and antiquities of the four Inns of Court.* See note 3 below.

2. W. S. Holdsworth, *A History of English Law*, vol. 2, p. 509 suggests that government regulation began earlier and that Dugdale was just unable to find the evidence.

3. G. Shaw Lefevre, "The Discipline of the Bar," in *Economic and Social Pamphlets*, vol. 74, no. 1, pp. 3–6, quotes Dugdale, note 1 above.

4. *Middle Temple Admission Register*, vol. 1 (1501–1781); *A Register of Admissions to Gray's Inn, 1521–1881; Records of the Honourable Society of Lincoln's Inn (Admissions and Chapel Registers)*, vol. 1. The Inner Temple admissions are only published for the years 1547–1660.

5. In 1604 all Lincoln's Inn entrants were described simply as "gen." and so they are not included in the table. There were, of course, no baronets in 1604 as the title was first granted in 1611.

6. John Evelyn, *Diary,* ed. de Beer, vol. 5, p. 358; quoted in Holdsworth, *History,* vol. 6, p. 483n.

7. *Admission Register,* vol. 1, p. 178.

8. *Register of Admissions,* p. 255.

9. J. Foster, *Alumni Oxonienses,* vol. 4, sub William Turnor [sic]; *Middle Temple Admission Register,* vol. 1, p. 179. See Roger North, *Lives of the Norths,* vol. 1, p. 50, concerning calls *ex gratia* granted because of influence.

10. Foster, *Alumni Oxonienses* and J. and J. A. Venn, *Alumni Contabrigienses,* pt. 1; both passim.

11. Holdsworth, *History,* vol. 6, p. 488n.

12. Dugdale, *History,* quoted in Lefevre, "Discipline of the Bar," p. 6; North, *Lives,* vol. 1, p. 50n. "Outer barrister" (or "utter barrister") was the term used in the Inns to describe those of their members who had been called to the bar. An "inner barrister" was a student who had not yet been called.

13. Edward Foss, *Memories of Westminster Hall,* passim.

14. North, *Lives,* vol. 1, p. 72. Vol. 1 and the first part of vol. 2 of this work tell the story of Lord Guilford's career. The remainder of the work describes the careers of the author's two other older brothers, Dudley and John.

15. Ibid., pp. 71–73, 81–83, 91–93.

16. Thomas Powell, "The Art of Thriving," *Somers Tracts,* vol. 7, p. 199.

17. *Somers Tracts,* pp. 199–200.

18. North, *Lives,* vol. 1, pp. 74, 76.

19. Ibid., p. 156.

20. Ibid., p. 161.

21. *Memoir of the Life of John Lord Somers,* p. 15. According to a contemporary (1696) estimate the average annual income of "persons in the law," including solicitors, notaries, etc. was £154. The average annual income of a skilled workman was £38. See G. N. Clark, *The Later Stuarts,* 2nd edition, pp. 25–26.

22. *DNB*

23. The book, which was in the library at Stanford Court in

Worcestershire, is reported on in some detail in *Notes and Queries,* 2nd series, vol. 7, p. 65.

24. Rebecca Warner, *Epistolary Curiosities,* pp. 103–104.

25. Roger North, *Examen,* p. 515.

26. These official salaries are taken from *CTB,* vols. 4, 5, and 6, passim.

27. *History,* vol. 6, pp. 473–74.

28. Ibid., p. 476.

29. Ibid., pp. 458–65.

30. *Lives,* vol. 1, pp. 148–49.

31. *History,* vol. 6, pp. 471–72.

32. Speech at Whitehall, 1609; quoted in ibid., p. 13n.

33. Edward Foss, *A Biographical Dictionary of the Judges of England, 1066–1870,* sub Edward Coke.

34. Quoted in Holdsworth, *Some Makers of English Law,* p. 113.

35. Holdsworth, ibid., p. 123–124; *Sources and Literature of English Law,* p. 94.

36. Edward Coke, *Institutes of the Laws of England,* vol. 4, p. 60.

37. Wm. Cobbett, ed., *Parliamentary History of England,* vol. 2, pp. 355, 357. In reading extracts from speeches in Cobbett and the other collections of parliamentary debates, it should be remembered that the speeches reported have usually been compiled from notes taken by a reporter often in longhand, hence the rather terse, and often disjointed, style. They should not be regarded as completely accurate word-for-word accounts of what was actually said.

38. Holdsworth, *Makers,* p. 117.

39. Holdsworth gives a fairly complete list of Selden's works in his *History,* vol. 5, pp. 408–409.

40. Ibid., vol. 6, pp. 24–25.

41. Ibid., p. 25n.

42. Francis Bacon, *Essays, or Counsels Moral and Civil,* ed. Wm. Willymot, vol. 1, pp. 345–46.

43. Ibid., p. 345.

44. C. Stephenson and F. G. Marcham, eds., *Sources of English Constitutional History,* p. 461.

45. *Declaration of the Lords and Commons, 27 May, 1642;*

quoted in Stephenson and Marcham, *Sources,* p. 488.

46. "The Humble Petition of the Gentlemen of the Four Innes of Court to the House of Commons," *Somers Tracts,* vol. 4, pp. 351–52.

47. The Lincoln's Inn reply. The other three Inns replied in similar terms. See Sir Simonds D'Ewes, *Journal,* ed. W. H. Coates, pp. 368, 376n, 378–80.

48. *The Political Writings of James Harrington,* ed. Chas. Blitzer, pp. xxxvii–xxxviii.

49. *The Elements of Law,* ed. F. Tonnies, pp. 85–86.

50. Ibid., pp. 91–92.

51. Holdsworth, *History,* vol. 6, p. 500. For the full text of Hale's reply see ibid., vol. 5, appendix 3. Sir Matthew Hale was chief justice of the King's Bench, 1671–1675.

52. Ibid., vol. 6, pp. 481–84.

53. Ibid., pp. 204–205.

54. Ibid., p. 205.

55. J. C. Gray, *The Nature and Sources of the Law,* pp. 448–67.

56. See his remarks on *Bonham's Case* (1610) in his *Eighth Report.*

57. C. H. McIlwain, *The High Court of Parliament and Its Supremacy,* chap. 7, passim.

58. *Examen,* p. 513.

59. Notably H. B. Irving in his *Life of Judge Jeffreys.*

60. Narcissus Luttrell, *A Brief Historical Relation of State Affairs from September 1678–April 1714,* vol. 1, pp. 99–100.

61. *History,* vol. 6, p. 502.

Chapter 2

1. *DNB*

2. In chap. 3, p. 70 and note.

3. See chap. 7, pp. 237–38.

4. *HMCR,* Thirteenth Report, app. 6, p. 120.

5. Information derived from *DNB; Le Neve's Pedigrees of the Knights,* ed. Geo. Marshall; the admission registers of the Inns of Court; J. Foster, *Alumni Oxonienses;* J. and J. A.

Venn, *Alumni Cantabrigienses;* Philip Yorke, *The Royal Tribes of Wales; et al.*

6. Foster, *Alumni; Middle Temple Admissions Register,* vol. I, p. 109; *Le Neve's Pedigrees,* p. 117.

7. *Middle Temple Admissions Register.*

8. Edward Foss, *A Biographical Dictionary of the Judges of England, 1066–1870.*

9. House of Commons, *Papers* (1878), vol. 62, pt. 1, p. 488.

10. *Somers Tracts,* vol. 4, pp. 218–22.

11. Ibid., pp. 349–51. A poem describing the impeachment proceedings, written by Strafford's nephew Lord Roscommon, noted that: "The Robe was summon'd, Maynard at the head / In legal murder none so deeply read." Quoted in D. P. Alford, "Four Tavistock Worthies of the Seventeenth Century," *Transactions of the Devonshire Association for the Advancement of Science,* vol. 21, p. 140.

12. *ST,* vol. 4, p. 320.

13. *DNB*

14. Foss, *Dictionary,* citing Clarendon's *History of the Great Rebellion.*

15. *ST,* vol. 4, p. 320.

16. Maynard was also recorder of Totnes, Devon, 1645–1687 and 1688–1691, *Trans. of the Devon Assocn.,* vol. 56, p. 222. English municipal corporations were, and are today, required to appoint a qualified barrister as their "recorder," to act as general legal adviser to the municipality and to preside over the "Quarter Sessions" of the magistrates. The office dates from the fourteenth century.

17. Commons, *Papers* (1878), vol. 62, pt. 1, pp. 513, 521.

18. *Le Neve's Pedigrees,* p. 117.

19. Ibid., Alford, "Tavistock Worthies," p. 141; J. J. Alexander, "Bere Alston as a Parliamentary Borough," *Trans. of the Devon. Assoc.,* vol. 41, pp. 153–54.

20. Venn, *Alumni;* Lincoln's Inn, *Admission Register,* p. 236. According to Foster, *Alumni,* Atkyns received a masters degree from Oxford in 1663.

21. Wm. Cobbett, ed., *Parliamentary History of England,* vol. 4, records only two speeches by him during this period, one

of which was in defense of the impeached Earl of Clarendon, ibid., p. 381.

22. Commons, *Papers* (1878), vol. 62, pt. 1, p. 520.

23. *Le Neve's Pedigrees*, p. 11.

24. Ibid., *CSPD* (1663–64), p. 268.

25. *CSPD* (1661–62), p. 404.

26. *CSPD* (1665–66), p. 125.

27. *HMCR*, Sixth Report, p. 368ᵃ.

28. *CSPD* (1671), p. 222.

29. *CTB*, vol. 4, pp. 148, 247.

30. *HMCR*, Buccleuch MSS vol. 1, p. 317.

31. *CSPD* (1671–72), p. 191.

32. *CSPD* (1663–64), p. 482; ibid. (1660–71), p. 435. Atkyns, as recorder, would be partially responsible for law enforcement in the city.

33. *HMCR*, Seventh Report, p. 467; or possibly because Atkyns joined with Ellis in dissenting from the majority opinion in the case of *Barnardiston* v. *Soame*, see chap. 3, p. 75.

34. *Domestick Intelligence*, Feb. 10, 1679/80.

35. Cobbett, *Parliamentary History*, vol. 5, pp. 307–308.

36. *Reg. of Admissions*, p. 244.

37. *Lives of the Norths*, vol. 1, p. 63.

38. *Diary*, ed. E. S. de Beer, vol. 3, p. 580.

39. *Examen*, p. 512.

40. Later Lord Chancellor and first Earl of Nottingham.

41. *Examen*, p. 515.

42. Ibid., pp. 515–16.

43. David Ogg, *England in the Reign of Charles II*, vol. 2, p. 542.

44. Evidently Henry O'Brien, eldest son and heir of the Irish Earl of Thomond, who predeceased his father in 1678. He was a personal friend of Williamson, who later married his widow. See G. E. Cokayne, *The Complete Peerage*, ed. Gibbs, vol. 12, pt. 1, pp. 710–11.

45. Chamberlain of the City and formerly head of the Honorable Artillery Company, from which latter position he had been dismissed because the Duke of York objected to him. See *DNB*.

46. *CSPD* (1675–76), pp. 562–63.

47. Ogg, *Charles II*, vol. 1, p. 101.

48. *Lives,* vol. 1, pp. 317–18. North claims that Jones half believed the threat and was made rather nervous by it.

49. *CSPD* (1675–76), p. 496.

50. Ogg, *Charles II*, pp. 101–102.

51. *Admissions Register,* p. 342.

52. Foss, *The English Judges,* vol. 7, p. 335. One could not plead in Westminster Hall until three years after being called to the bar (see chap. 1, p. 18).

53. Middle Temple, *Register of Admissions;* Foster, *Alumni.* Treby was made a Bencher of his Inn in 1681, held the office of Reader in 1686, and was made treasurer in 1689.

54. *CSPD* (1677–78), pp. 17, 36; *CJ,* vol. 9, p. 401.

55. *HMCR,* Thirteenth Report, app. 6, pp. 6–7.

56. Otherwise they could not have been admitted to their respective Inns (see chap. 1, pp. 14–15).

57. *Lives,* vol. 2, p. 23.

58. Ibid., p. 9.

59. *DNB*

60. *HMCR,* Thirteenth Report, app. 6, p. 7.

61. *CSPD* (1677–78), pp. 446, 449. This work by Nathaniel Bacon, Master of Requests under the Protectorate, was originally published in 1647. Starkey published it again in 1682 (when it was again suppressed) and in 1689 (British Museum, *General Catalogue of Printed Books, sub* Bacon, Nathaniel).

62. Foster, *Alumni; Register of Admissions; DNB.*

63. Yorke, *Royal Tribes,* p. 112.

64. Sir Peter Leicester, quoted in Anthony à Wood, *Athenae Oxonienses,* ed. P. Bliss, vol. 4, p. 720. Shakerley's letter is in *CSPD* (1667), p. 25.

65. *CSPD* (1667), p. 44.

66. *The Rolls of the Freemen of the City of Chester* (Lancashire and Cheshire Record Society, 1906), pt. 1, p. 154.

67. *HMCR,* Eighth Report, p. 389ᵇ.

68. *CTB,* vol. 2, p. 876.

69. *HMCR,* Eighth Report, p. 389ᵇ.

70. *CSPD* (1672–73), pp. 505–506.

71. *CSPD* (1675–76), p. 124.

72. *CSPD* (1672–73), p. 587.

73. *CSPD* (1675–76), pp. 124–25.
74. *DNB*, but he is not listed in Foster *Alumni.*
75. *Register of Admissions,* vol. 1, p. 158.
76. *Memoir of the Life of John Lord Somers,* p. 10.
77. In chap. 1, p. 21.
78. Ibid.
79. *DNB*
80. *Le Neve's Pedigrees*
81. *CTB,* vol. 4, p. 453.
82. *HMCR,* Portland MSS, vol. 3, p. 342.
83. *Le Neve's Pedigrees,* p. 282.
84. *CTB,* vol. 4, p. 342.
85. *Notes and Queries,* 2nd series, vol. 7, p. 65.
86. 4 Edward III, c. 14.
87. *CSPD* (1677–78), p. 216; *ST,* vol. 6, pp. 1276–94.

Chapter 3

1. Wm. Cobbett, *Parliamentary History of England,* vol. 4, p. 1017.
2. *CJ,* vol. 9, p. 530.
3. Cobbett, *Parliamentary History,* vol. 4, p. 1017n.
4. *CJ,* vol. 9, p. 530.
5. Ibid., passim.
6. Ibid.
7. Anchitell Grey, *Debates of the House of Commons, 1667–1694,* vol. 6; pp. 261–62.
8. Cobbett, *Parliamentary History,* vol. 4, p. 848.
9. *Lives of the Norths,* vol. 1, pp. 99–100.
10. British Museum, Additional MSS, 38,847, fol. 230–37.
11. For a discussion of the state of the law at this time in regard to witnesses in treason trials, see W. S. Holdsworth, *A History of English Law,* vol. 4, p. 499.
12. *ST,* vol. 7, pp. 159–230.
13. Ibid., pp. 1–78; Grey, *Debates,* vol. 6, p. 295.
14. *HMCR,* Eighth Report, p. 390^b.
15. Ibid.
16. Ibid.
17. Cobbett, *Parliamentary History,* vol. 4, p. 1038.

18. Armand Baschet, quoted in B. Behrens, "The Whig Theory of the Constitution in the Reign of Charles II," *Cambridge Historical Journal,* vol. 7, p. 43.

19. Sir John Dalrymple, *Memoirs,* vol. 2, app. 1, p. 196; J. R. Jones, *The First Whigs,* p. 28.

20. Member for Marlborough and one of the more extreme Whigs. See Jones, *Whigs,* p. 156.

21. Cobbett, *Parliamentary History,* vol. 4, p. 1061.

22. For the full text, see Cobbett, *Parliamentary History,* vol. 4, app. 15. Gilbert Burnet, *History of His Own Time* (1734 ed.) vol. 1, p. 500, says that Sir Algernon Sidney prepared the first draft of the *Vindication* and that it was later revised by Somers and Jones. It was published anonymously in 1681, and republished in 1689 with the title *The Design of Enslaving England Discovered* and signed "W. J." See *DNB,* sub Algernon Sidney and sub William Jones, also British Museum, *Catalogue of Printed Books* sub William Jones. Burnet, loc. cit., is the only authority (though probably a good one) for Sidney's and Somers' role in its composition.

23. Cobbett, *Parliamentary History,* vol. 4, p. 1065.

24. *CJ,* vol. 9, p. 560.

25. Ibid., pp. 561–562.

26. *LJ,* vol. 13, p. 431.

27. Narcissus Luttrell, *A Brief Historical Relation of State Affairs from September 1678 to April 1714,* vol. 1, p. 6; House of Commons, *Papers* (1878), vol. 62, pt. 1, p. 539.

28. *HMCR,* Thirteenth Report, app. 6, pp. 11–12.

29. *CJ,* vol. 9, p. 568; *DNB.*

30. David Ogg, *England in the Reign of Charles II,* vol. 2, p. 586.

31. Cobbett, *Parliamentary History,* vol. 4, p. 1085.

32. Ibid., p. 1110.

33. Ibid., p. 1107.

34. *CJ,* vol. 9, pp. 568, 572; *HMCR,* Ormond MSS, new series, vol. 5, p. 9.

35. Jones, *Whigs,* p. 51.

36. *CJ,* vol. 9, p. 571.

37. Ibid., p. 577.

38. *ST,* vol. 6, pp. 1068–76.

39. Ibid., pp. 1076–1117, where he is referred to as "late one of the Judges of the Common Pleas." The text is also to be found in R. Atkyns, *Parliamentary and Political Tracts,* pp. 130–76.

40. *Tracts,* pp. 137–42.

41. Ibid., pp. 160–61.

42. Ibid., p. 137.

43. *CJ,* vol. 9, pp. 609ff. The only major piece of legislation passed by this parliament was the Habeas Corpus Act (31 Charles II, c. 2).

44. Ibid., pp. 568, 579.

45. Ibid., p. 571.

46. Edward and Annie Porritt, *The Unreformed House of Commons,* vol. 1, p. 516. By the end of the nineteenth century the House had given up the struggle and all members of the bar were excused from committee work, ibid., p. 519. The order had to be repeated a few weeks later, *CJ,* vol. 9, p. 602.

47. C. H. McIlwain *The High Court of Parliament and its Supremacy,* pp. 214–15.

48. *CTB,* vol. 5, entry for Apr. 29, 1679.

49. *HMCR,* Thirteenth Report, app. 6, p. 17.

50. Ibid.

51. Ibid., p. 23.

52. *LJ,* vol. 13, p. 471.

53. *HMCR,* Tenth Report, vol. 4, p. 130.

54. *CJ,* vol. 9, p. 574.

55. Nottingham's arguments prepared on Danby's behalf were published twelve years later: *A Treatise on the King's Powers of granting pardons in cases of impeachment* (London, 1691).

56. Burnet, *History* (1734 ed.) vol. 1, p. 460.

57. Ibid., pp. 576, 630–31.

58. Burnet, *History of My Own Time* (ed. Wm. Airey, 1900), vol. 2, p. 257.

59. Grey, *Debates,* vol. 6, p. 148.

60. In 1681 John Somers published a tract entitled *A Brief History of the Succession* in which he pointed out, quite rightly, that the English throne had by no means always devolved in accordance with the strict laws of inheritance. It was repub-

lished several times in the following century. See B. M., *Catalogue*, sub John Somers.

61. *CJ*, vol. 9, p. 620.

62. Cobbett, *Parliamentary History*, vol. 4, pp. 1133–34.

63. *CJ*, vol. 9, p. 620.

64. *HMCR*, Ormond MSS, new series, vol. 3, p. 509.

65. D. Milne and A. Browning, "An Exclusion Bill Division List," *Bulletin of the Institute of Historical Research*, vol. 23, pp. 205–25, provides the fullest information. Another list can be found in K. Feiling, *History of the Tory Party*, app. 1.

66. *HMCR*, Seventh Report, pp. 472^b, 473^a; ibid., Ormond MSS, new series, vol. 5, pp. 456–57.

67. Cobbett, *Parliamentary History*, vol. 4, p. 959.

68. Ibid., p. 986.

69. Ibid., p. 1046.

70. *CJ*, vol. 9, p. 358.

71. Ibid., pp. 540, 552 and passim.

72. Ibid., p. 544.

73. Williams-Wynn MSS, quoted in *ST*, vol. 13, pp. 1439–40.

74. Ibid.

75. Michael Macdonagh, *The Speaker of the House*, pp. 3–4.

76. *CJ*, vol. 9, p. 253.

77. Ibid., pp. 463–64.

78. Cobbett, Parliamentary History, vol. 4, pp. 1112–13.

79. Arthur Dasent, *The Speakers of the House of Commons*, p. 228.

80. Cobbett, *Parliamentary History*, vol. 4, pp. 957, 1112–13.

81. Macdonagh, *Speaker*, p. 249.

82. Grey, *Debates*, vol. 7, p. 349.

83. *HMCR*, Eighth Report, p. 391^b.

84. Ibid., Twelfth Report, vol. 9, p. 103.

85. T. H. Escott, *Gentlemen of the House of Commons*, vol. 2, p. 107.

86. *CJ*, vol. 9, p. 668.

87. *Diary*, ed. E. S. de Beer, vol. 4, p. 234.

88. James Manning. *The Lives of the Speakers of the House of Commons*, p. 379. In the interval between the first and second Exclusion parliaments (May, 1679 to October, 1680) the Whigs

had organized petitions calling for a new parliament to be summoned immediately because of the Popish threat. Wythens and other Tories had organized counter-petitions "abhorring" the Whig attempts to dictate to the king how he should exercise his prerogative right to summon a parliament when he chose.

89. Cobbett, *Parliamentary History*, vol. 4, p. 1233. Peyton had allegedly participated in the Dangerfield Plot, a "sham Presbyterian" plot allegedly engineered by the Catholics in order to discredit the Whigs. See chap. 6, p. 184.

90. Luttrell, *Relation*, vol. 1, p. 65.

91. Cobbett, *Parliamentary History*, vol. 4, p. 764.

92. *HMCR*, Ormond MSS, new series, vol. 5, p. 106.

93. See chap. 2, p. 50.

94. *Examen*, pp. 508–509; Burnet, *History* (Airey), vol. 2, p. 106.

95. Elkanah Settle in *Absalom Senior*. See H. W. Jones, *Anti-Achitophel (1682), Three Verse Replies to Absalom and Achitophel*, p. 50.

96. *HMCR*, Ormond MSS, new series, vol. 3, p. 569.

97. Ibid., new series, vol. 5, p. 454.

98. Quoted in North, *Lives*, vol. 1, p. 103n.

99. Commons, *Papers* (1878), vol. 62, pt. 1, p. 541.

100. Sir William Temple, *Works*, vol. 2, pp. 532–33.

101. Jones, *Whigs*, p. 138.

102. Cobbett, *Parliamentary History*, vol. 4, pp. 1168–70.

103. Grey, *Debates*, vol. 7, pp. 418–20.

104. *Salus populi, supreme lex* was traditionally supposed to have been one of the rules inscribed on the twelve tablets of the original laws of ancient Rome.

105. Cobbett, *Parliamentary History*, vol. 4, pp. 1208–11.

106. *CJ*, vol. 9, pp. 646–48, 651.

107. Cobbett, *Parliamentary History*, vol. 4, p. 1215.

108. Helen Foxcroft, *The Life and Letters of George Savile, Marquess of Halifax*, vol. 1, pp. 246–48. Unfortunately no record of this debate seems to have been preserved.

109. *CJ*, vol. 9, pp. 655, 676, 692, 697.

110. Ibid., pp. 677, 682, 686, 695, 701.

111. 35 Elizabeth I, c. 1. See *CJ*, vol. 9, pp. 646, 681.

112. Evelyn, *Diary,* vol. 4, pp. 229–33; *CJ,* vol. 9, pp. 655, 662–63, 667–71.

113. *HMCR,* Ormond MSS, new series, vol. 5, pp. 561–63.

114. Williams-Wynn MSS, quoted in *ST,* vol. 13, p. 1440.

115. *HMCR,* Ormond MSS, new series, vol. 5, pp. 561–63.

116. Luttrell, *Relation,* vol. 1, pp. 61, 64, 67; *Protestant Domestick Intelligence,* Jan. 25, 1680/81 and Feb. 8, 1680/81. There is no evidence that Charles actively favored Treby for the post.

117. *CJ,* vol. 9, p. 702.

118. Jones, *Whigs,* pp. 153–54.

119. *Smith's Protestant Intelligence,* Mar. 17–21, 1680/81.

120. *Protestant Domestick Intelligence,* Feb. 4, 18, 1680/81.

121. *Smith's Protestant Intelligence,* Feb. 1, 1680/81; *Protestant Oxford Intelligence,* Mar. 14–17, 1680/81.

122. Cobbett, *Parliamentary History,* vol. 4, pp. 1305–06.

123. *CJ,* vol. 9, p. 708.

124. Ibid., p. 711.

125. Ibid., p. 708.

126. Ogg, *Charles II,* vol. 2, p. 615.

127. Cobbett, *Parliamentary History,* vol. 4, pp. 1324–25. 1 Henry VII, c. 1 states that: "all the pre-eminence and dignity royal . . . , with the appurtenances thereto in any wise due or pertaining, be, rest, remain, and abide in the most royal person of our now sovereign lord, King Henry VII, and in the heirs of his body lawfully coming, perpetually with the grace of God, so to endure, and in none other," (C. Stephenson and F. C. Marcham, eds., *Sources of English Constitutional History,* p. 299). It is a basic principle of English common law that any office or relationship carries with it certain inalienable rights and duties.

128. Ogg, *Charles II,* vol. 2, pp. 614, 619.

Chapter 4

1. *Leviathan,* chap. 19.

2. *CSPD* (1680–81), p. 660.

3. *CSPD* (1680–81), p. 232. The following June the same

informer was petitioning Secretary Jenkins from jail for financial assistance (ibid., p. 317).

4. *HMCR*, Thirteenth Report, app. 6, p. 24.

5. *CSPD,* (1680–81), pp. 256, 257.

6. Ibid., pp. 278–80. Charles told this delegation to go home and mind their own business. (Reginald Sharpe, *London and the Kingdom*, vol. 2, p. 466).

7. *CSPD* (1680–81), p. 505.

8. Ibid., p. 561.

9. Ibid., p. 39. But Bushell's case (1670) had been very similar, and then it had been established that a jury could not be punished for bringing in a verdict that was clearly against the weight of the evidence (W. S. Holdsworth, *History of English Law*, vol. 6, p. 388).

10. *ST,* vol. 8, p. 550; A. F. Havighurst, "The Judiciary and Politics in the Reign of Charles II and James II," *Law Quarterly Review*, vol. 66, p. 241.

11. *CSPD* (1680–81), pp. 509–10.

12. Ibid., p. 521.

13. Ibid., p. 525; Havighurst, "Judiciary," p. 243. It was at about this time that John Somers wrote and published anonymously his pamphlet entitled *The Security of Englishmen's Lives,* which stressed the importance of the jury system as a bulwark of English liberty (British Museum, *Catalogue of Printed Books*).

14. Sir John Reresby, *Memoirs,* quoted in Havighurst, "Judiciary," p. 243.

15. *CSPD* (1680–81), p. 521.

16. *ST*, vol. 8, p. 759.

17. Quo Warranto: Action by writs of this type (issued by Chancery and answerable before the King's Bench) was prescribed by the Statute of Gloucester (6 Edward I), and was originally used to question the feudal rights exercised by the barons. "It is a writ of right, a civil remedy to try the mere right to the franchise or office, where the person in possession never had a right to it or had forfeited it by neglect or abuse" (Blackstone, quoted in *Bouvier's Law Dictionary*).

18. J. H. Sacret, "The Restoration Government and Municipal Corporations," *English Historical Review,* vol. 45, p. 234.

Sacret's article gives a very good account of Charles II's attacks on municipal corporations prior to 1681.

19. *CSPD* (1628–29), p. 555.

20. Sacret, "Corporations," p. 235.

21. Ibid., quoting *CSPD* (1660–61), p. 582.

22. *CSPD* (1660–61), p. 608.

23. 13 Charles II, c. 1.

24. *CJ*, vol. 8, pp. 310–12; Sacret, "Corporations," pp. 249–50.

25. Clause 8.

26. Clause 14.

27. David Ogg, *England in the Reign of Charles II*, vol. 2, p. 315; Wm. Cobbett, *Parliamentary History of England*, vol. 4, p. 378, the fourteenth article.

28. Preamble to the Corporations Act.

29. *CSPD* (1679–80), pp. 499–500.

30. *ST*, vol. 8, p. 1042, quoting Roger North, *Examen*.

31. Sharpe, *London*, vol. 2, pp. 18–19.

32. Ibid., p. 403.

33. Roger Morrice, unpublished diary in the Morrice MSS, Dr. Williams Library, London, p. 321 (Dec. 27, 1681). Hilary Term lasts from Jan. 23 to Feb. 21. The other common law terms are: Michaelmas (Oct. 29–Nov. 28), Easter (eighteen days after Easter to the Monday after Ascension Day), and Trinity (the Wednesday after Trinity Sunday to the Wednesday two weeks later).

34. *ST*, vol. 8, pp. 1039–40.

35. In his capacity as recorder, Treby had headed the delegation that carried it to the king. Charles rebuffed it, saying that he was sure of London's loyalty but that he wished they would not let others influence them into meddling in affairs that did not concern them (Morrice diary, p. 294).

36. *ST*, vol. 8, pp. 1039–86.

37. Diary, p. 321.

38. Oliver Wynne to Lord Preston, *HMCR* Seventh Report, p. 359^b.

39. *ST*, vol. 7, pp. 1079–85.

40. Ibid., pp. 1085–86.

41. Corporation of London, Journal, vol. 50, p. 2. The opin-

ion was signed by Treby, Williams, Winnington, Richard Wallop, and two other lawyers.

42. *ST*, vol. 8, pp. 1087, 1099; Narcissus Luttrell, *A Brief Historical Relation of State Affairs from September 1678 to April 1714,* vol. 1, p. 249.

43. *CSPD* (1682–83), pp. 222–23; Luttrell, *Relation,* vol. 1, p. 249. *ST*, vol. 8, pp. 1143, 1213, is wrong in dating both these last two hearings, Apr. 27, 1682.

44. *ST*, vol. 8, p. 1267.

45. Havighurst, "Judiciary," p. 76.

46. Ibid., pp. 229–30.

47. Ibid., pp. 244–45.

48. John Pollock, *Cambridge Modern History* (1907–11), vol. 5, sec. 9, p. 229.

49. Francis Gwynne to the Earl of Conway, *CSPD* (1682–83), pp. 222–23.

50. *ST*, vol. 8, pp. 1087–99.

51. Ibid., pp. 1099–1145.

52. Luttrell, *Relation,* vol. 1, p. 256; *CSPD* (1682–83), p. 222.

53. *ST,* vol. 8, pp. 1147–1213.

54. Ibid., pp. 1213–63.

55. Clause 3.

56. *ST*, vol. 8, pp. 1264–72.

57. Ibid., p. 1244.

58. Ibid., p. 1214.

59. Ibid., p. 1240.

60. Ibid.

61. Ibid., p. 1090.

62. Ibid., pp. 1148–49.

63. Sharpe, *London,* vol. 2, p. 476.

64. *CSPD* (1680–81), p. 478, from a newsletter of Sept. 29, 1681.

65. Sharpe, *London,* vol. 2, p. 476.

66. *CSPD* (1680–81), p. 660.

67. North, *Examen,* quoted in *ST,* vol. 9, p. 189.

68. Sharpe, *London,* vol. 2, pp. 471–72.

69. For his biography see North, *Lives of the Norths,* vol. 2.

70. *CSPD,* (1682–83), p. 263.

71. Sharpe, *London,* vol. 2, p. 480.

72. Ibid., p. 481n; London newsletter (from an unpublished collection in the Library of Congress), July 8, 1682.

73. Luttrell, *Relation,* vol. 1, p. 204; London newsletter (L.C.), July 8, 1682.

74. Sharpe, *London,* vol. 2, pp. 482–85.

75. *CSPD* (1682), p. 441.

76. Sharpe, *London,* vol. 2, pp. 487–88.

77. London newsletter (L.C.), Oct. 7, 1682. On October 21 Williams and Sir Robert Clayton, representing the Common Council, appeared before the King's Bench and lodged a charge against Moore. They also procured a writ of *Mandamus* ordering that Papillon and Dubois be recognized as sheriffs. But it would seem that nothing ever came of either action. (Ibid., Oct. 25, 1682.)

78. *CSPD* (1682–83), p. 317.

79. *ST,* vol. 8, pp. 1273–74.

80. Ibid., pp. 1276–81.

81. Ibid., p. 1282.

82. *Examen,* quoted in ibid. p. 1051.

83. Sharpe, *London,* vol. 2, p. 500.

84. Corporation of London, Journal, vol. 50, p. 101.

85. *CSPD* (1683), p. 424.

86. Sharpe, *London,* vol. 2, p. 504.

87. North, *Examen,* quoted in *ST,* vol. 8, pp. 1058–59.

88. 2 William and Mary, c. 8.

89. John Evelyn, *Diary,* ed. E. S. de Beer, vol. 4, p. 342; Luttrell, *Relation,* vol. 1, p. 295.

90. *CSPD* (1683–84), p. 13.

91. Quoted in *ST,* vol. 8, p. 1067.

92. "Abstract of the charters granted by Charles II, 1680–85," *HMCR,* Twelfth Report, vol. 6, p. 298.

93. Ibid.; Morrice diary, Oct. 27, 1683.

94. *ST,* vol. 8, pp. 1043–66.

95. Humphrey Prideaux, *Letters to John Ellis,* ed. E. Thompson, p. 104.

96. Mandamus: a writ from a high court to a corporation, individual person, or inferior court within its jurisdiction requiring them to do some particular, specified thing which apper-

tains to their particular duty. It is used where the law has established no specific remedy and where, "in justice and good government there ought to be one" (Lord Mansfield in *Bouvier's, Law Dictionary*).

97. *CSPD* (1682), pp. 1, 35, 57.
98. Ibid., p. 279.
99. *CSPD* (1684, p. 2), p. 65.
100. Dr. John Lloyd, *CSPD* (1683–84), p. 303.
101. *CSPD* (1684, pt. 2), p. 65; *HMCR*, Twelfth Report, vol. 6, p. 298.
102. *CSPD* (1684, pt. 1), p. 396.
103. Ibid. (1684–85), p. 231 (William Lawson to the Duke of Newcastle).
104. Morrice diary, p. 430.
105. Atkyns' argument before the King's Bench in *Rex v. Atkyns, Modern Reports*, vol. 3, p. 23.
106. *CSPD* (1680–81), p. 137. A number of contemporary lists, however, attest that Atkyns was that same month elected to the seat for the county of Middlesex vacated by the expelled Sir Robert Peyton (note in the files of the History of Parliament Trust, London).
107. *Protestant Domestick Intelligence,* issues of Mar. 11 and 15, 1680/81.
108. Ibid., Mar. 15, 1680/81.
109. Luttrell, *Relation,* vol. 1, p. 127.
110. *CSPD* (1682), p. 500.
111. Luttrell, *Relation,* vol. 1, p. 294; *CSPD* (1683, pt. 1), p. 142; *Modern Reports,* vol. 3, pp. 3–23.
112. *CSPD* (1682), p. 563.
113. A first cousin once removed of his famous namesake the future Duke of Marlborough. He was later to serve as Master of the Rolls, January-March, 1685 (*DNB*).
114. *CSPD* (1682), pp. 566, 573, 578.
115. Ibid., p. 581.
116. Ibid. (1683, pt. 1), p. 9.
117. See chap. 2, p. 49.
118. *Protestant Domestick Intelligence,* Mar. 11, 1680/81.
119. *CSPD* (1683, pt. 1), pp. 141–42.
120. Ibid., p. 160.

121. Ibid. (1683–84), p. 248.

122. Ibid., p. 85.

123. "Abstract of the charters," *HMCR,* Twelfth Report, vol. 6, p. 298.

124. *CSPD* (1682), p. 280.

125. *HMCR,* Seventh Report, p. 533^b; Edward Parry, *Royal Visits and Progresses to Wales and the Border Counties,* pp. 409–10; J. P. Earwaker, "The 'Progress' of the Duke of Monmouth in Cheshire, in September 1682," *Transactions of the Historic Society of Lancashire and Cheshire,* new series, vol. 10, pp. 71–96.

126. Ibid., the latter two.

127. *HMCR,* Seventh Report, p. 533^b.

128. *CSPD* (1682), p. 402.

129. Ibid., p. 406.

130. Ibid., p. 467.

131. Ibid., p. 427.

132. Ibid., p. 440.

133. Ibid., p. 439.

134. Ibid., p. 475.

135. The Shakerleys to Jenkins, October 9 and 11, Ibid., pp. 465, 467.

136. London newsletter (L.C.), Oct. 5, 1682.

137. *CSPD* (1682), p. 440.

138. Ibid., pp. 439–40.

139. Ibid., p. 449.

140. Ibid., pp. 471–72.

141. Ibid. (1683, pt. 1), p. 213.

142. Ibid. (1683, pt. 2), p. 188.

143. Ibid., pp. 294, 393.

144. Ibid., p. 265.

145. Ibid., p. 293. On May 6, 1682 the frigate Gloucester, bringing the Duke of York, his family, and retinue from Edinburgh to London, had been shipwrecked off the Norfolk coast with a loss of more than two hundred lives. The Mayor and citizens of Chester seem to have been rather tardy with their congratulations.

146. Ibid., p. 190.

147. Colonel Werden and P. Shakerley to Jenkins, *CSPD* (1683–84), pp. 165–66.

148. Ibid., p. 200.

149. *CSPD* (1684–85), p. 38; H. T. Dutton, "The Stuart Kings and Chester Corporation," *Journal of the Chester and North Wales Architectural, Archeological and Historic Society,* vol. 28, pp. 194–195.

150. *CSPD* (1684–85), p. 214; "Abstract of the Charters," *HMCR*, Twelfth Report, vol. 6, p. 298; James Hall, Royal Charters and Grants to the City of Chester," *Journal of the Chester and North Wales . . . Historic Society,* new series, vol. 18, pp. 65–72.

151. Hall, ibid.; *HMCR*. Eighth Report, p. 561^b.

Chapter 5

1. For the Text of his confession see *ST,* vol. 8, pp. 223–26.

2. Ibid., p. 227.

3. *The Protestant Oxford Intelligence,* Mar. 10–14, 1680/81.

4. *ST,* vol. 8, pp. 231–32.

5. Gilbert Burnet, *History of His Own Time* (1734), vol. 1, p. 498.

6. *ST,* vol. 8, p. 233.

7. Ibid., p. 234.

8. Ibid., pp. 236–42.

9. Armand Baschet, quoted in David Ogg, *England in the Reign of Charles II,* vol. 2, p. 624.

10. On April 11, Robt. Beatson, *A Political Index,* vol. 2, p. 281.

11. *ST,* vol. 8, pp. 234–49.

12. Ibid., pp. 249–54.

13. Ibid., pp. 254–63.

14. John Ellis' suggestion in a letter of May 7, 1681 (*HMCR*, Ormond MSS, New series vol. 6, p. 59) that Williams seemed not to want to take the case was apparently wrong in view of his strenuous efforts in it later.

15. Wm. Cobbett, *Parliamentary History of England,* vol. 4, p. 1355.

16. *ST,* vol. 8, pp. 263–81.

17. Ibid., p. 281.

18. Narcissus Luttrell, *A Brief Historical Relation of State Affairs from September 1678 to April 1714,* vol. 1, p. 80; *CSPD* (1680–81), p. 270.

19. Cf. the debate on Danby's pardon in Chap. 3, pp. 77–79.

20. *ST,* vol. 8, pp. 281–96; *CSPD* (1680–81) p. 270.

21. Ibid., p. 296.

22. Ibid., pp. 296–303.

23. Ibid., pp. 303–11.

24. Ibid., pp. 311–18.

25. *CSPD* (1680–81), p. 270.

26. *ST,* vol. 8, pp. 318–22.

27. Ibid., pp. 322–33.

28. Ibid., pp. 326–30.

29. Ibid.

30. Ibid.

31. *CSPD* (1680–81), p. 271.

32. *ST,* vol. 8, pp. 330–99.

33. Ibid., pp. 399–426.

34. Ibid., p. 250; *HMCR,* Ormond MSS, new series, vol. 6, p. 48.

35. Diary, vol. 4, pp. 180–81.

36. See chap. 4, p. 118.

37. *CSPD* (1682), p. 40.

38. *HMCR,* Ormond MSS, new series, vol. 6, p. 114.

39. Gilbert Burnet, *History of My Own Time,* ed. Wm. Airey, vol. 2, p. 343 (note by Arthur Onslow); Roger North, *Examen,* p. 509. A newsletter of May 4, 1682 says Jones died in his chambers in Gray's Inn (*CSPD* [1682], p. 198). Luttrell says that he died at his home in Southampton Square, London (*Relation,* vol. 1, p. 181). However, a letter written by Lord Fauconberg from Sutton Court and dated May 4, 1682 reporting Jones' death "here yesterday" seems to substantiate the reports of North and Onslow (*HMCR,* Astley MSS, p. 51). Arthur Onslow, of the notable Whig family of that name, served as Speaker of the House of Commons under George II (*DNB*).

40. Burnet (Airey), vol. 2, p. 343, note by Onslow. Thomas, Lord Trevor (1658–1730), lawyer and politician, served successively as solicitor general, attorney general, chief justice of the Common Pleas, and finally, Lord Privy Seal under William and Mary, Anne, and George II (*DNB*).

41. *Examen*, p. 509, says Jones reportedly expressed his contempt for Shaftesbury's alleged attempts, during his imprisonment in 1681, to negotiate with the government for his freedom in return for a promise to refrain from all future political activities.

42. *Examen*, p. 509.

43. Ogg, *Charles II*, vol. 2, p. 646.

44. *HMCR*, Astley MSS, p. 51.

45. Ibid., Hastings MSS, p. 392.

46. Ibid., Ormond MSS, new series, vol. 6, p. 209; *CSPD* (1682), p. 105.

47. *CSPD* (1683), p. 274.

48. *DNB*, sub Thomas Thynne; *ST*, vol. 9, pp. 1–126.

49. *ST*, vol. 9, pp. 127–86.

50. Ibid., pp. 299–352.

51. Ibid., pp. 219–91.

52. Ibid., pp. 299–352.

53. Ibid., vol. 10, pp. 321–71.

54. *Charles II*, vol. 2, p. 637.

55. The proceedings against Russell are reported in *ST*, vol. 9, pp. 577–635.

56. Lady Russell had petitioned the King, on July 3, that these three and one other be assigned to assist her husband, which was allowed (*CSPD* [1683, pt. 2], pp. 17, 25).

57. For his letter of complaint to Secretary Jenkins, see ibid., pp. 402–403.

58. *DNB*, sub Hugh Speke; *CSPD* (1683, pt. 2), pp. 108–109.

59. *ST*, vol. 9, p. 719.

60. *CSPD* (1683, pt. 2), p. 127; *ST*, vol. 9, p. 722.

61. *HMCR*, Various Collections, vol. 4, p. 188; Sir John Dalrymple, *Memoirs*, vol. 1, pp. 91–93. Both these sources claim that Treby was a member of the Commission that tried Russell;

however, his name is not mentioned in the account of the trial given in the *State Trials*.

62. For the text see *ST*, vol. 9, pp. 685–95.

63. Ibid., p. 519.

64. Ibid., pp. 709–16.

65. Ibid., p. 716.

66. Ibid., p. 718.

67. Ibid., p. 787.

68. Ibid., pp. 725–42, 744.

69. Ibid., pp. 741–56.

70. Ibid., pp. 483–94.

71. Ibid., pp. 755–72.

72. Ibid., pp. 695–96.

73. Evidently a republican in his political beliefs, Sidney (1622–83) returned to England in 1677 from a self-imposed exile on the Continent that had lasted since the Restoration. He was active in the Whig cause in the next five years and acted as a go-between for the Whigs and the French government (*DNB*).

74. *CSPD* (1683–84), p. 64; *ST*, vol. 9, pp. 818ff.

75. Williams' notes are reproduced in full in *ST*, vol. 9, pp. 825–35.

76. Dalrymple, *Memoirs*, vol. 1, pp. 96–97.

77. *ST*, vol. 9, pp. 1054–1126.

78. Luttrell, *Relation*, vol. 1, p. 299; *DNB*, sub Hugh Speke and Laurence Braddon. It was perhaps while searching Speke's house that some of Atkyns' letters concerning Russell's trial were discovered which would explain their presence among the secretary of state's papers (*CSPD* [1683, pt. 2], pp. 108–109, 127). For an account of Braddon's and Speke's trial, see *ST*, vol. 9, pp. 1127–1224.

79. *History of My Own Time* (Supplement, ed. Foxcroft), p. 122; but Atkyns showed himself rather cautious in his letters to Speke (see above, p. 161).

80. *ST*, vol. 9, p. 1169.

81. 21–22 James I, c. 3; C. Stephenson and F. G. Marcham, *Sources of English Constitutional History*, p. 434.

82. *Collection of Parliamentary Debates in England, 1668–1740*, vol. 1, p. 366.

83. For Holt's speech, see *ST*, vol. 10, pp. 371–83.

84. For Treby's speech see ibid., pp. 383–405.

85. John Shaw, ed., *Charters Relating to the East India Company from 1600 to 1761*, pp. 69–73.

86. Ibid., pp. 70–71.

87. For Finch's speech see *ST*, vol. 10, pp. 405–14.

88. For Pollexfen's speech, see ibid., pp. 414–54. Jeffreys chaffed Pollexfen at the conclusion of his speech for attacking corporations when he had so strenuously defended that of London the year before.

89. For Sawyer's speech see *ST*, vol. 10, pp. 457–95.

90. For Williams' speech see ibid., p. 495–516.

91. For Jeffreys' statement see ibid., pp. 519–54.

Chapter 6

1. David Ogg, *England in the Reign of Charles II*, vol. 2, pp. 650–51.

2. *HMCR*, Thirteenth Report, app. 6, p. 25.

3. *CSPD* (1685), item 38.

4. *ST*, vol. 10, pp. 1166–67, 1170–72, 1310. Wallop had joined Treby and Williams in refusing to aid Oates in February, 1685 (*HMCR*, Thirteenth Report, app. 6, p. 25).

5. *CSPD* (1685), item 1840. Lord Brandon was convicted in November 1685 (on the evidence of Lord Grey of Werke, who, following Howard's example after the Rye House Plot, turned informer in return for a pardon). He was sentenced to death, but later was granted a reprieve. Lord Delamere, despite the extreme partiality of Jeffreys who as Lord High Steward was presiding over his trial, was acquitted by his fellow peers in January, 1686 (David Ogg, *England in the Reigns of James II and William III*, p. 155; *DNB*).

6. *Lives of the Norths*, vol. 2, p. 23.

7. Thomas, Lord Macaulay, *History of England*, vol. 1, p. 372; *ST*, vol. 11, pp. 493–502.

8. See note 5 above.

9. Sir Edward Parry, *The Bloody Assize*, p. 196, excuses Pollexfen on these grounds, which certainly seems reasonable.

10. *ST*, vol. 10, pp. 316ff.

11. *A Brief Historical Relation of State Affairs from September 1678 to April 1714,* vol. 1, p. 311.

12. *ST,* vol. 13, pp. 1369–90.

13. *CJ,* vol. 9, p. 649.

14. *ST,* vol. 13, p. 1349.

15. *History of His Own Time* (1734), vol. 1, p. 592.

16. *Lives,* vol. 2, p. 21.

17. Ogg, *Charles II,* vol. 2, p. 634.

18. *Lives,* vol. 2, p. 21.

19. In the *DNB,* et al.

20. Ibid.

21. *The Life of Judge Jeffreys,* pp. 126–27.

22. *CJ,* vol. 9, p. 653.

23. Ibid., pp. 656–67.

24. *HMCR,* Fourteenth Report, app. 4, p. 264.

25. *CSPD* (1684–85), p. 183.

26. Ibid., pp. 309–10.

27. For the Text see *ST,* vol. 13, pp. 1380–1436.

28. *CTB,* vol. 8, p. 1067.

29. Anchitell Grey, *Debates of the House of Commons,* vol. 8, p. 374. James himself claimed that "there were not above forty Members but such as he himself wished for" (Burnet, *History,* quoted in Grey, *Debates,* vol. 8, p. 343n).

30. *DNB,* Grey, *Debates,* vol. 8, p. 359.

31. *HMCR,* Thirteenth Report, app. 6, p. 26. *CJ,* vol. 9, p. 726 and index.

32. *CJ,* vol. 9, p. 732.

33. Morrice diary, pp. 491, 522.

34. Ibid., pp. 533–34.

35. *HMCR,* Tenth Report, app. 6, p. 97.

36. *DNB,* sub Edward Herbert.

37. *ST,* vol. 13, pp. 1346–47.

38. *HMCR,* Downshire MSS, app. 1, p. 169; Morrice diary, p. 538.

39. Williams-Wynn MSS, quoted in *DNB.*

40. Lord John Campbell, *Speeches,* p. 290.

41. Ibid.

42. Ibid., p. 287.

43. Sir John Bramston, *Autobiography,* p. 399.

44. Dated from Gloucester.

45. Samuel Singer, ed., *The Correspondence of Henry Hyde, Earl of Clarendon, and of . . . Laurence Hyde, Earl of Rochester,* vol. 1, pp. 496–97.

46. Macaulay, *History,* vol. 2, pp. 56, 57n.

47. North, *Lives,* vol. 1, editor's introduction.

48. Macaulay, *History,* vol. 2, pp. 63–64.

49. Ibid.

50. Ibid., p. 260.

51. M. M. Verney, *Memoirs of the Verney Family, 1660–1696,* vol. 4, p. 412; Bramston, *Autobiography,* p. 303.

52. Sir John Reresby, *Memoirs,* ed. Browning, pp. 422–23.

53. William Cobbett, *Parliamentary History of England,* vol. 5, p. 337.

54. *Speeches,* p. 290.

55. *CTB,* vol. 8, p. 841.

56. Ibid., p. 865.

57. Ibid., pp. 831, 871, 938.

58. Williams-Wynne MSS, quoted in *ST,* vol. 13, p. 1440.

59. Ibid., p. 1438.

60. Singer, *Clarendon Correspondence,* vol. 1, p. 497.

61. Luttrell, *Relation,* vol. 1, p. 380.

62. *CSPD* (1686), pp. 619–20.

63. *ST,* vol. 13, pp. 1347, 1348n.

64. Laurence Echard, *The History of the Revolution,* p. 78. For a general discussion of James' policy in this regard, see J. R. Jones, "James II's Whig Collaborators," *Historical Journal,* vol. 3, pp. 65–73.

65. A. M. Dodd, *Studies in Stuart Wales,* pp. 221–22; Matthew Henry, "A Short Account of the Beginning and Progress of our Congregation" (1710), *Cheshire Sheaf,* vol. 57, para. 10,927.

66. Henry, "A Short Account," para. 10,927.

67. Ibid.; *DNB,* sub Grosvenor.

68. Henry, loc. cit.; James Hall, "Royal Charters and Grants to the City of Chester," *Journal of the Chester and North Wales Architectural, Archeological and Historic Society,* new series, vol. 10, pp. 65–67.

69. Joseph Hunter, ed., *The Diary of Dr. Thomas Cartwright, Bishop of Chester,* p. 75.

70. Ibid., p. 77.

71. *DNB*

72. *London Gazette,* Dec. 19, 1687, datelined: "Whitehall, December 11."

73. *Poems on Affairs of State,* vol. III, p. 174.

74. North, *Lives,* vol. 2, p. 20 (editor's note by H. Roscoe).

75. P. 339.

76. *History,* vol. 2, p. 261.

77. *DNB*

78. George Savile, Marquess of Halifax, *Miscellanies,* pp. 88–89.

79. Cobbett, *Parliamentry History,* vol. 4, p. 933.

80. Ogg, *Charles II,* vol. 2, pp. 465–66.

81. Philip Yorke, *The Royal Tribes of Wales,* p. 176 (original in Latin).

82. One Whig M. P., Colonel John Birch, expressed sympathy for Williams in a speech to the House of Commons on Mar. 9, 1689, saying: "he did take upon him the . . . place . . . because he did not know any way to get his Fine again, but by such an Office" (Grey, *Debates,* vol. 9, p. 146).

83. Pp. 128–29.

84. Irving, *Jeffreys,* p. 339.

85. *DNB*

86. Irving, *Jeffreys,* p. 339.

87. Ibid.

88. Ogg, *James II and William III,* p. 168.

89. Atkyns, *Parliamentary and Political Tracts,* pp. 177–82. For a full account of the trial, see *ST,* vol. 11, pp. 1186–1200.

90. *HMCR,* Ninth Report, app. 2, p. 28ᵃ (note).

91. *ST,* vol. 11, p. 1200n; *HMCR,* Downshire MSS, vol. 1, p. 184.

92. Page 191.

93. *ST,* vol. 11, p. 1200. Northey later served as attorney general, 1701–07 and 1710–18.

94. Pows' speech is in *ST,* vol. 11, pp. 1191–95. See also Paul Birdsall, " 'Non-Obstante'—a Study of the Dispensing

Power of English Kings," *Essays in History and Political Theory,* pp. 71–73.

95. In his *Seventh Report,* quoted in Birdsall, " 'Non-Obstante,' " pp. 52–53.

96. Coke, loc. cit.; Serjeant Edmund Plowden, in his *Commentaries* (1578); Lord Chief Justice Sir John Vaughan in his *Reports* (ed. E. Vaughn, 1677) et al. See Birdsall " 'Non-Obstante,' " pp. 53–66; W. S. Holdsworth, *History,* vol. 6, pp. 218–19, 223.

97. Holdsworth, *History,* vol. 6, p. 223; Birdsall, " 'Non-Obstante,' " p. 74n.

98. *ST,* vol. 11, pp. 1195–99.

99. Atkyns, *Tracts,* pp. 177–282.

100. Advt. in the *London Gazette,* Jan. 14–17, 1680/81; British Museum, *Catalogue of Printed Books.*

101. *CSPD* (1686), p. 619.

102. *HMCR,* Eleventh Report, app. 2, pp. 300, 309; Singer, *Clarendon Correspondence,* vol. 2, pp. 157, 164, 170, 205.

103. Ibid., p. 150.

104. Holdsworth, *History,* vol. 6, pp. 220–23.

105. Leopold von Ranke, *A History of England,* vol. 4, p. 356.

106. Reresby, *Memoirs,* quoted in *ST,* vol. 11, p. 192n.

107. Macaulay, *History,* vol. 2, p. 289.

108. Ibid., p. 286.

109. Burnet, *History* (1734), vol. 1, p. 742; Bramston, *Autobiography,* p. 310; Robert Price to the Duke of Beaufort, quoted in *ST,* vol. 12, p. 200n.

110. Singer, *Clarendon Correspondence,* vol. 2, p. 177.

111. *Abridgment of the Trials 1678–1688,* p. 938; Macaulay, *History,* vol. 2, p. 289.

112. J. Mackintosh, *A History of the Revolution in England in 1688,* p. 369.

113. Macaulay, *History,* vol. 2, p. 285.

114. Burnet, *History* (1734), vol. 1, p. 742; Mackintosh, *History,* p. 370; Campbell, *Speeches,* p. 291.

115. *History,* p. 364.

116. This and all subsequent references to the Bishops' trial are derived from the account of it in *ST,* vol. 12, pp. 189–439.

117. Cobbett, *Parliamentary History,* vol. 5, p. 263.
118. E. Ranke, *History,* vol. 4, p. 357.
119. Singer, *Clarendon Correspondence,* vol. 2, p. 180.
120. Ogg, *James II and William III,* pp. 203–204; but the writs were recalled on Sept. 28.
121. Williams-Wynne MSS, quoted in *DNB.*
122. Yorke, *Royal Tribes,* p. 113.
123. *ST,* vol. 12, p. 125.
124. Luttrell, *Relation,* vol. 1, p. 468.
125. Ogg, *James II and William III,* p. 211.
126. *HMCR,* Fourteenth Report, app. 9, p. 448.
127. Vol. 4, p. 609.

Chapter 7

1. *Somers Tracts,* vol. 10, pp. 321–22; Reginald Sharpe, *London and the Kingdom,* vol. 2, pp. 531, 536–37.
2. *The London Intelligence,* Jan. 19, 1688/89.
3. Samuel Singer, ed., *The Correspondence of Henry Hyde, Earl of Clarendon, and of, . . . Laurence Hyde, Earl of Rochester,* vol. 2, p. 228; *The London Courant* (no. 3), Dec. 18, 1688.
4. Singer, *Clarendon Correspondence,* vol. 2, p. 228.
5. Ibid., pp. 225–26.
6. He was so described by Thomas, Lord Macaulay (*History of England,* vol. 2, p. 286).
7. Under the Protectorate more county seats were created and many of the smaller boroughs were disfranchised.
8. *The London Mercury . . . ,* Dec. 24, 1688, says "Bradford" and "Atkinson" were summoned, but it has not been possible to trace any lawyers with those names in this period. Edward Foss, *A Biographical Dictionary of the Judges of England, 1066–1870,* says Bradbury was summoned on this occasion. Called to the bar from the Middle Temple in May, 1667, Bradbury became a cursitor baron of the Exchequer in July, 1689 and served in that capacity till his death in February, 1696.
9. David Ogg, *England in the Reigns of James II and William II,* p. 223.

10. *CSPD* (1689–90), p. 9. Lord John Campbell, *Lives of the Lord Chancellors,* vol. 5, pp. 2–3. Rawlinson was called to the bar from Gray's Inn in 1667 and was made a Serjeant-at-law in 1686. He was reportedly a man "of good repute." Keck was a bencher of the Inner Temple, and had made his reputation as a Chancery advocate (Foss, *Dictionary*).

11. Singer, *Clarendon Correspondence,* vol. 2, pp. 223, 226; Narcissus Luttrell, *A Brief Historical Relation of State Affairs from September 1678 to April 1714,* vol. 1, p. 481.

12. Campbell, *Lord Chancellors,* vol. 5, p. 2n.

13. Ibid., vol. 5, p. 3n. *Le Neve's Pedigrees of the Knights,* p. 414.

14. *CSPD* (1689–90), p. 59.

15. *Correspondence,* vol. 2, p. 273. Perhaps they were unwilling to give up a successful barrister's ample fees for a judge's salary; or perhaps they simply feared a Jacobite Restoration. Ward, of the Inner Temple, was Thomas Papillon's son-in-law (Foss, *Dictionary*).

16. *CSPD* (1689–90), p. 76; Robert Beatson, *A Political Index,* vol. 2, p. 298.

17. Beatson, *Index,* vol. 2, pp. 291, 308. Holt had been appointed a King's Serjeant in April, 1686 (ibid., p. 337).

18. *History,* vol. 3, p. 18.

19. *CSPD* (1689–90), pp. 65–66.

20. He is listed as "Sir Francis Winningham."

21. Beatson, *Index,* vol. 2, pp. 295, 313.

22. Luttrell, *Relation,* vol. 1, p. 329.

23. *CSPD* (1689–90), p. 271. A *Custos Rotulorum* ("keeper of the rolls") performs the same functions for a county as a recorder does for a town or city. Williams held the office for six months.

24. See *HMCR,* Thirteenth Report, app. 5, passim.

25. *ST,* vol. 12, pp. 927–48. Luttrell, *Relation,* vol. 1, p. 336.

26. Luttrell, *Relation,* vol. 1, p. 449.

27. *The London Intelligence,* Jan. 24, 1688/89. William Petyt (1636–1707), "archivist and antiquary," became Treasurer of his Inn, the Middle Temple, in 1701 (*DNB*).

28. Letter to Treby, Dec. 24, 1689, *HMCR*, Thirteenth Report, app. 6, p. 26.

29. House of Commons, *Papers*, (1878), vol. 62, pt. 1, p. 558.

30. *CTB*, vol. 8, item 2010.

31. Ibid., vol. 9, items 145, 158; vol. 10, item 438.

32. Commons, *Papers* (1878), vol. 62, pt. 1, p. 563.

33. Ibid., p. 562.

34. *CJ*, vol. 10, pp. 9, 11.

35. Ibid., p. 14.

36. The account of this debate is taken from Anchitell Grey, *Debates of the House of Commons, 1667–1694*, vol. 9, pp. 7–25.

37. Speech to both Houses at Whitehall, March 21, 1609. See chap. 1, p. 25.

38. *CJ*, vol. 10, p. 14.

39. *HMCR*, Twelfth Report, app. 6, pp. 14–17.

40. Daniel Finch (1647–1730), 2nd Earl of Nottingham, elder brother of Sir Heneage Finch who was solicitor general, 1678–1686.

41. See chap. 3, p. 97.

42. *HMCR*, Twelfth Report, app. 6, p. 17.

43. *Collection of the Parliamentry Debates in England* (1741), vol. 2, p. 184.

44. The account of the conference is taken from ibid., pp. 189–258.

45. Campbell, *Lord Chancellors*, vol. 5, p. 83n.

46. Except for Pollexfen's remark to Clarendon (see above, p. 220).

47. E.g. Campbell, *Lord Chancellors*, vol. 5, p. 83.

48. Cobbett, *Parliamentary History of England*, vol. 5, p. 108.

49. Ibid., p. 53; Ogg, *James II and William III*, p. 225.

50. *DNB* and Macaulay, *History*, vol. 2, p. 500, both say that Somers was chairman; but *CJ*, vol. 10, p. 17, and an account in British Museum, Additional MSS 35,838, fol. 309, both say that it was Treby who delivered the committee's report to the House, which was always done by the chairman.

51. Campbell, *Lord Chancellors*, vol. 5, p. 82; *DNB*.

52. Campbell, *Lord Chancellors,* vol. 5, p. 85.

53. The Declaration of Rights of February, 1689 was enacted into law by the Bill of Rights, which incorporated it, in December, 1689. See C. Stephenson and F. C. Marcham, *Sources of English Constitutional History,* pp. 599–605.

54. In March, 1689 Holt and a majority of the justices reportedly advised the House of Lords that in common law the Crown did have a dispensing power (*HMCR,* Seventh Report, p. 759*). It should be noted that the prohibition in the Bill of Rights refers to the power of dispensing with laws, "as it hath been assumed and exercised of late, . . ." However, the prohibition has ever afterwards been regarded as total.

Conclusion

1. "The English Revolution and Locke's 'Two Treatises of Civil Government,' " *Cambridge Historical Journal,* vol. 12, no. 1, pp. 40ff.

2. B. Behrens points out this essential difference between the reasoning of the lawyers and that of other rationalists of the age ("The Whig theory of the Constitution in the Reign of Charles II," *Cambridge Historical Journal,* vol. 7, pp. 46–47n).

3. *Works,* vol. 2, pp. 292–93.

4. Rather paradoxically, many of those who today sympathize with the Whig lawyers in their opposition to "big government' may also, because they are worried by the present so-called "breakdown of law and order" in the cities and on the campuses, find themselves rather in sympathy with Lord Keeper North's denunciation in 1683 of the disaffected elements in London. See chap. 3, p. 121.

Bibliography of Works Cited

PRIMARY SOURCES

Atkyns, Robert. *Parliamentary and Political Tracts*. London: R. Gosling, 1734.

Bacon, Francis. *Essays or Counsels Moral and Civil*. Edited by William Willymott. London: H. Parson, etc., 1720.

Bramston, Sir John. *Autobiography*. London: Camden Society, 1845.

Burnet, Gilbert. *History of His Own Time*. 2 vols. London: Thos. Ward, 1724, 1734.

————. *History of My Own Time*. Edited by William Airey, 2 vols. Oxford: Clarendon Press, 1897, 1900.

————. *History of My Own Time* (supplement to Airey's edition above). Edited by H. C. Foxcroft. Oxford: Clarendon Press, 1902.

Cobbett, William, ed. *A Complete Collection of State Trials . . . from the earliest to the Present time . . . compiled by T. B. Howell*. 34 vols. London: R. Bagshaw; Longmans & Co., 1809–1828.

————. *Parliamentary History of England*, 12 vols. London: R. Bagshaw; Longmans & Co., 1806–1812.

Coke, Edward. *The Institutes of the Laws of England*. 4 vols. London: E. & R. Brooke, 1797.

A Collection of the Parliamentary Debates in England from the year MDCLXVIII to the present time. 21 vols. London: J. Torbuck, 1741.

Dalrymple, Sir John. *Memoirs of Great Britain and Ireland.* 3 vols. Edinburgh: 1771–1788.

D'Ewes, Simonds. *Journal.* Edited by W. H. Coates. New Haven: Yale University Press, 1942.

Evelyn, Sir John. *Diary.* Edited by E. S. de Beer. 8 vols. Oxford: Clarendon Press, 1955.

Finch, Heneage [1st Earl of Nottingham]. *A treatise on the king's power of granting pardons in cases of impeachment.* London: 1691.

Great Britain. *Calendars of State Papers, Domestic Series.* London: Her Majesty's Stationery Office.

Great Britain. *Calendars of the Treasury Books.* London: Her Majesty's Stationery Office.

Great Britain. Courts. *Modern Reports.* vol. 3. London: 1725.

Great Britain. *Historical Manuscripts Commission Reports.* London: Her Majesty's Stationery Office.

Great Britain. House of Commons. *Journal.* Vols. 9 and 10.

Great Britain. House of Commons. *Papers.* (1878), Vol. 62. Pt. 1.

Great Britain. House of Lords. *Journal.* Vol. 13.

Grey, Anchitell. *Debates of the House of Commons, 1667 to 1694.* 10 vols. London: 1763.

Harrington, James. *The Political Writings—Representative Selections.* Edited by Charles Blitzer. New York: Liberal Arts Press, 1955.

Henry, Matthew. "A Short Account of the Beginning and Progress of Our Congregation." *The Cheshire Sheaf.* 3rd series. Vol. 57, 10, 925–10, 930.

Hobbes, Thomas. *The Elements of Law.* Edited by F. Tonnies (Cambridge English Classics). Cambridge: University Press, 1928.

———*Leviathan.*

Hunter, Joseph, ed. *The Diary of Dr. Thomas Cartwright, Bishop of Chester.* London: Camden Society, 1843.

Jones, Harold, ed. *"Anti-Achitophel" (1682), Three Verse Replies to "Absolom and Achitophel" by John Dryden.* Gainesville: University of Florida Press, 1961.

Lefevre, G. S. "The Discipline of the Bar." *Economic and Social Pamphlets.* (Collection in the University of Wisconsin Library, Madison). Vol. 74, No. 1.

Le Neve's Pedigrees of the Knights. (Harleian Society Publications," vol. 8) London: 1873.

London. British Museum Library. Additional Manuscripts Collection.

London. British Museum Library. The Burney Collection of Early Newspapers: *The Domestick Intelligence,* 1680. *The London Courant,* 1688–1689. *The London Gazette,* 1687–1689. *The London Intelligence,* 1689. *The London Mercury or Moderate Intelligencer,* 1689. *The Protestant Domestick Intelligence,* January–March 1681. *The Protestant Oxford Intelligence,* March, 1681. *Smith's Protestant Intelligence,* 1681.

London. British Museum. *General Catalogue of Printed Books.*

London. Corporation of the City. "Journal." Vol. 50.

London. Dr. Williams Library. Morris Manuscripts. Unpublished Diary of Roger Morrice.

London. Inns of Court. *The Register of Admissions to Grays Inn, 1521–1889.* (1889). *Students admitted to the Inner Temple, 1571–1660.* (2 vols. 1868, 1878). *Records of the Honourable Society of Lincoln's Inn. Admissions (and Chapel Registers).* (2 vols., 1896). *The Register of Admissions to the Honourable Society of the Middle Temple.* (3 vols., 1949).

Luttrell, Narcissus. *A Brief Historical Relation of State Affairs from September 1678 to April 1714.* 6 vols. Oxford: University Press, 1857.

Milne, D. and Browning A., eds. "An Exclusion Bill Division List." *Bulletin of the Institute of Historical Research.* Vol. 23, pp. 205–25.

N——, P. *An Exact Abridgment of All the Trials . . . Relating to the Popish and Pretended Presbyterian Plots.* London: 1690.

North, Roger. *Examen.* London: F. Gyles, 1740.

————. *Lives of the Norths.* 3 vols. London: H. Colburn, 1826.

Poems on Affairs of State. 3 vols. London: 1710.

Powell, Thomas. "The Art of Thriving, or the Plaine Pathway to Preferment." *Somers Tracts* (1809–1815). Vol. 7, pp. 187–209.

Prideaux, Humphrey. *Letters . . . to John Ellis.* Edited by E. Thompson. London: Camden Society, 1875.

Reresby, Sir John. *Memoirs.* Edited by A. Browning. Glasgow: Jackson, Son & Co., 1936.

The Rolls of the Freemen of the City of Chester. Part 1 (1392–1700). Chester: Record Society for the Publication of Original Documents Relating to Lancashire and Cheshire, 1906.

Savile, George [1st Marquis of Halifax]. *Miscellanies.* London: 1704.

Shaw, John, ed. *Charters Relating to the East India Company from 1600 to 1761.* Madras: Government Press, 1887.

Singer, Samuel, ed. *The Correspondence of Henry Hyde, Earl of Clarendon, and of his brother, Laurence Hyde, Earl of Rochester, with the Diary of Lord Clarendon, from 1687 to 1690.* 2 vols. London: 1828.

Somers Tracts ("A Collection of Scarce and Valuable Tracts"). Edited by Sir Walter Scott. 13 vols. London: 1809–1815.

Stephenson, Carl, and Marcham, F. G. *Sources of English Constitutional History.* New York: Harper & Row, 1937.

Temple, Sir William. *Works.* 4 vols. London: 1770.

Verney, M. M. *Memoirs of the Verney Family from the*

Restoration to the Revolution. 4 vols. London: 1892–1899.

Warner, Rebecca. *Epistolary Curiosities* . . . consisting of unpublished letters, illustrative of the Herbert Family. London: 1818.

Washington, D.C. Library of Congress. Collection of unpublished London newsletters of the year 1682.

SECONDARY SOURCES

Alexander, J. J. "Bere Alston as a Parliamentary Borough." *Reports and Transactions of the Devonshire Association for the Advancement of Science,* vol. 41, pp. 152–78.

Alford, D. P. "Four Tavistock Worthies of the Seventeenth Century." *Reports and Transactions of the Devonshire Association for the Advancement of Science,* vol. 21, pp. 138–47.

Behrens, B. "The Whig Theory of the Constitution in the Reign of Charles II." *Cambridge Historical Journal,* vol. 7, pp. 42–71.

Birdsall, Paul, " 'Non-Obstante'—A Study of the Dispensing Power of English Kings." *Essays in History and Political Theory in honor of Charles Howard McIlwain.* Cambridge, Mass.: Harvard University Press, 1936.

Burke, Edmund. *Works.* 6 vols. London: George Bell & Sons, 1901.

Campbell, Baron John. *Lives of the Lord Chancellors and Keepers of the Great Seal.* 10 vols. London: John Murray, 1868.

———. *Speeches as Lord Chancellor of Ireland and at the Bar and in the House of Commons.* Edinburgh; A. & C. Black, 1842.

Clark, G. N. *The Later Stuarts.* (Oxford History of England.) Oxford: Clarendon Press, 1956.

Dasent, Arthur. *The Speakers of the House of Commons.* New York: John Lane, 1911.

Dodd, A. H. *Studies in Stuart Wales.* Cardiff: University of Wales Press, 1952.

Dugdale, Sir Wm. *History and antiquities of the four Inns of Court.* London: 1780.

Dutton, Hugh. "The Stuart Kings and Chester Corporation." *Journal of the Chester and North Wales Architectural, Archeological and Historic Society,* new series, vol. 28, pt. 2, pp. 180–210.

Earwaker, J. P. "The 'Progress' of the Duke of Monmouth in Cheshire in September 1682." *Transactions of the Historic Society of Lancashire and Cheshire,* new series, vol. 10. Liverpool: 1895.

Echard, Laurence. *The History of the Revolution and of the Establishment of England.* London: 1725.

Escott, T. H. *Gentlemen of the House of Commons.* 2 vols. London: Hurst & Blackett, 1902.

Feiling, Keith. *A History of the Tory Party, 1640–1714.* Oxford: Clarendon Press, 1924.

Foss, Edward. *The English Judges.* 9 vols. London: Longman, Brown, Green, & Longmans, 1848–1864.

———. *Memories of Westminster Hall.* 2 vols. Jersey City, n.d.

Foxcroft, H. C. *The Life and Letters of George Savile, First Marquis of Halifax.* 2 vols. London: Longmans & Co., 1898.

Gray, J. C. *The Nature and Sources of the Law.* New York: Columbia University Press, 1909.

Hall, James. "Royal Charters and Grants to the City of Chester." *Journal of the Chester and North Wales Architectural, Archeological and Historic Society,* new series, vol. 18, pp. 26–76.

Havighurst, A. F. "The Judiciary and Politics in the Reigns of Charles II and James II." *Law Quarterly Review,* vol. 66, pp. 62–78, 229–52.

Holdsworth, W. S. *Essays in Law and History.* Oxford: Clarendon Press, 1946.

————. *A History of English Law.* 16 vols. London: Methuen & Co., Ltd., Sweet and Maxwell, 1966.

————. *Some Makers of English Law.* Cambridge: University Press, 1938.

————. *The Sources and Literature of English Law.* Oxford: Clarendon Press, 1925.

Irving, H. B. *The Life of Judge Jeffreys.* New York: Longmans, Green & Co., 1906.

Jones, J. R. *The First Whigs, The Politics of the Exclusion Crisis, 1678–1683.* London: Durham University Publication, 1961.

————. "James II's Whig Collaborators." *Historical Journal,* vol. 3, pp. 65–73.

Laslett, Peter. "The English Revolution and Locke's 'Two Treatises of Government.' " *Cambridge Historical Journal,* vol. 12, pp. 40–55.

Macaulay, Lord Thomas. *History of England from the Accession of James II.* 5 vols. New York: Harper & Brothers, 1856.

Macdonagh, Michael. *The Speaker of the House.* London: Methuen & Co., 1914.

McIlwain, C. H. *The High Court of Parliament and its Supremacy.* New Haven: Yale University Press, 1910.

Mackintosh, James. *History of the Revolution in England in 1688.* Philadelphia: Carey, Lea & Blanchard, 1835.

Manning, James. *The Lives of the Speakers of the House of Commons.* London: 1850.

Memoir of the Life of John Lord Somers. London: 1716.

Notes and Queries. Second series, vol. 7. London: 1859.

Ogg, David. *England in the Reign of Charles II.* 2 vols. Oxford: Clarendon Press, 1934.

————. *England in the Reigns of James II and William III.* Oxford: Clarendon Press, 1955.

Parry, Edward. *Royal Visits and Progresses to Wales and the Border Counties . . . From the First Invasion of*

Julius Caesar to the Friendly Visit of Her Most Gracious Majesty Queen Victoria. Chester: 1850.

Parry, Sir Edward. *The Bloody Assize.* London: E. Benn, Ltd., 1929.

Pollock, John. "The Policy of Charles II and James II (1667–1687)." *The Cambridge Modern History* (1907–1911), vol. 5, section 9.

Porritt, Edward, and Annie. *The Unreformed House of Commons, parliamentary representation before 1832.* 2 vols. Cambridge: University Press, 1903.

Ranke, Leopold von. *A History of England, Principally in the Seventeenth Century.* 6 vols. Oxford: 1875.

Sacret, J. H. "The Restoration Government and Municipal Corporations." *English Historical Review,* vol. 45, pp. 232–59.

Sharpe, Reginald. *London and the Kingdom.* 3 vols. London: Longmans & Co., 1894–1895.

Trevelyan, G. M. *The English Revolution, 1688–1689.* New York: H. Holt & Co., 1939.

Wood, Anthony à. *Athenae Oxonienses.* Edited by P. Bliss. 4 vols. London: F. C. & J. Rivington, 1813–1820.

Yorke, Philip. *The Royal Tribes of Wales.* Wrexham: 1799.

REFERENCE WORKS

Beatson, Robert. *A Political Index.* 3 vols. London: Longman & Co., 1806.

Bouvier's Law Dictionary. Baldwin's Students Edition. Cleveland: 1934.

Cokayne, G. E. *The Complete Peerage of England, Scotland, Ireland and the United Kingdom.* Edited by Vicary Gibbs *et al.* 13 vols. London: St. Catherine Press, 1910–1940.

The Dictionary of National Biography. Edited by Sir Leslie Stephen and Sir Sidney Lee. 22 vols. London: Oxford University Press, 1937–1938.

Foss, Edward. *A Biographical Dictionary of the Judges of England, 1066–1870.* London: J. Murray, 1870.

Foster, J. *Alumni Oxonienses: The Members of the University of Oxford, 1500–1714.* 4 vols. Oxford: 1891.

Venn, J. and J. A. *Alumni Cantabrigienses.* 4 vols. Cambridge: University Press, 1922.

Index